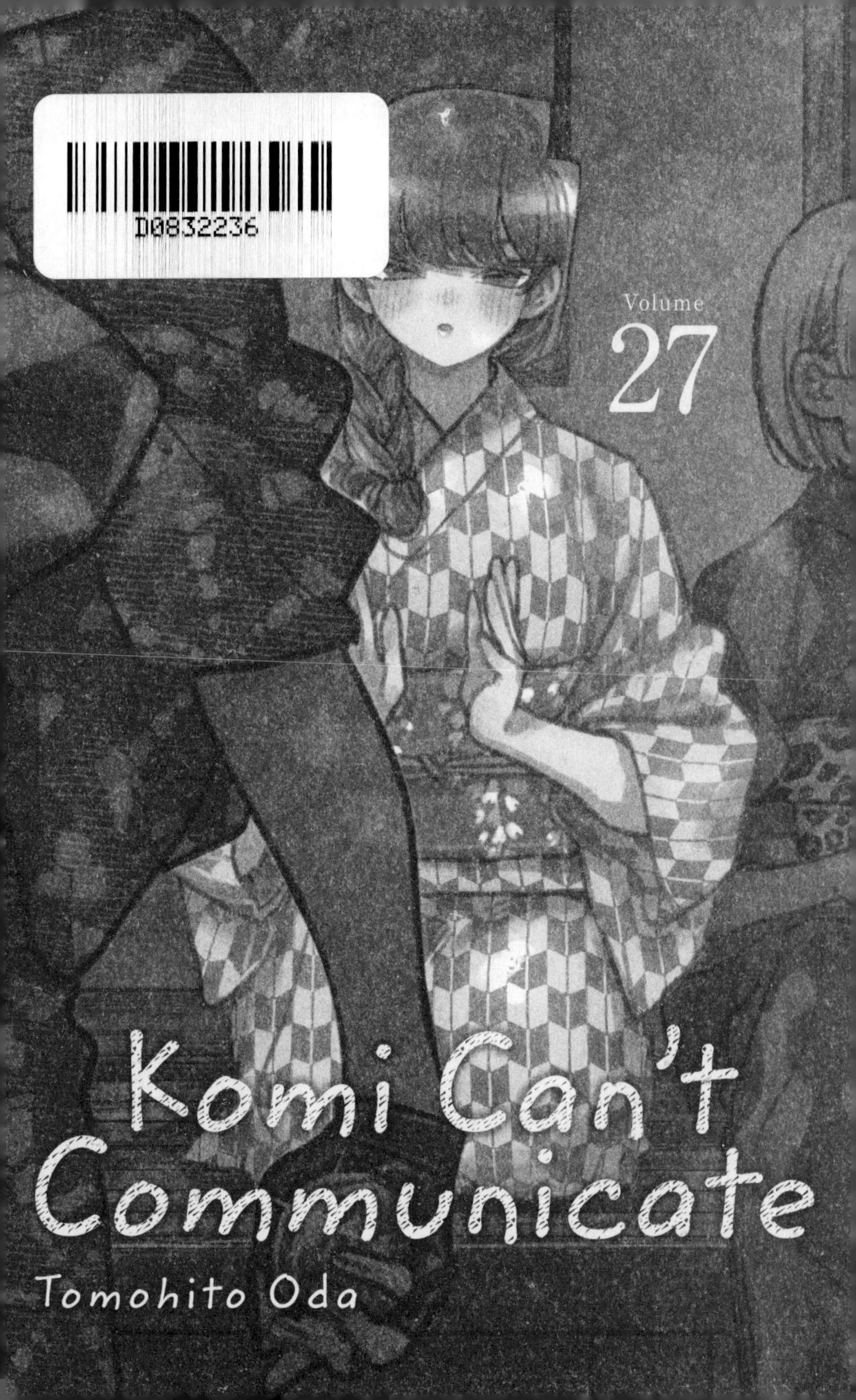
Volume
27
Komi Can't Communicate
Tomohito Oda

Contents

27

Komi Can't Communicate

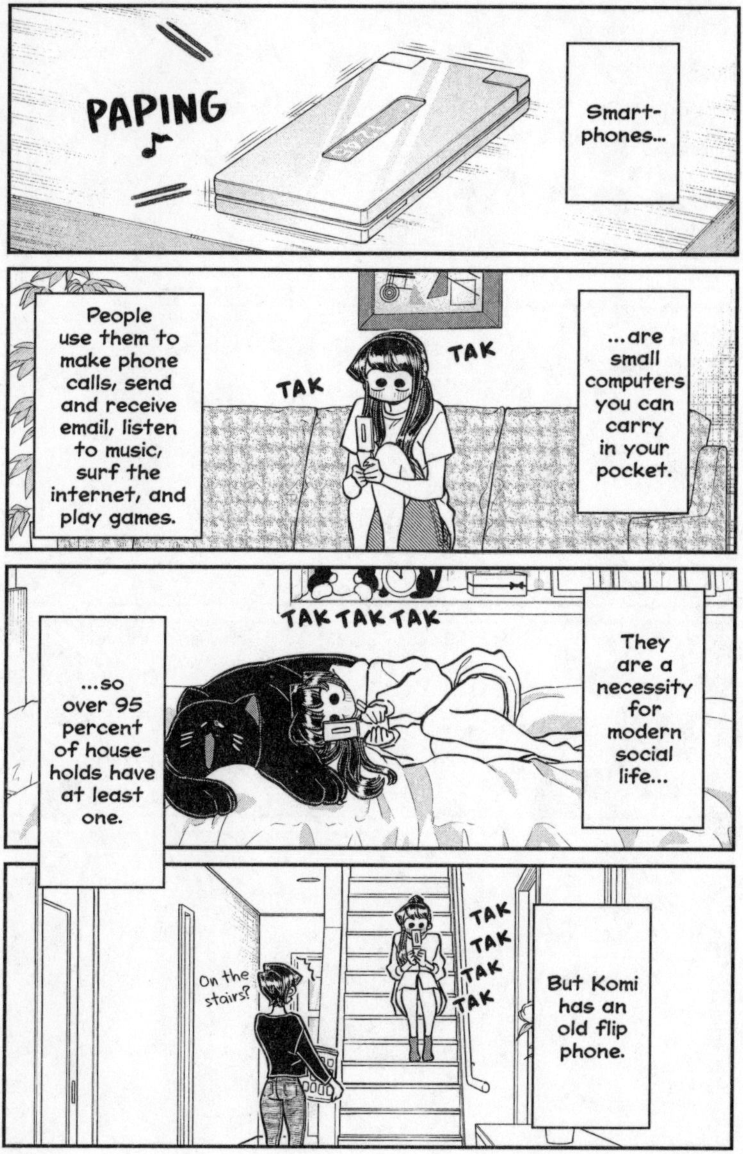
Smart-
phones...
PAPING ♪
...are small computers you can carry in your pocket.
TAK
TAK
People use them to make phone calls, send and receive email, listen to music, surf the internet, and play games.
They are a necessity for modern social life...
TAK TAK TAK
...so over 95 percent of house-holds have at least one.
But Komi has an old flip phone.
TAK
TAK
TAK
TAK
On the stairs?

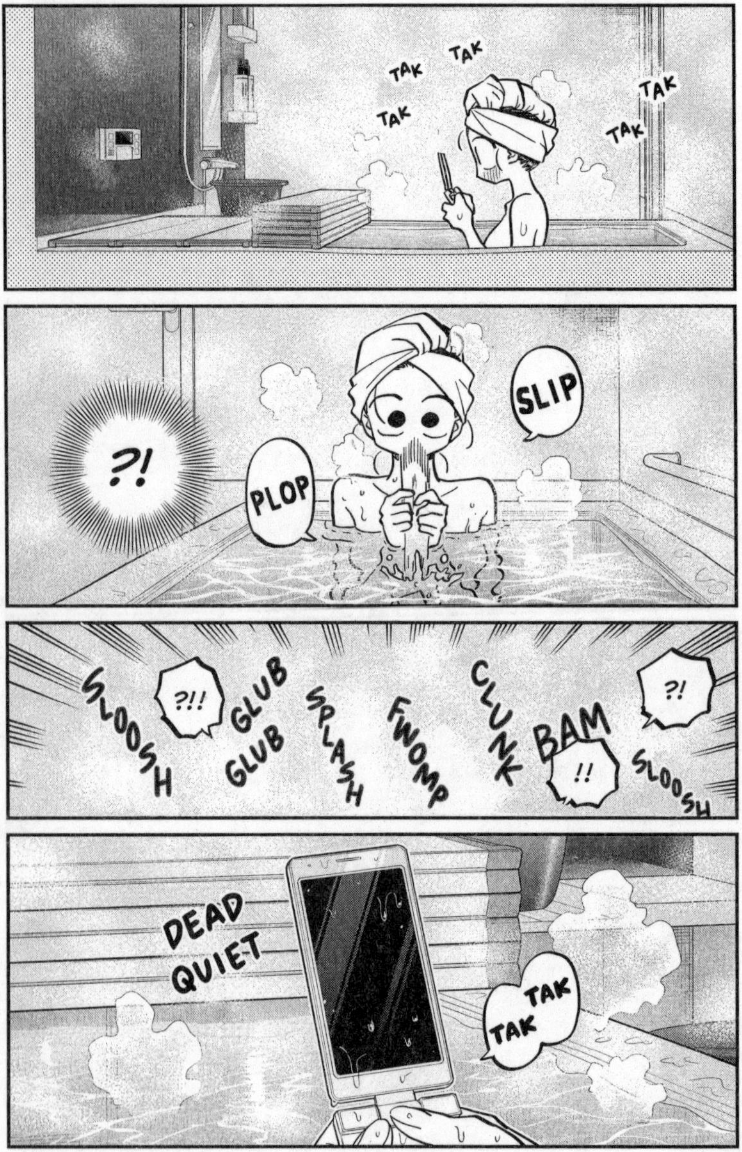
TAK
TAK
TAK
TAK
TAK
SLIP
PLOP
?!
?!
SLOOSH
BAM
!!
CLUNK
FWOMP
SPLASH
GLUB GLUB
?!!
SLOOSH
TAK TAK
DEAD QUIET

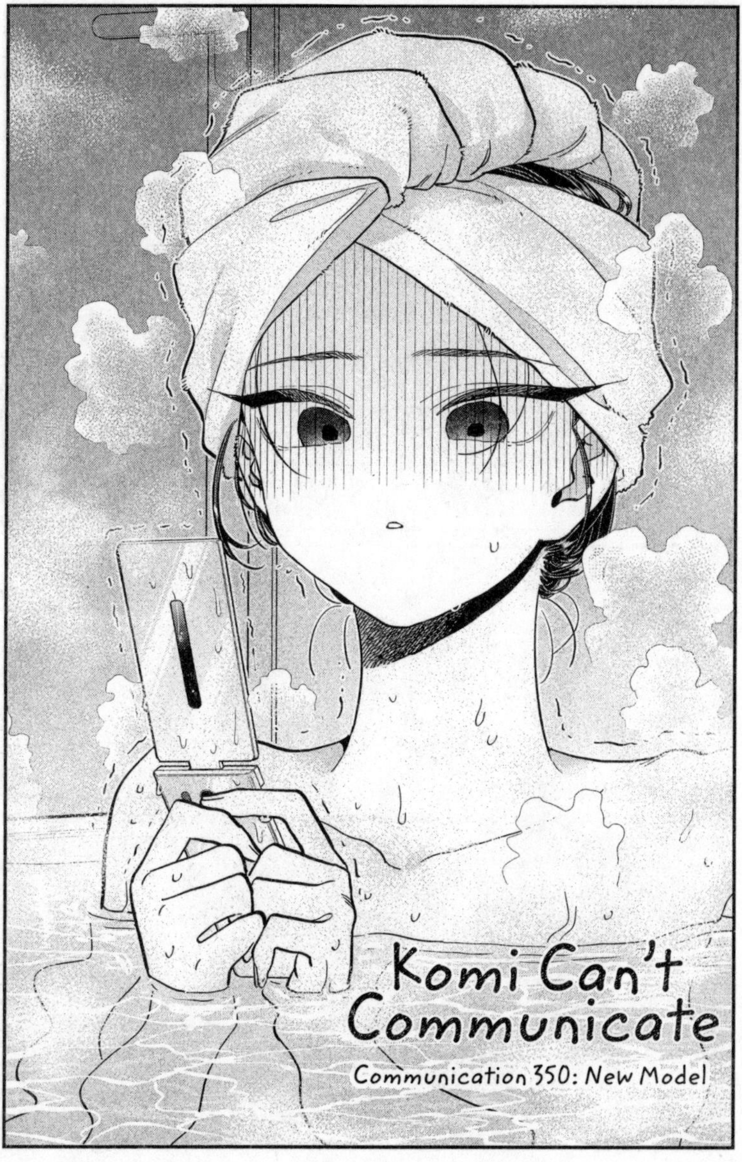
Komi Can't Communicate
Communication 350: New Model

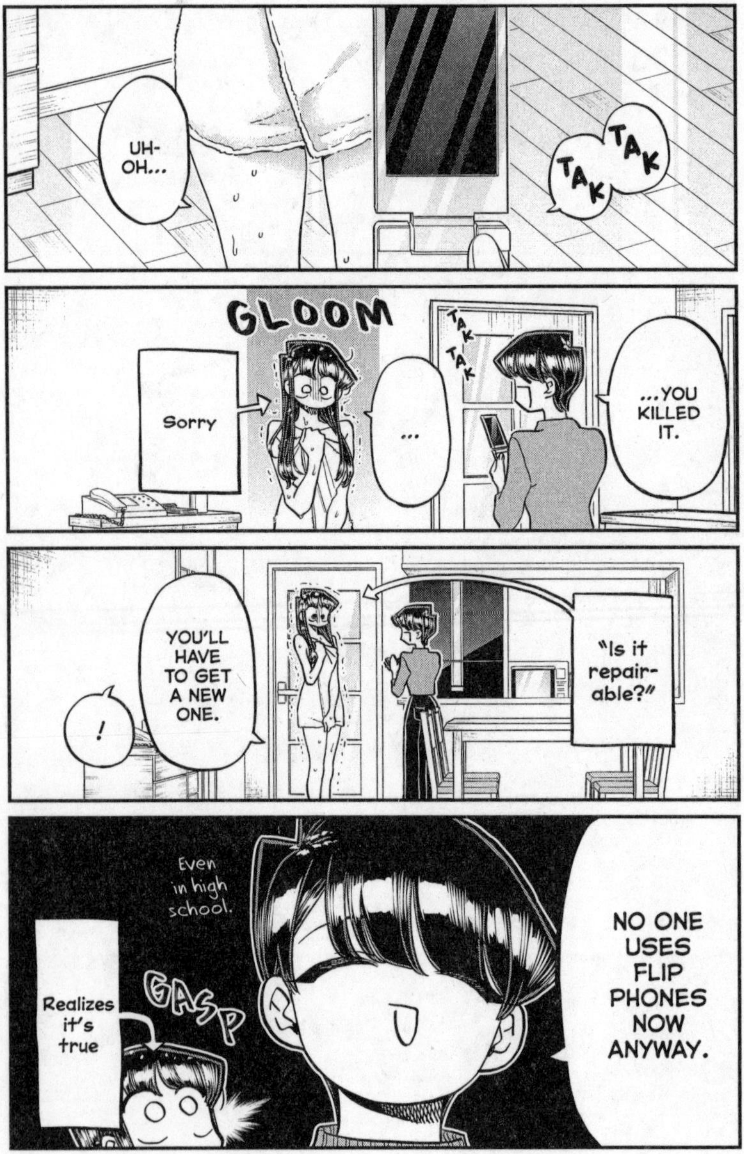
TAK TAK
UH-OH...
...YOU KILLED IT.
TAK TAK
...
GLOOM
Sorry
"Is it repairable?"
YOU'LL HAVE TO GET A NEW ONE.
!
NO ONE USES FLIP PHONES NOW ANYWAY.
Even in high school.
GASP
Realizes it's true

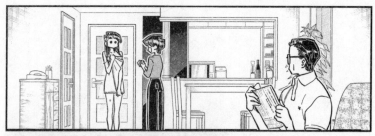

I CAN'T BELIEVE YOUR FATHER BOUGHT THAT.

*Vol. 1, page 135.

A flip phone!

BUT YOU SEEMED OKAY WITH IT.

HMPH HMPH

*Vol. 1, page 135.

She's okay with that?

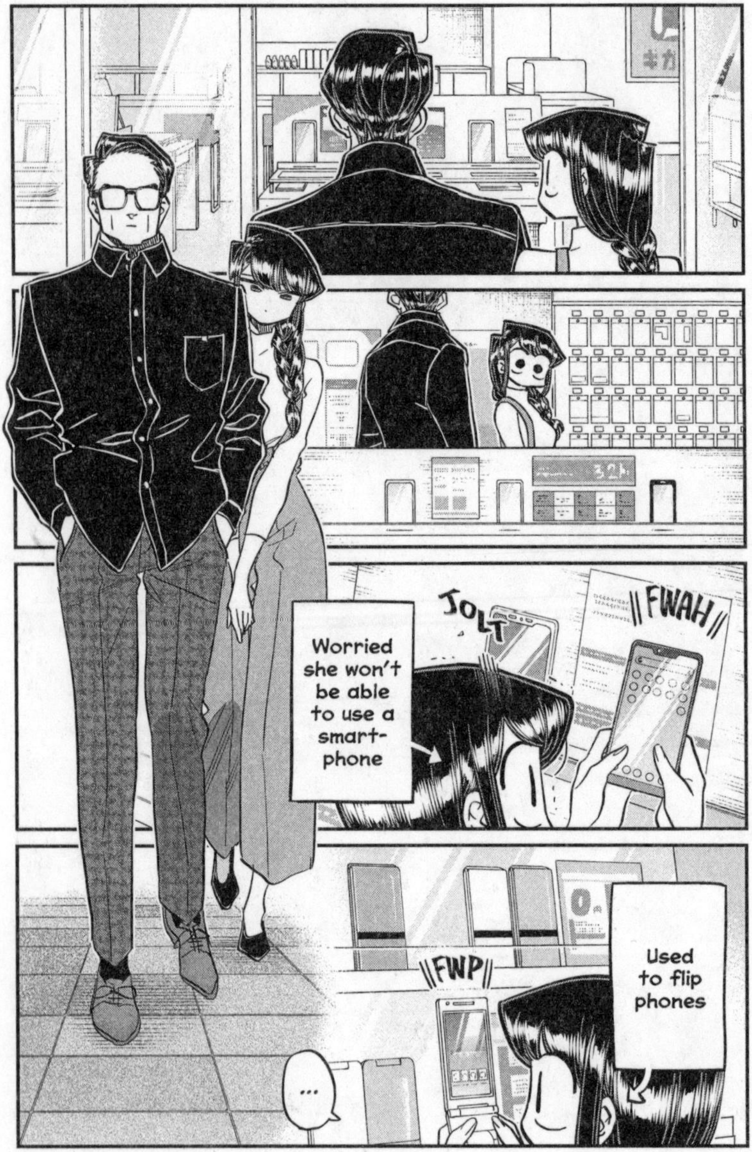
JOLT
FWAH
Worried she won't be able to use a smartphone
FWP
Used to flip phones
...

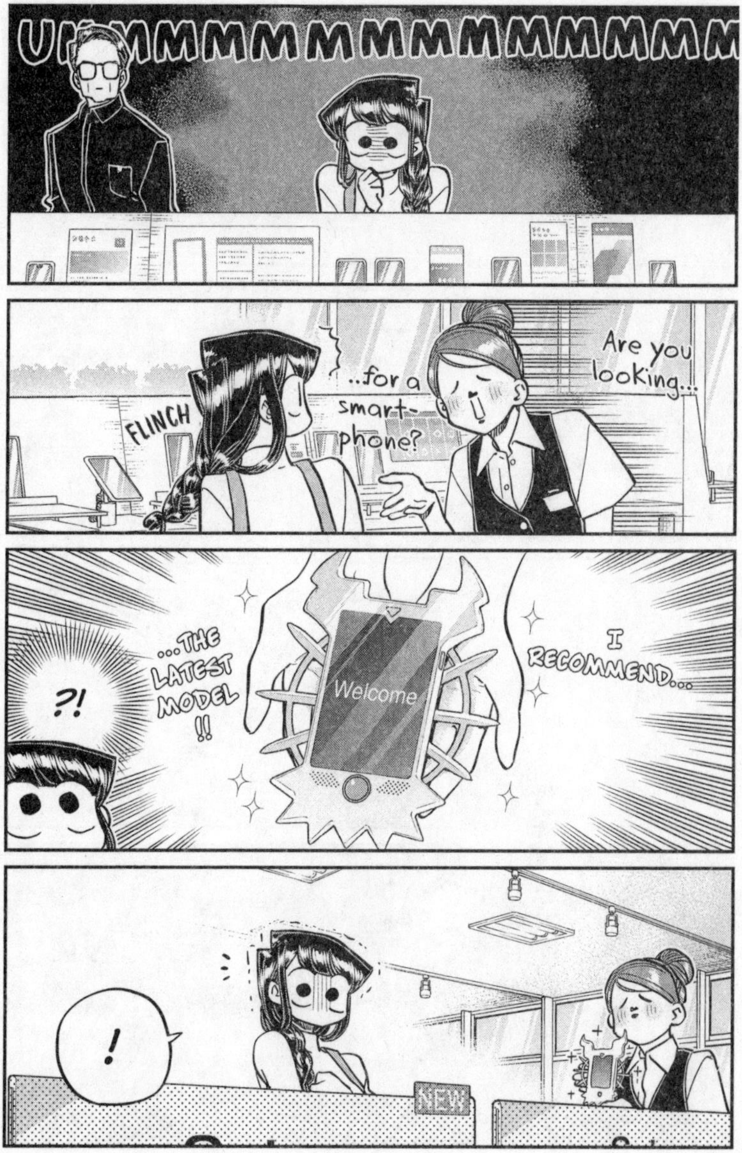
UMMMMMMMMMMMMMMMMM
Are you looking...
...for a smart-phone?
FLINCH
I RECOMMEND...
...THE LATEST MODEL!!
Welcome
?!
NEW
!

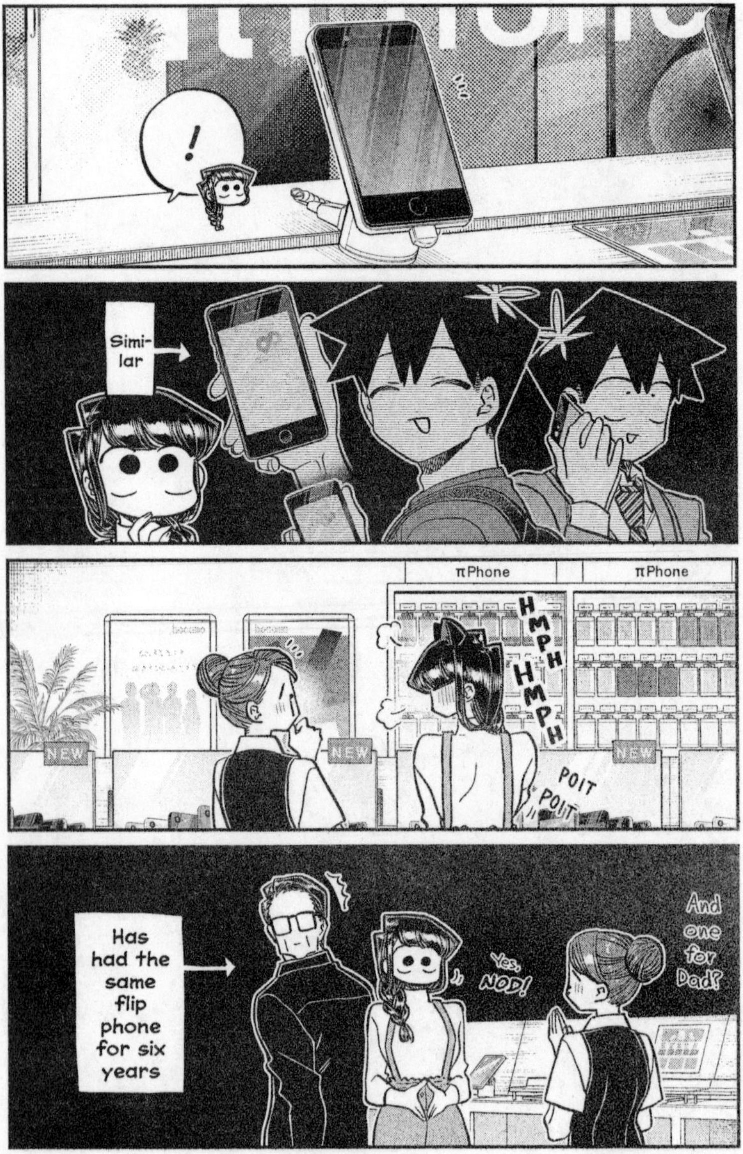
!
Similar
πPhone
πPhone
HMPH HMPH
NEW
POIT POIT
NEW
NEW
And one for Dad?
Yes. NOD!
Has had the same flip phone for six years

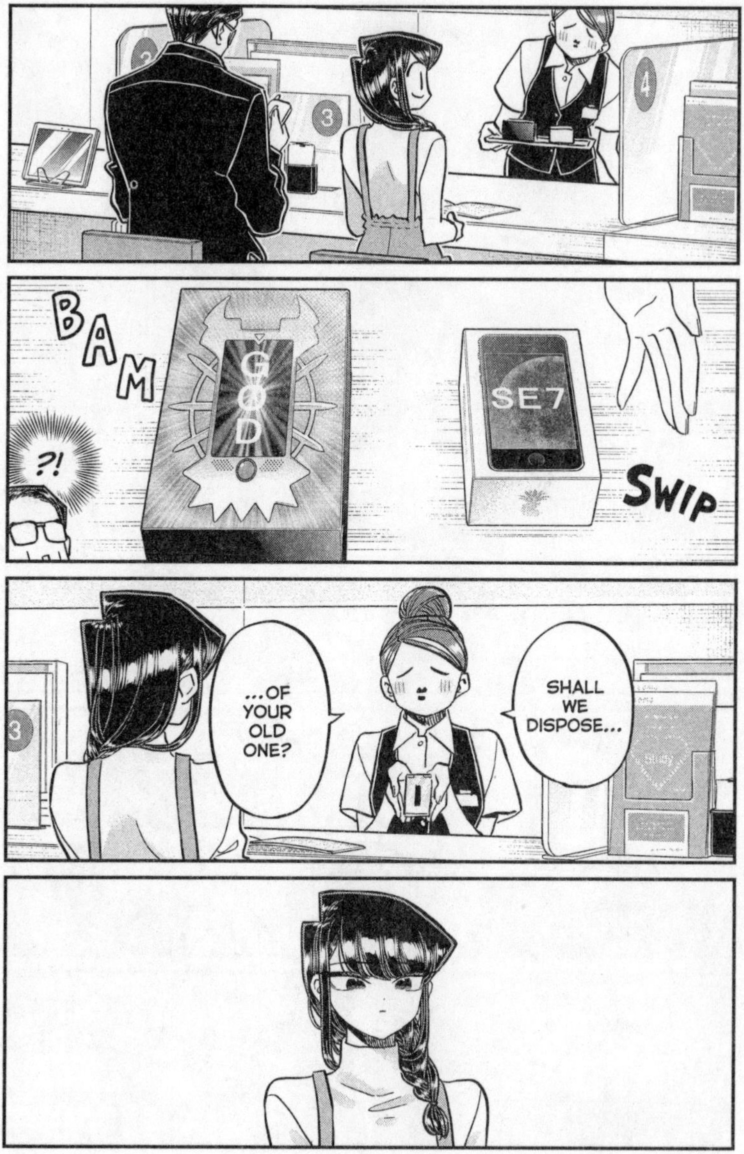
SE7
SWIP
GOD
BAM
?!
SHALL WE DISPOSE...
...OF YOUR OLD ONE?

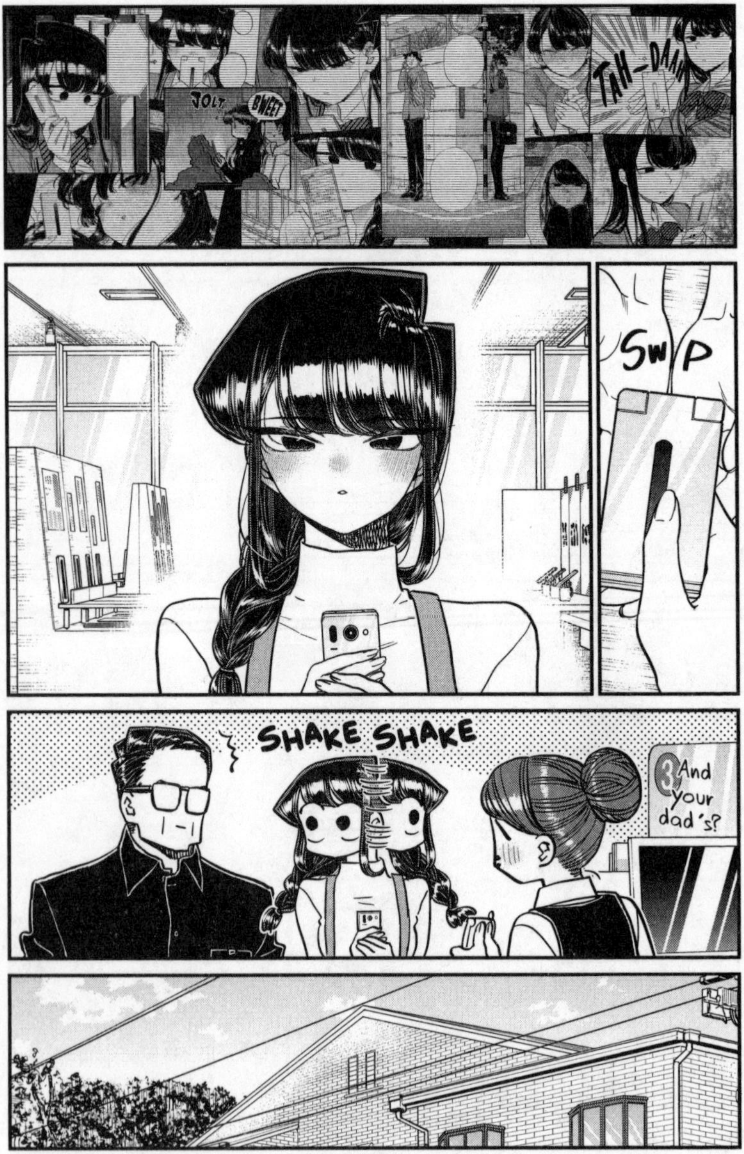
TAH-DAAH
JOLT
BWEET
SW P
3 And your dad's?
SHAKE SHAKE

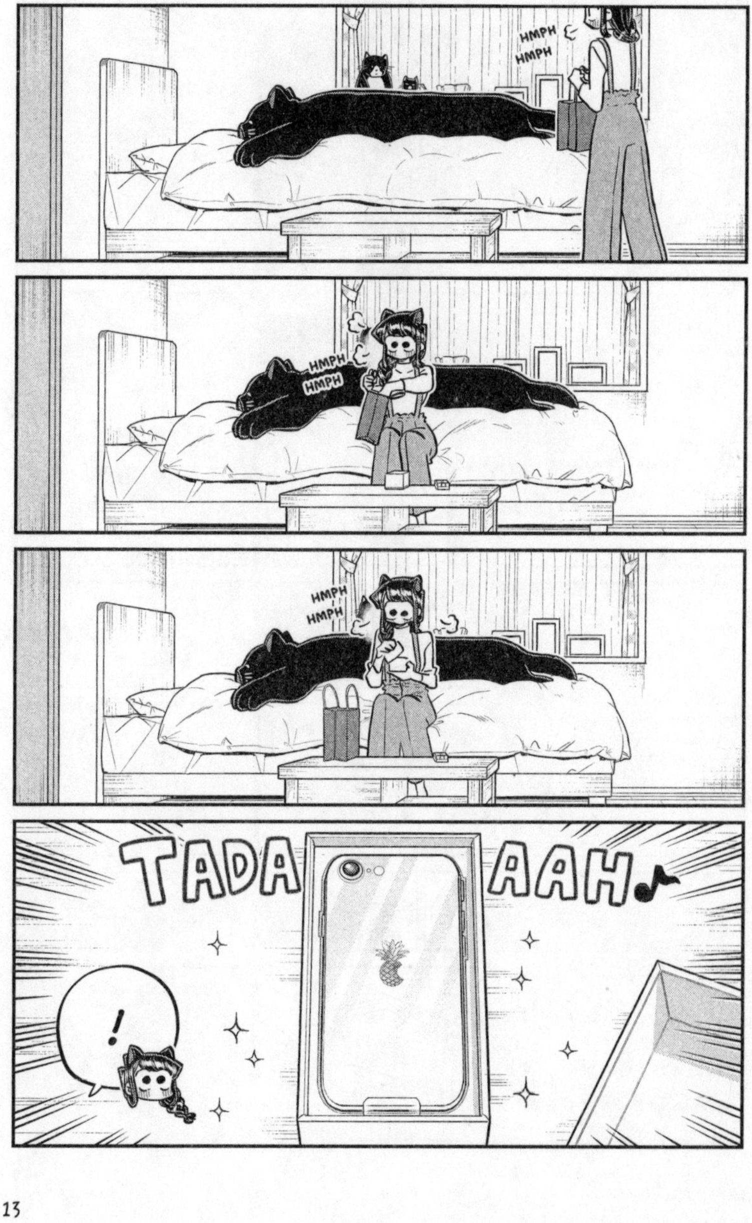
HMPH
HMPH
HMPH
HMPH
HMPH
HMPH
TADA
AAH♪
!

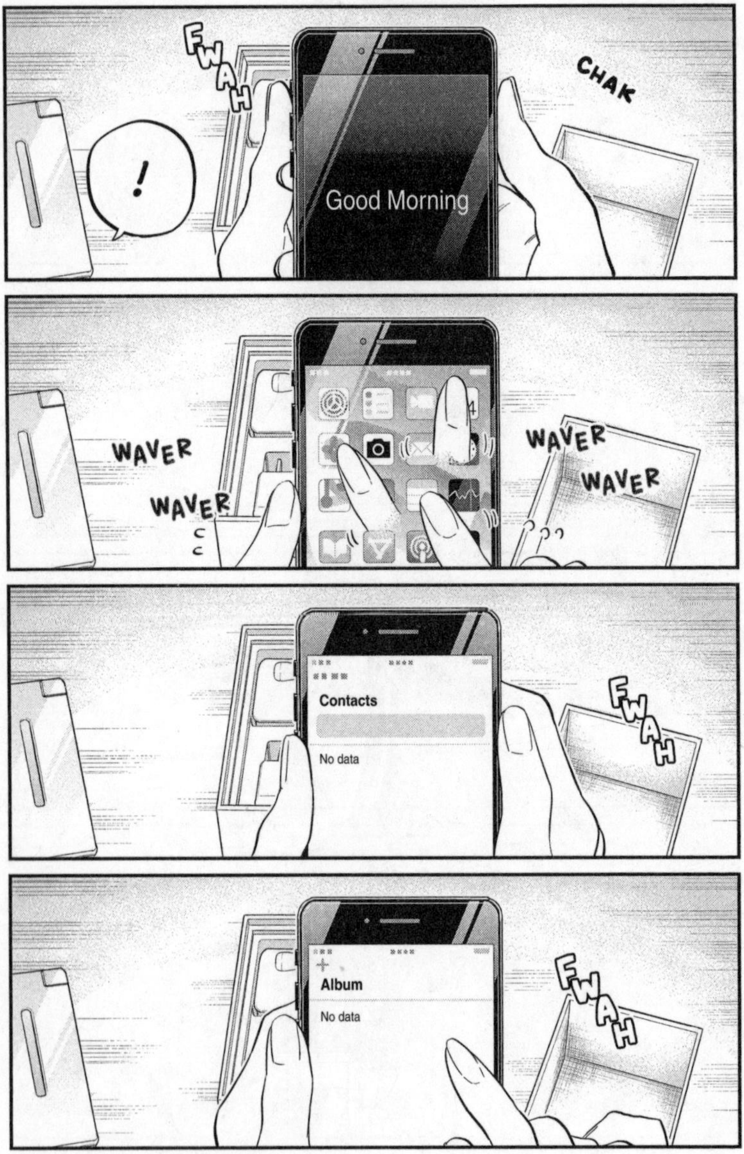
CHAK
FWAH
Good Morning
!
WAVER
WAVER
WAVER
WAVER
FWAH
Contacts
No data
FWAH
Album
No data

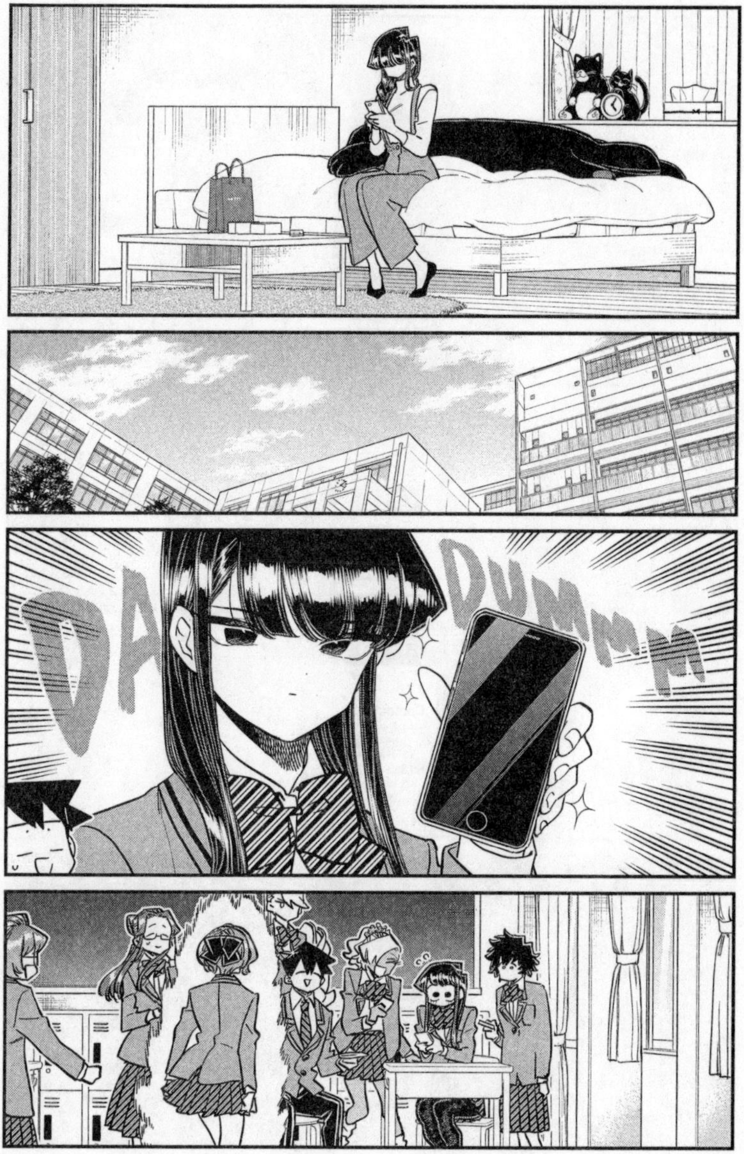
DADUMMM

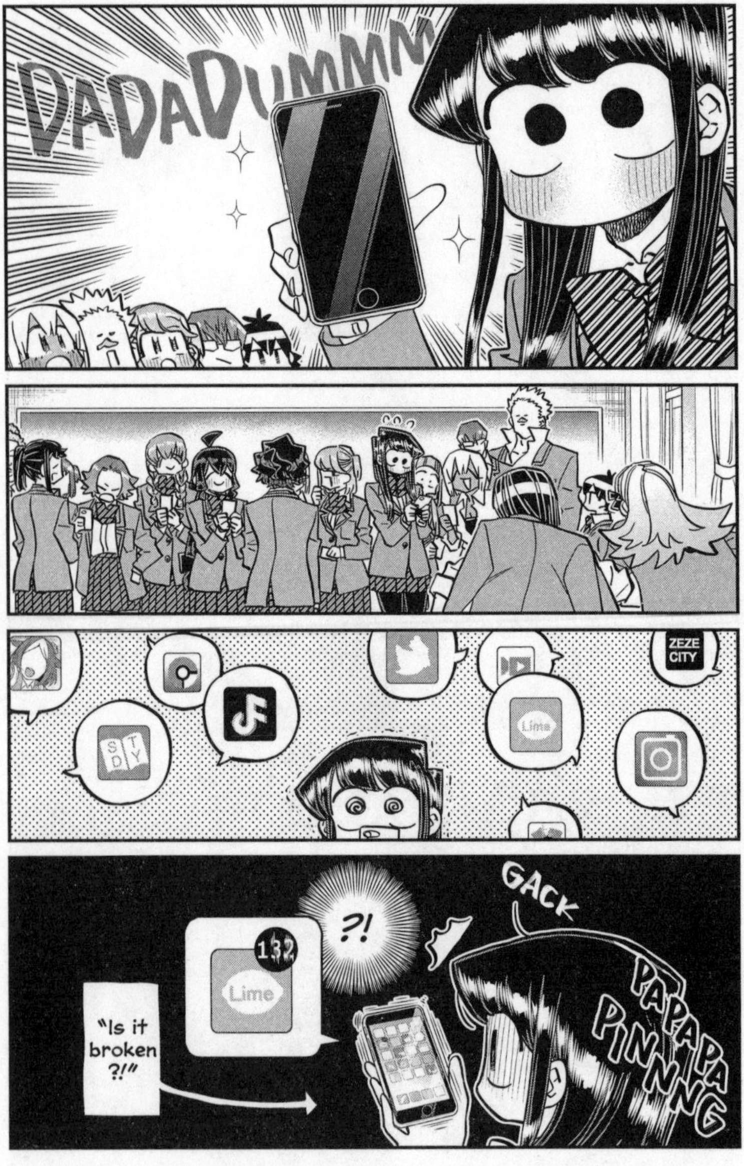
DADADUMMM
ZEZE CITY
Lime
GACK
PAPAPA PINNNG
?!
132
Lime
"Is it broken ?!"

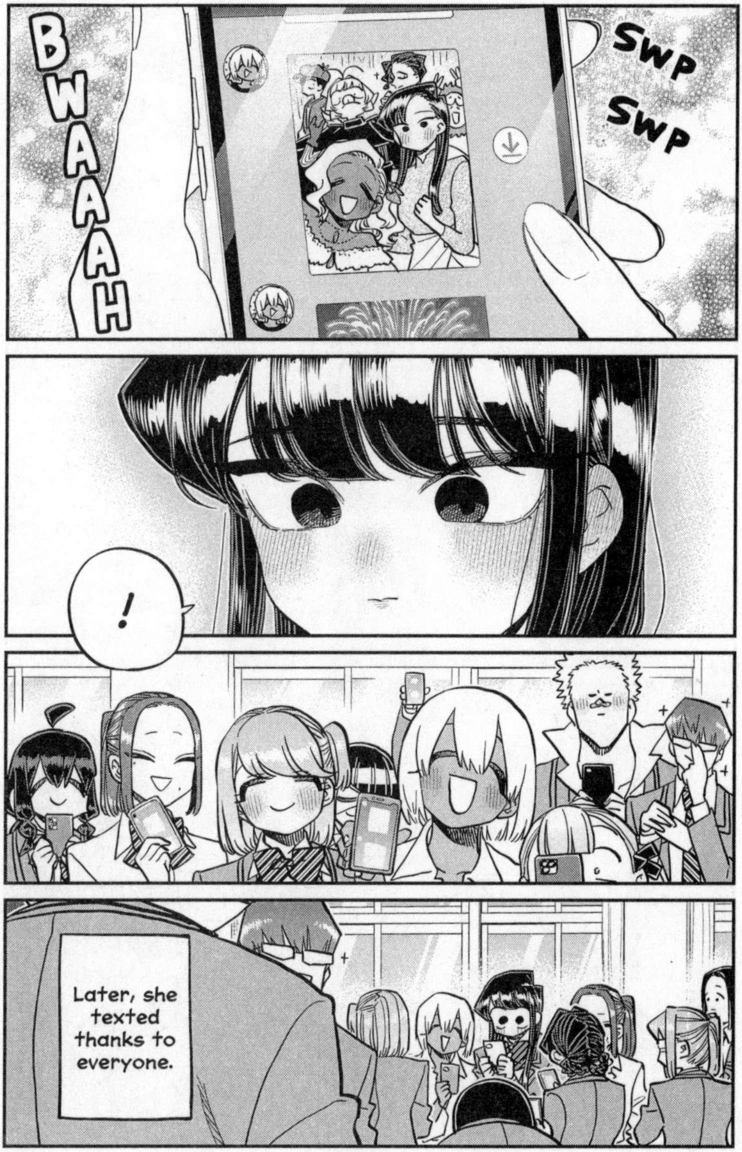
SWP
SWP
BWAAAH
!
Later, she texted thanks to everyone.

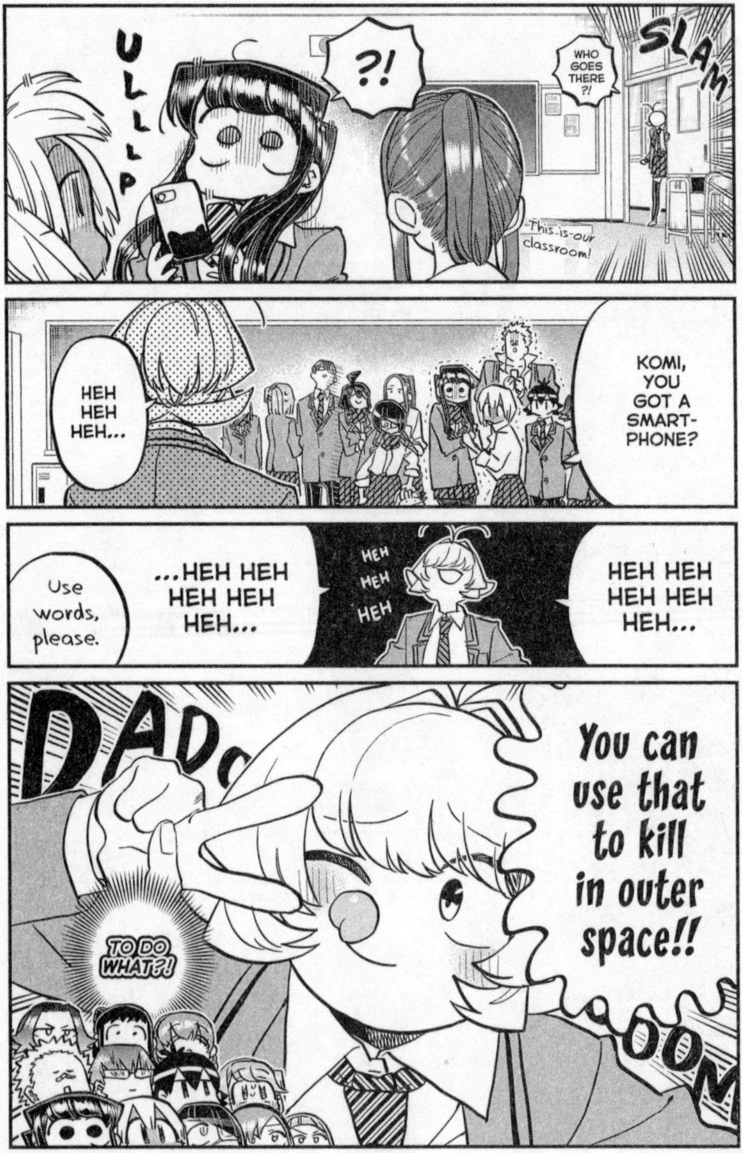
SLAM
WHO GOES THERE ?!
This-is-our classroom!
?!
ULLLP
KOMI, YOU GOT A SMARTPHONE?
HEH HEH HEH...
HEH HEH HEH HEH HEH...
HEH HEH HEH
...HEH HEH HEH HEH HEH...
Use words, please.
You can use that to kill in outer space!!
DADOOOM
TO DO WHAT?!

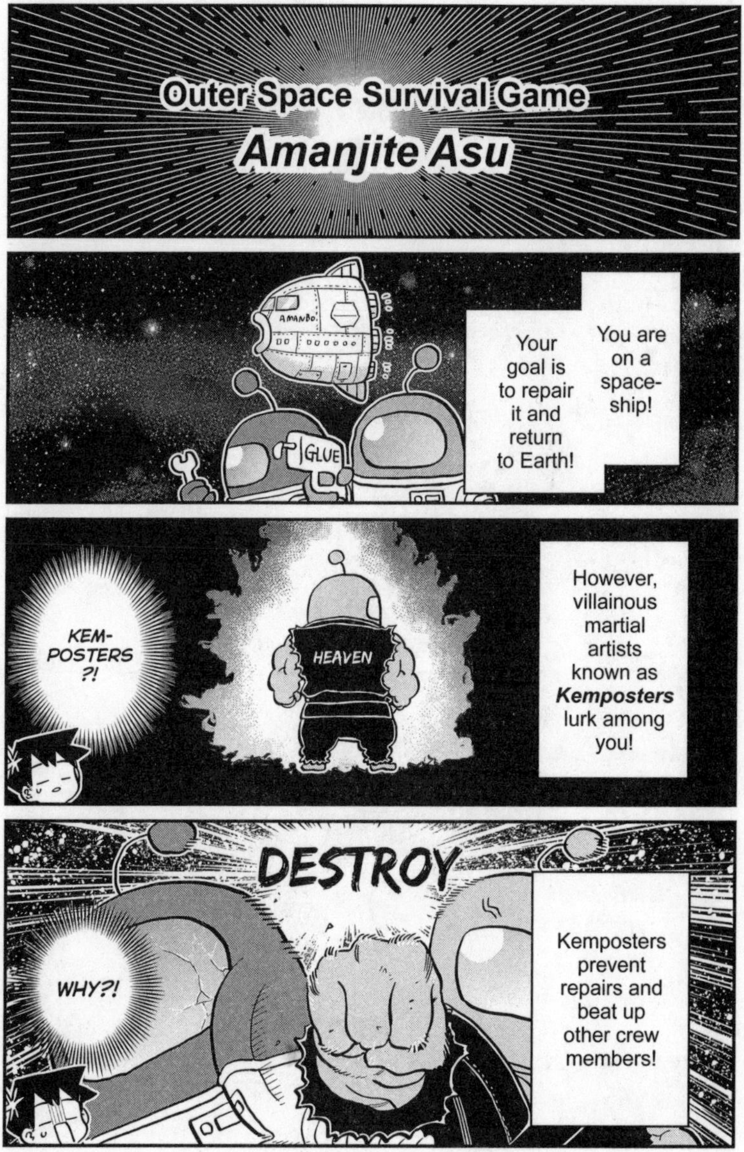
Outer Space Survival Game
Amanjite Asu
AMANBO
GLUE
You are on a spaceship!
Your goal is to repair it and return to Earth!
However, villainous martial artists known as ***Kemposters*** lurk among you!
HEAVEN
KEM-POSTERS?!
Kemposters prevent repairs and beat up other crew members!
DESTROY
WHY?!

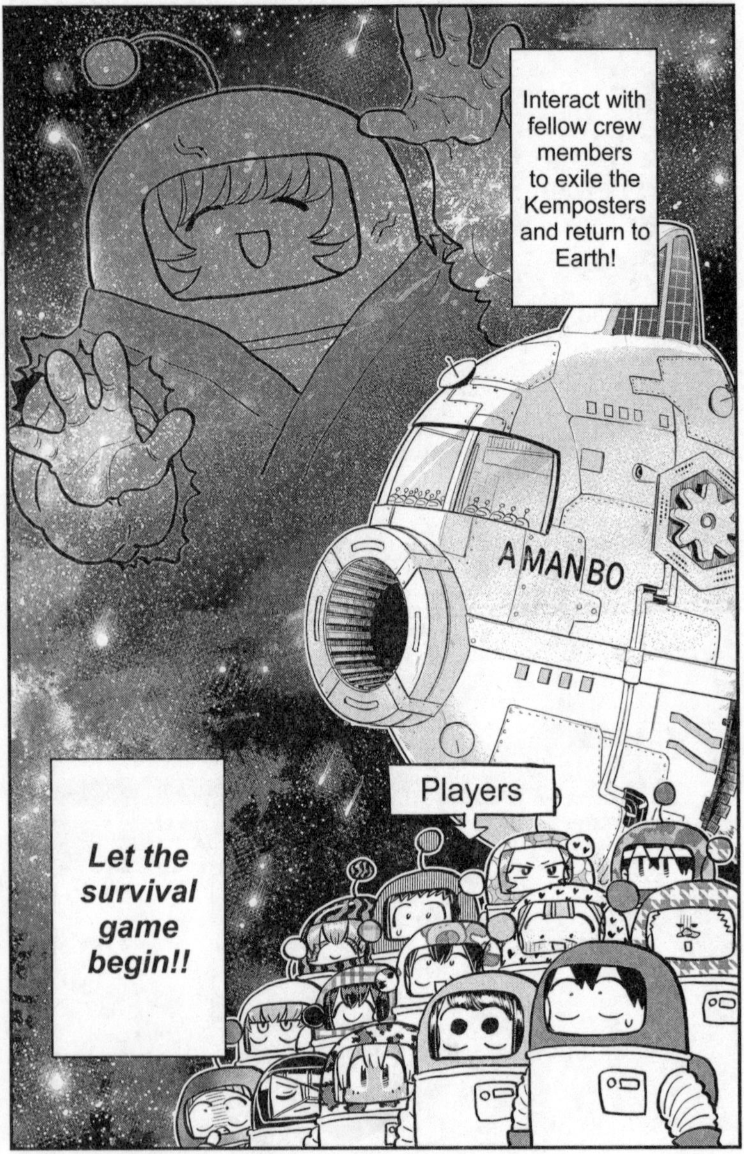
Interact with fellow crew members to exile the Kemposters and return to Earth!
AMANBO
Players
Let the survival game begin!!

Communication 350 — The End

A
surprisingly
comfy
grip

Komi Can't Communicate

Komi Can't Communicate

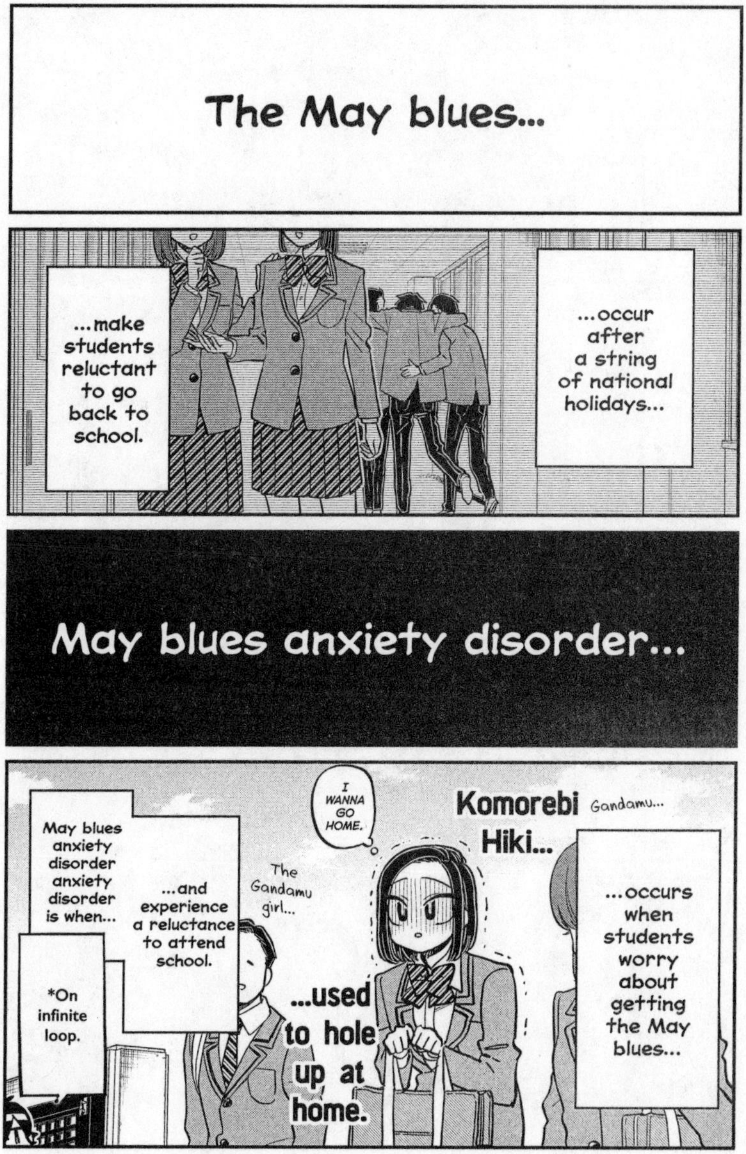

The May blues...
...occur after a string of national holidays...
...make students reluctant to go back to school.
May blues anxiety disorder...
...occurs when students worry about getting the May blues...
Gandamu...
Komorebi Hiki...
I WANNA GO HOME.
...used to hole up at home.
The Gandamu girl...
...and experience a reluctance to attend school.
May blues anxiety disorder anxiety disorder is when...
*On infinite loop.

Communication 351: Mountain-Stream Fishing

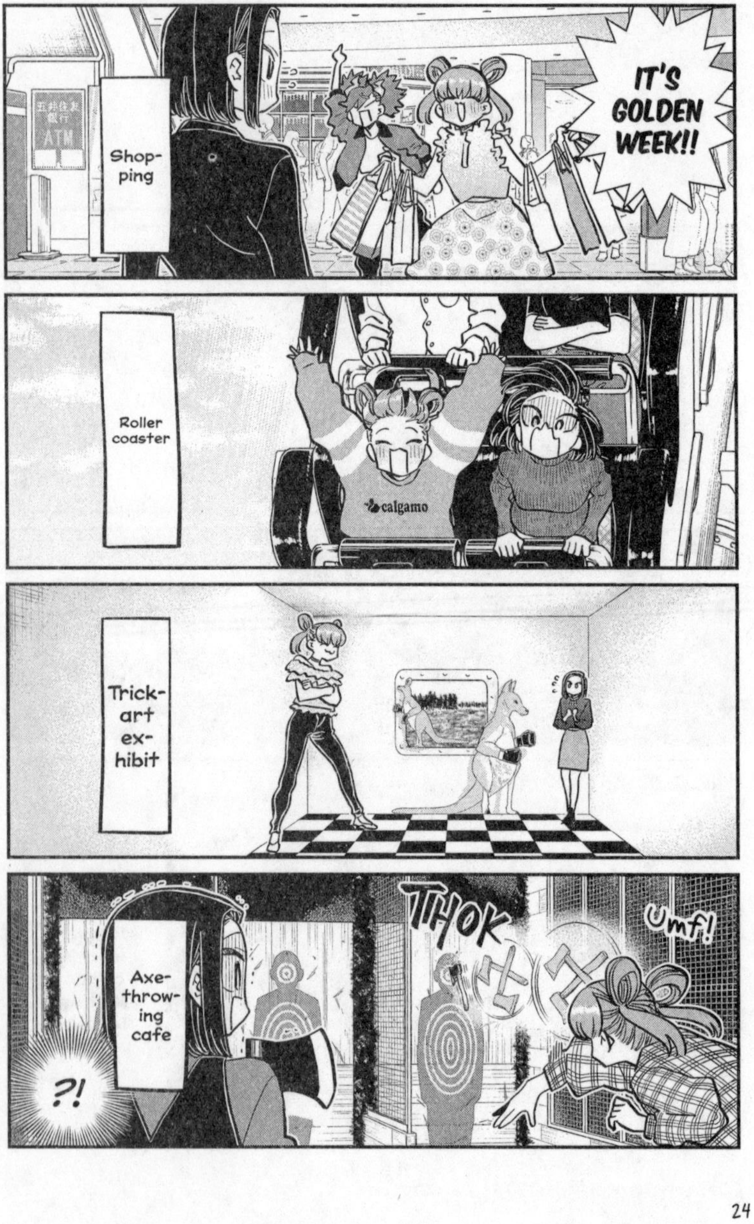
IT'S GOLDEN WEEK!!
Shop-ping
Roller coaster
calgamo
Trick-art ex-hibit
Umf!
THOK
Axe-throw-ing cafe
?!

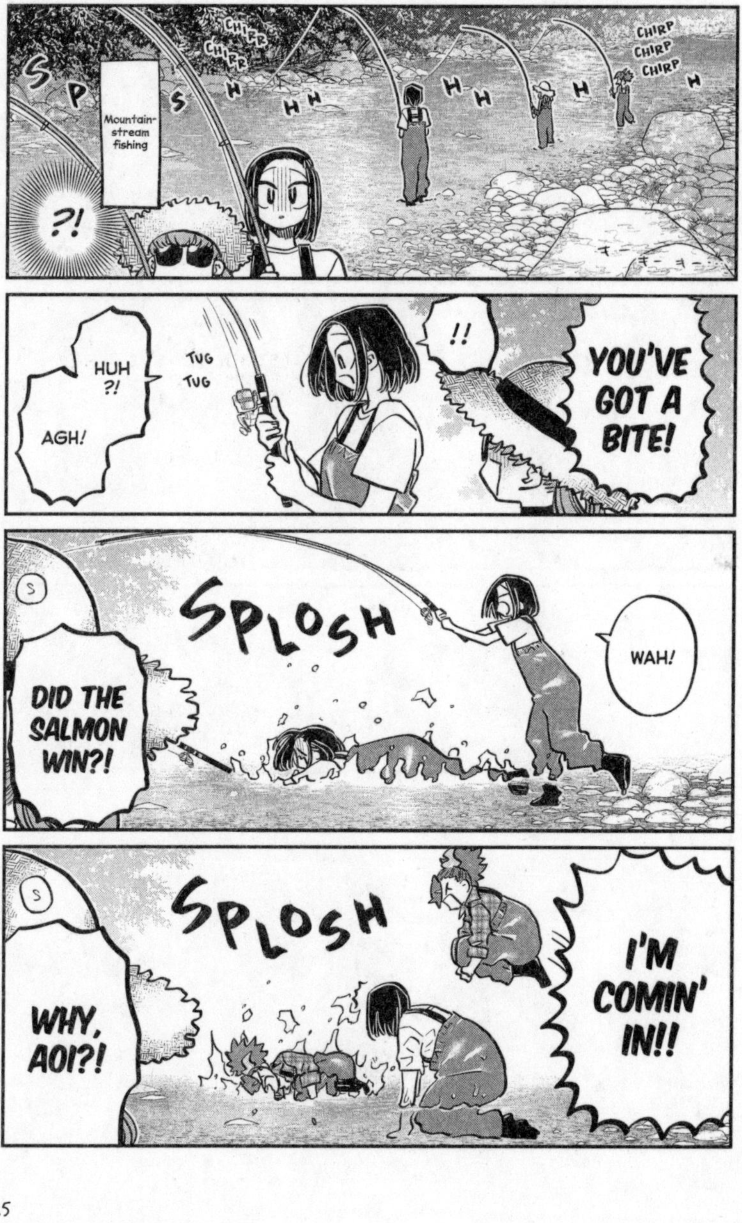
CHIRP
CHIRP
CHIRP
CHIRR
CHIRR
SPSHHHHHHH
Mountain-stream fishing
?!
!!
YOU'VE GOT A BITE!
TUG
TUG
HUH ?!
AGH!
WAH!
SPLOSH
S
DID THE SALMON WIN?!
I'M COMIN' IN!!
SPLOSH
S
WHY, AOI?!

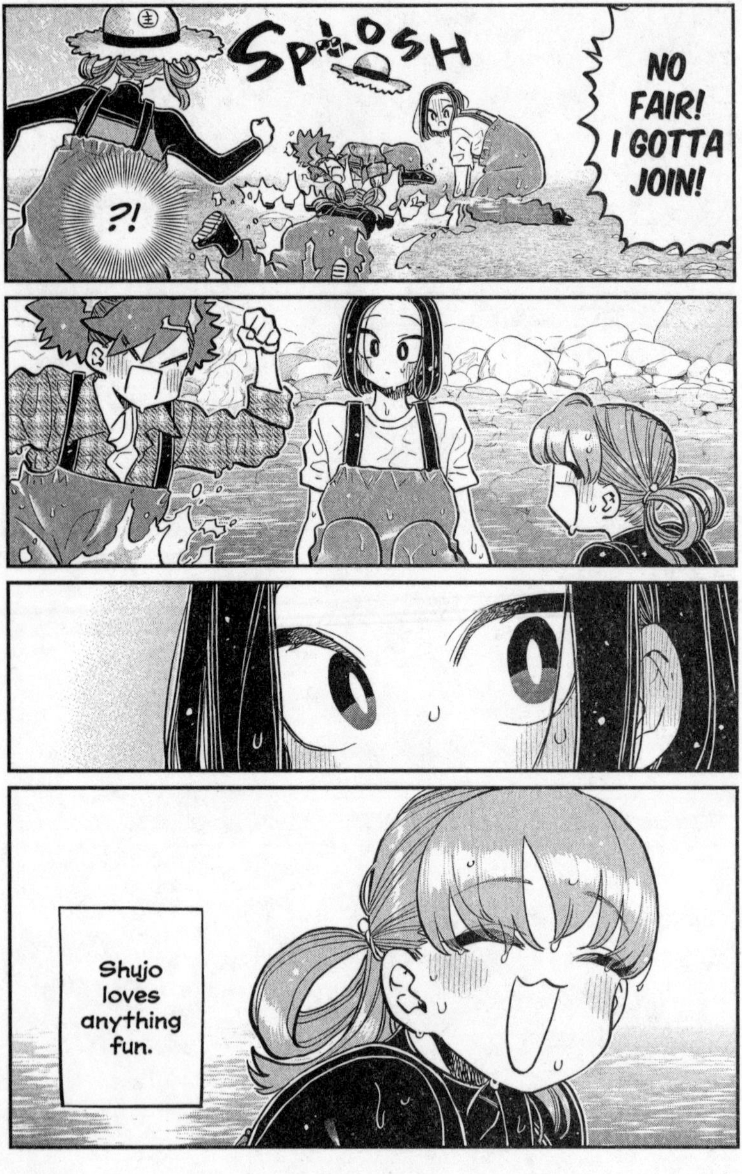
NO FAIR! I GOTTA JOIN!
SPLOSH
?!
Shujo loves anything fun.

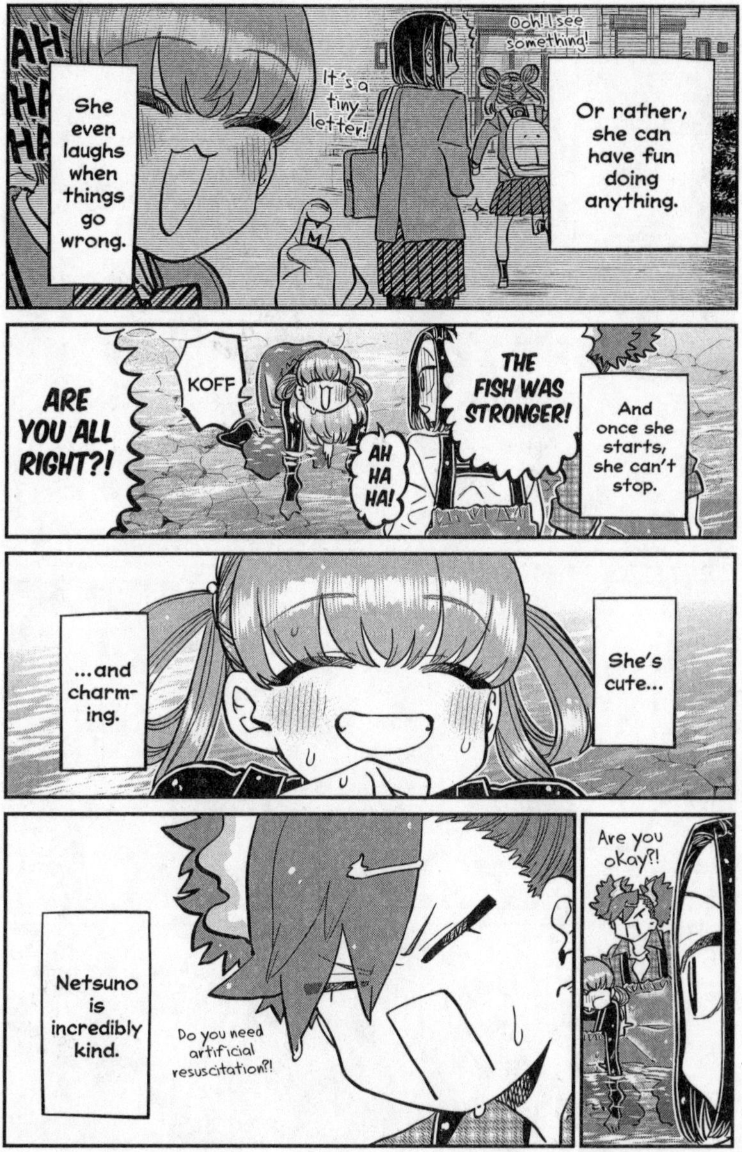
Ooh! I see something!
Or rather, she can have fun doing anything.
It's a tiny letter!
She even laughs when things go wrong.
AH HA HA
And once she starts, she can't stop.
THE FISH WAS STRONGER!
AH HA HA!
KOFF
ARE YOU ALL RIGHT?!
She's cute...
...and charming.
Are you okay?!
Do you need artificial resuscitation?!
Netsuno is incredibly kind.

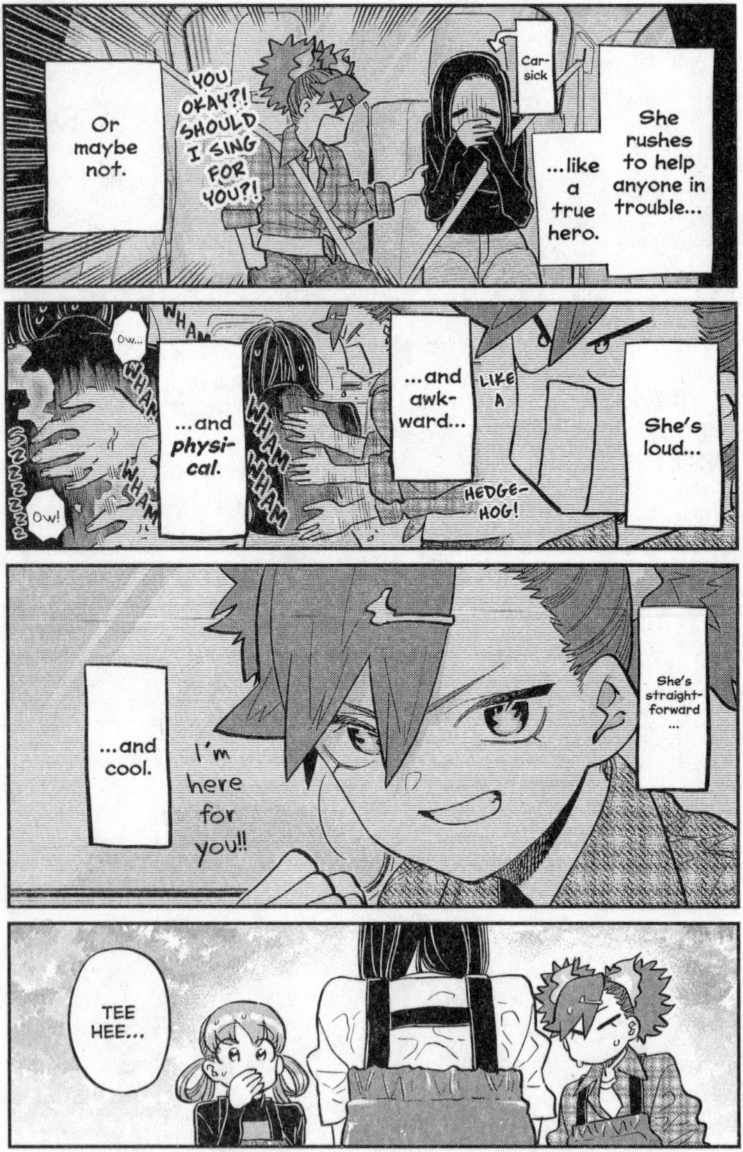
She rushes to help anyone in trouble...
...like a true hero.
Car-sick
YOU OKAY?! SHOULD I SING FOR YOU?!
Or maybe not.
She's loud...
LIKE A HEDGEHOG!
...and awkward...
WHAM WHAM
...and *physical*.
Ow...
WHAM
WHAM
WHAM
Ow!
ZZZZZZZ
She's straightforward...
I'm here for you!!
...and cool.
TEE HEE...

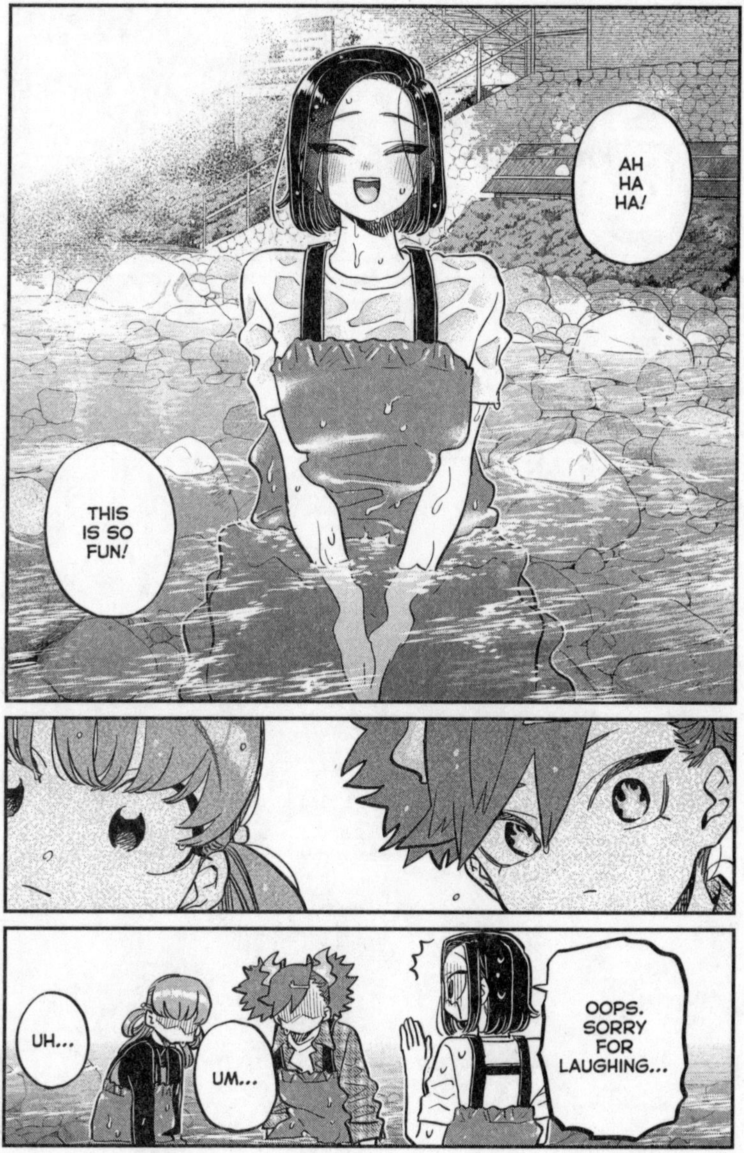
AH HA HA!
THIS IS SO FUN!
OOPS. SORRY FOR LAUGHING...
UM...
UH...

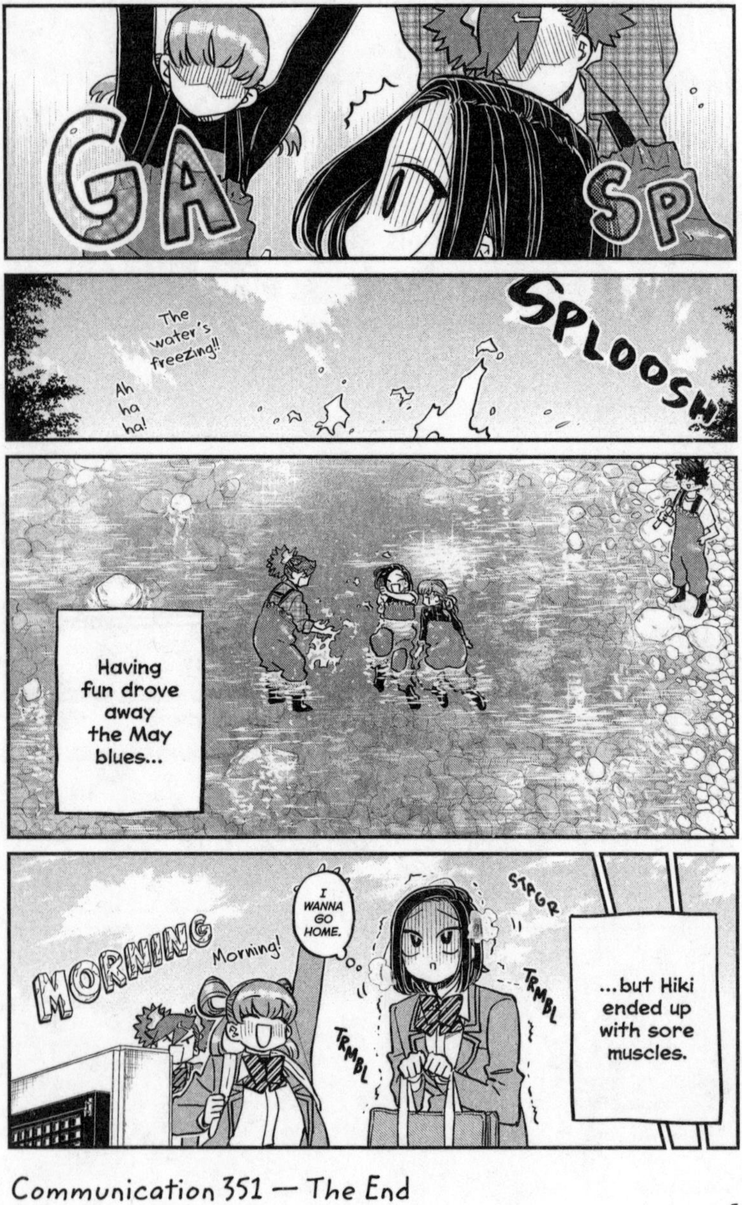
GASP
SPLOOSH
The water's freezing!!
Ah ha ha!
Having fun drove away the May blues...
...but Hiki ended up with sore muscles.
STAGR
TRMBL
I WANNA GO HOME.
Morning!
MORNING
TRMBL

Communication 351 — The End

Komi Can't Communicate

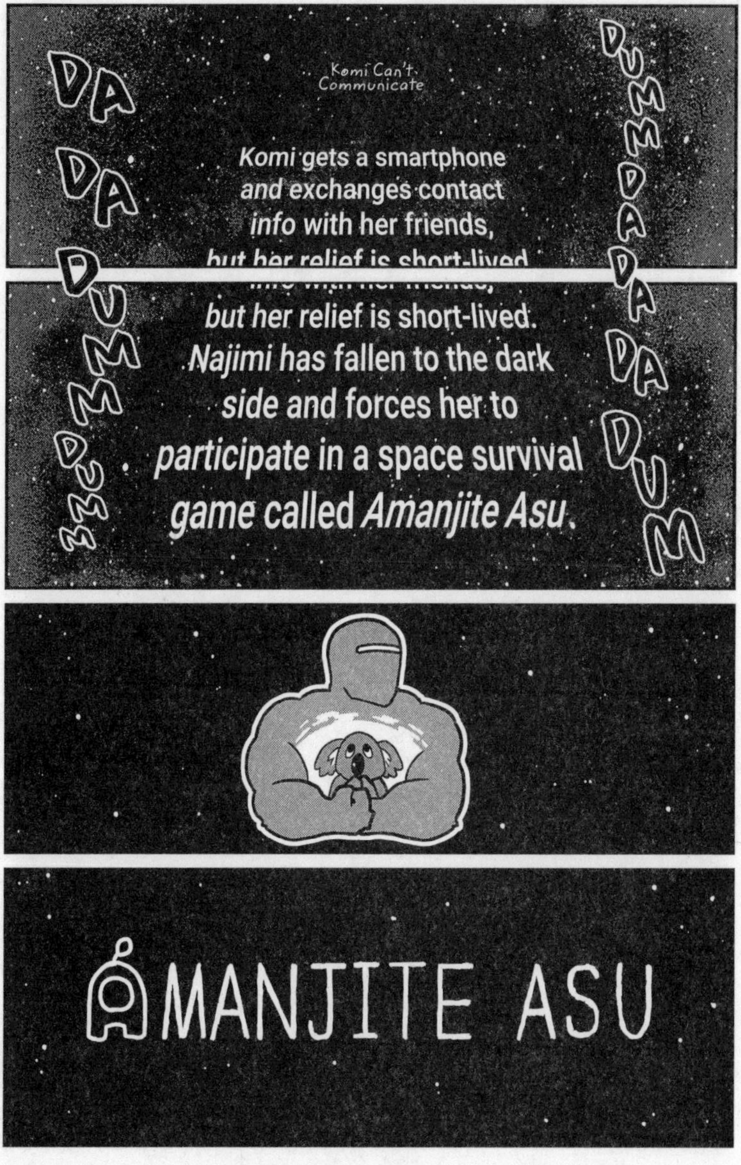
DUMMM DA DA DA DUM
DA DA DUMMM DUMMM
Komi Can't Communicate
Komi gets a smartphone and exchanges contact info with her friends, but her relief is short-lived. Najimi has fallen to the dark side and forces her to participate in a space survival game called Amanjite Asu.
AMANJITE ASU

Communication 352: The Players

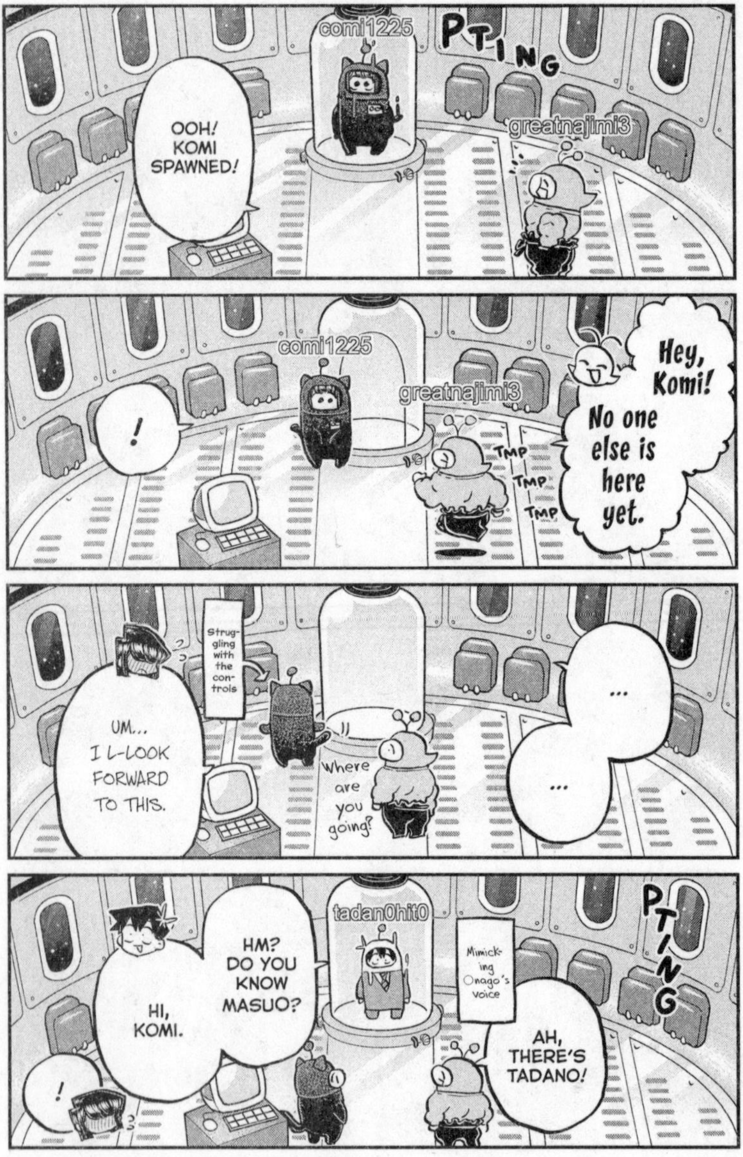
PTING
comi1225
greatnajimi3
OOH! KOMI SPAWNED!
Hey, Komi!
No one else is here yet.
TMP TMP TMP
greatnajimi3
comi1225
!
...
...
Where are you going?
Strug-gling with the con-trols
UM... I L-LOOK FORWARD TO THIS.
PTING
Mimick-ing Onago's voice
AH, THERE'S TADANO!
tadan0hit0
HM? DO YOU KNOW MASUO?
HI, KOMI.
!

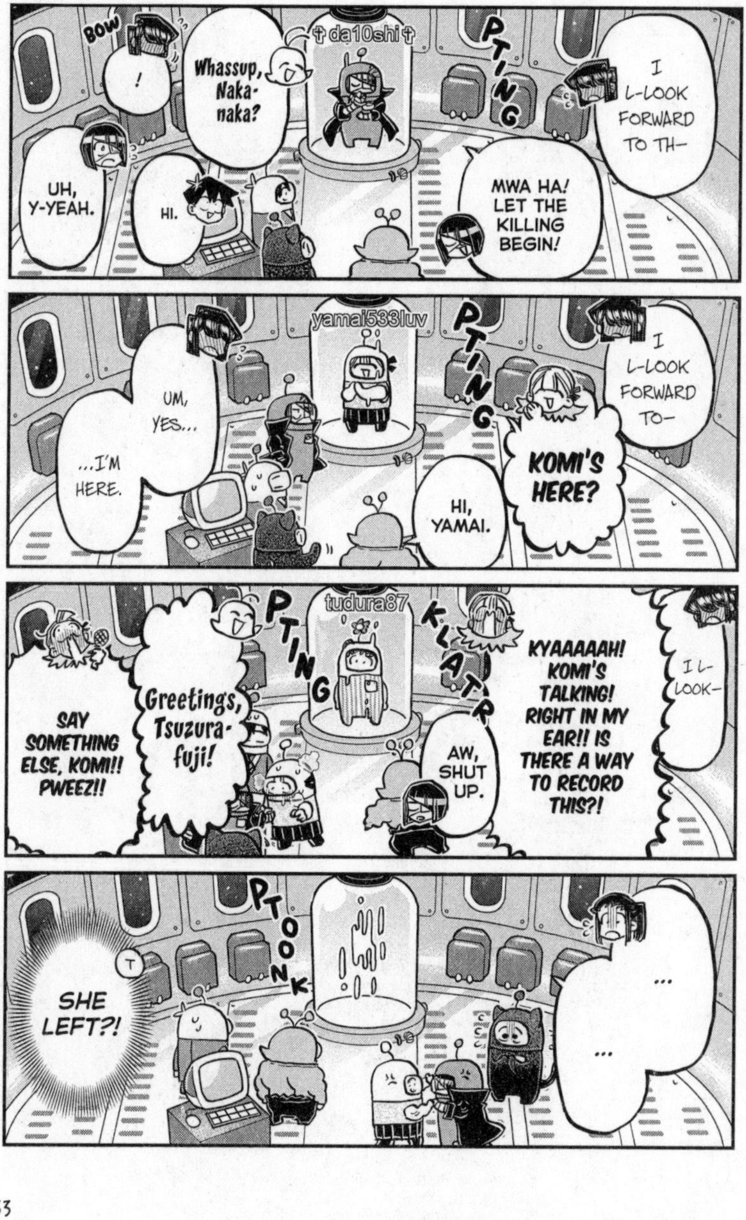
I L-LOOK FORWARD TO TH—
PTING
MWA HA! LET THE KILLING BEGIN!
†da10shi†
Whassup, Naka-naka?
BOW
!
HI.
UH, Y-YEAH.
I L-LOOK FORWARD TO—
PTING
yamai533luv
KOMI'S HERE?
HI, YAMAI.
UM, YES...
...I'M HERE.
I L-LOOK—
KYAAAAAH! KOMI'S TALKING! RIGHT IN MY EAR!! IS THERE A WAY TO RECORD THIS?!
KLATR
tudura87
PTING
AW, SHUT UP.
Greetings, Tsuzura-fuji!
SAY SOMETHING ELSE, KOMI!! PWEEZ!!
...
...
PTOONK
T
SHE LEFT?!

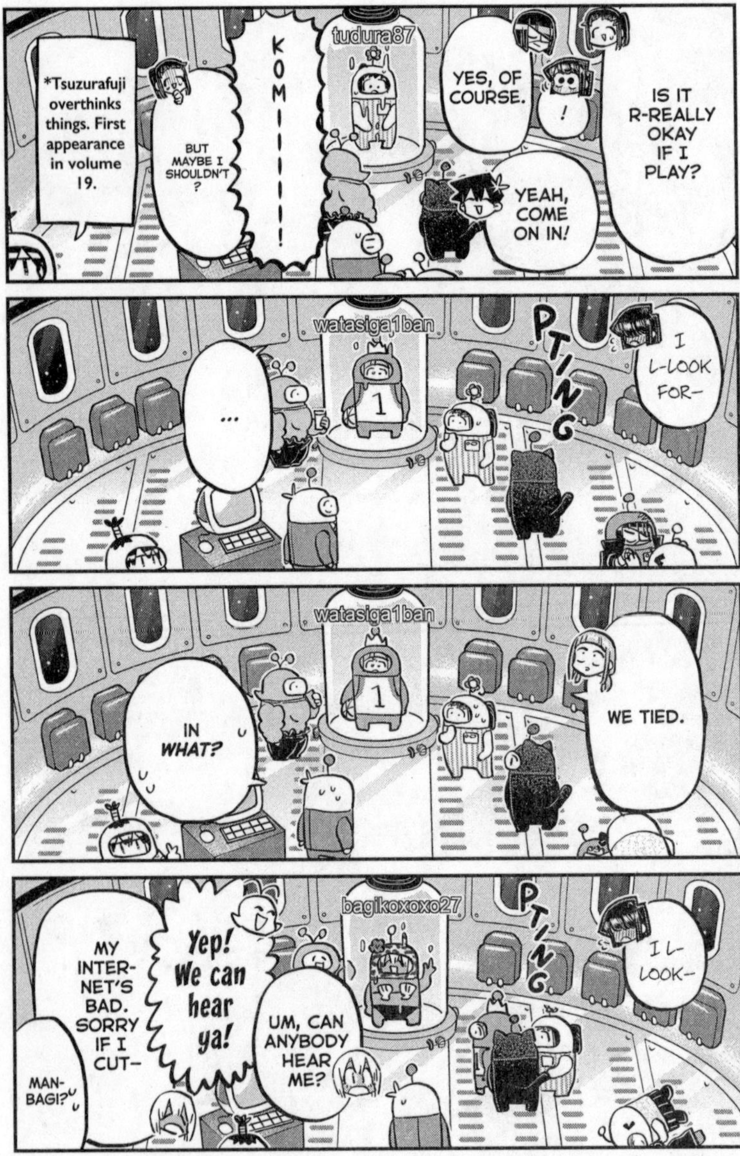
IS IT R-REALLY OKAY IF I PLAY?
!
YES, OF COURSE.
YEAH, COME ON IN!
tudura87
KOMI---!
BUT MAYBE I SHOULDN'T?
*Tsuzurafuji overthinks things. First appearance in volume 19.
I L-LOOK FOR-
PTING
watasiga1ban
...
WE TIED.
watasiga1ban
IN WHAT?
I L-LOOK-
PTING
bagikoxoxo27
UM, CAN ANYBODY HEAR ME?
Yep! We can hear ya!
MY INTERNET'S BAD. SORRY IF I CUT-
MANBAGI?

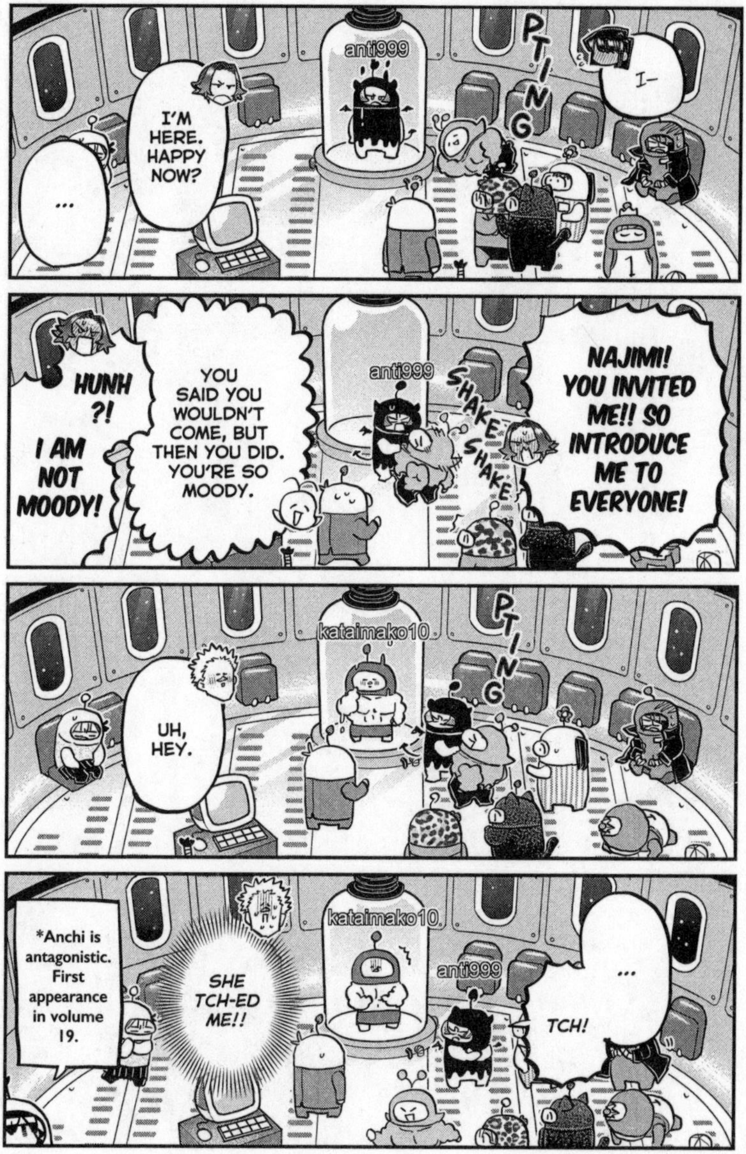
I–
PTING
anti999
I'M HERE. HAPPY NOW?
...
NAJIMI! YOU INVITED ME!! SO INTRODUCE ME TO EVERYONE!
SHAKE SHAKE
anti999
YOU SAID YOU WOULDN'T COME, BUT THEN YOU DID. YOU'RE SO MOODY.
HUNH ?! I AM NOT MOODY!
PTING
kataimako10
UH, HEY.
...
TCH!
anti999
kataimako10
SHE TCH-ED ME!!
*Anchi is antagonistic. First appearance in volume 19.

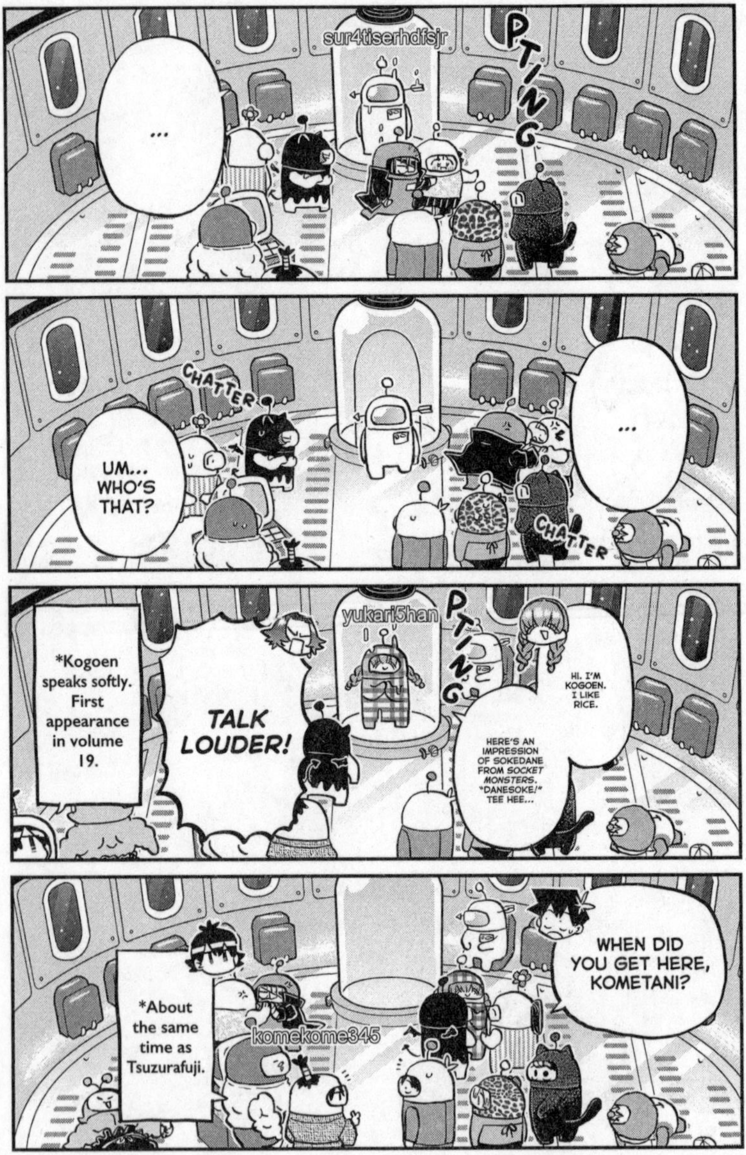
PTING
sur4tiserhdfsjr
...
...
CHATTER
CHATTER
UM... WHO'S THAT?
PTING
yukari5han
HI. I'M KOGOEN. I LIKE RICE.
HERE'S AN IMPRESSION OF SOKEDANE FROM SOCKET MONSTERS. "DANESOKE!" TEE HEE...
TALK LOUDER!
*Kogoen speaks softly. First appearance in volume 19.
WHEN DID YOU GET HERE, KOMETANI?
komekome345
*About the same time as Tsuzurafuji.

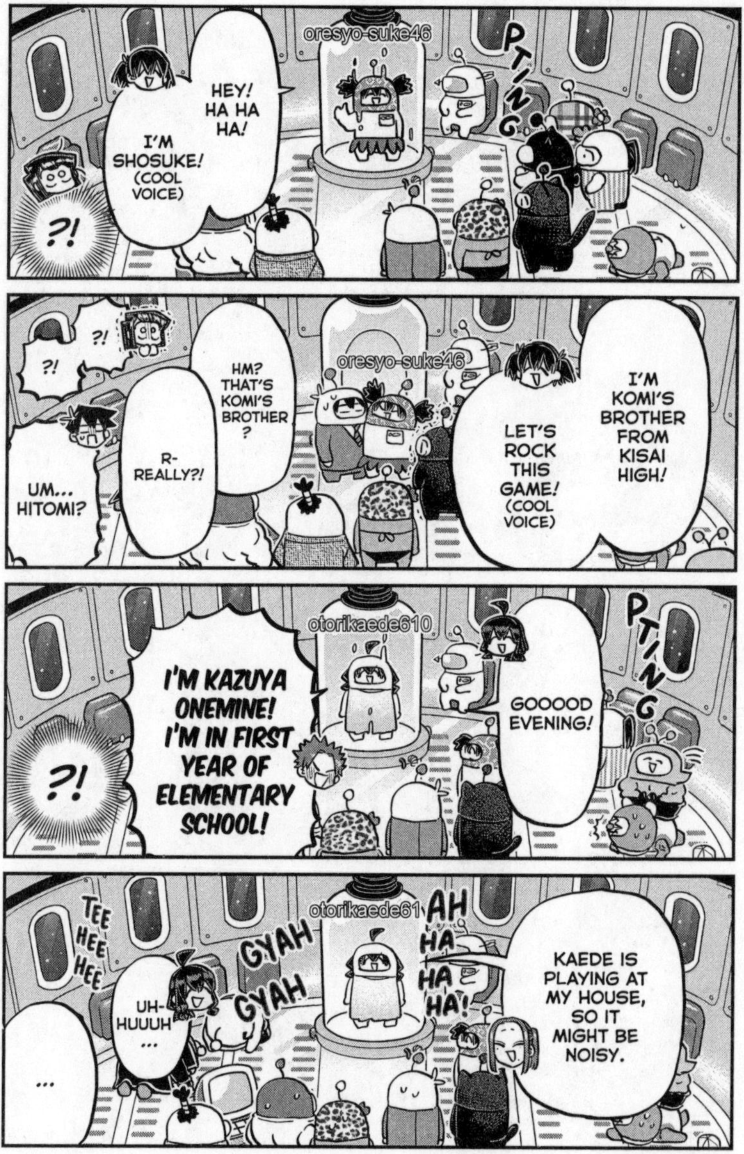
PTING
oresyo-suke46
HEY! HA HA HA!
I'M SHOSUKE! (COOL VOICE)
?!
I'M KOMI'S BROTHER FROM KISAI HIGH!
LET'S ROCK THIS GAME! (COOL VOICE)
oresyo-suke46
HM? THAT'S KOMI'S BROTHER?
R- REALLY?!
?!
?!
UM... HITOMI?
PTING
GOOOOD EVENING!
otorikaede610
I'M KAZUYA ONEMINE! I'M IN FIRST YEAR OF ELEMENTARY SCHOOL!
?!
KAEDE IS PLAYING AT MY HOUSE, SO IT MIGHT BE NOISY.
AH HA HA HA!
otorikaede61
GYAH GYAH
UH-HUUUH...
TEE HEE HEE
...

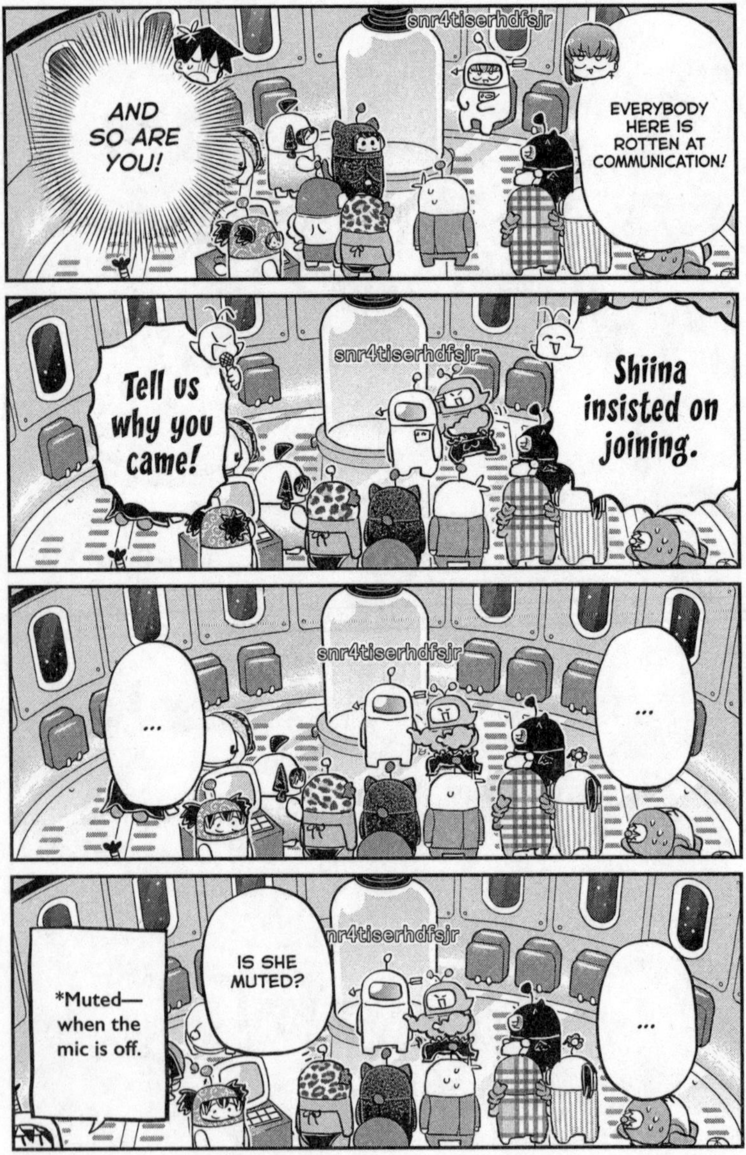
EVERYBODY HERE IS ROTTEN AT COMMUNICATION!
AND SO ARE YOU!
Shiina insisted on joining.
Tell us why you came!
...
...
...
IS SHE MUTED?
*Muted—when the mic is off.

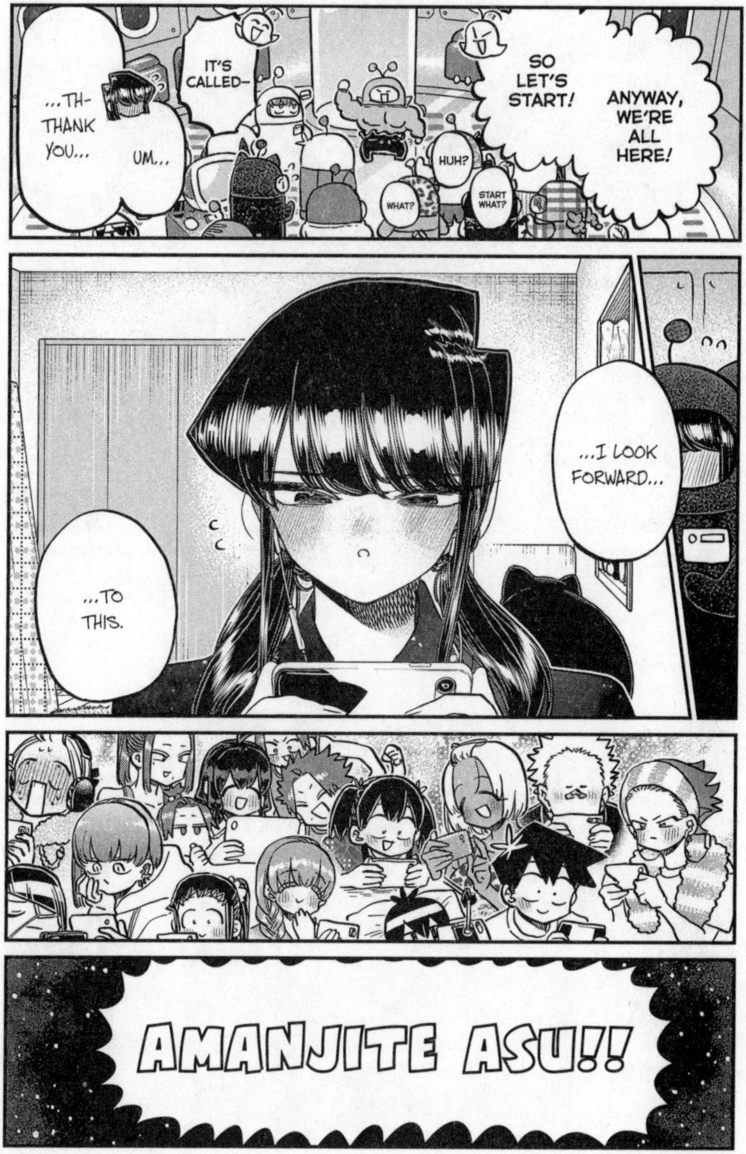
ANYWAY, WE'RE ALL HERE!
SO LET'S START!
START WHAT?
HUH?
WHAT?
IT'S CALLED—
UM...
...TH-THANK YOU...
...I LOOK FORWARD...
...TO THIS.
AMANJITE ASU!!

Communication 352 — The End

Communication 353: The First Casualty

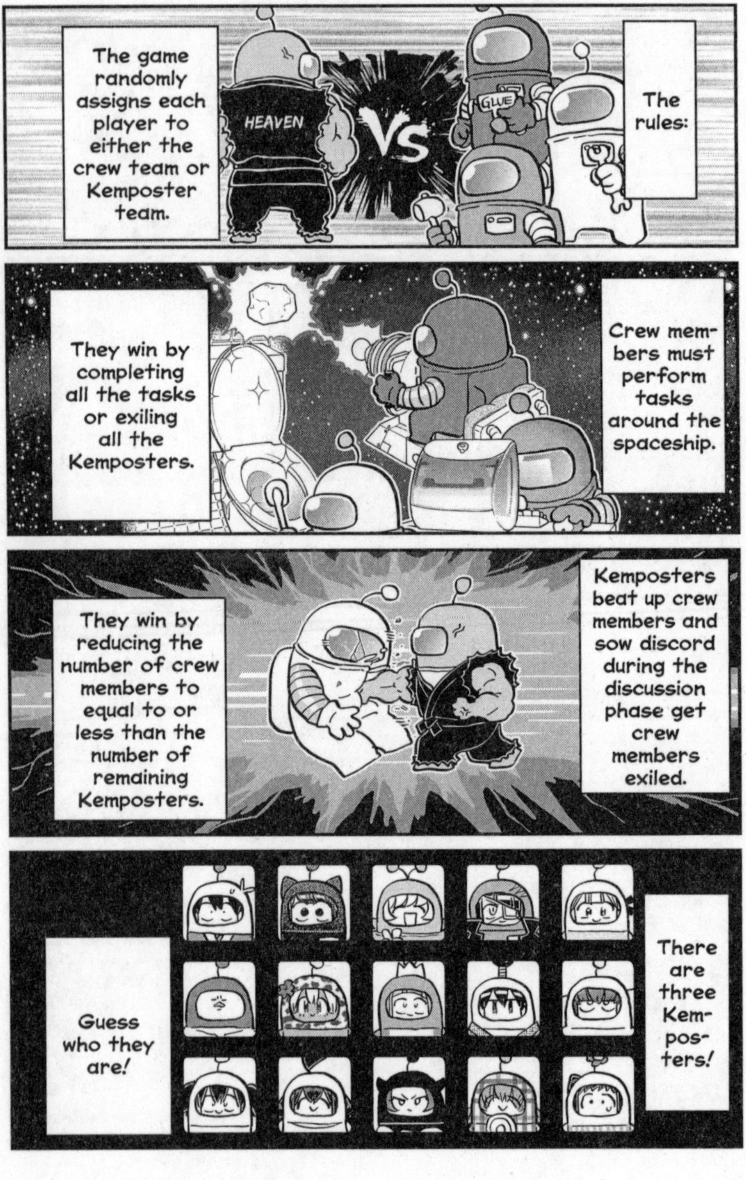
The rules:
GLUE
The game randomly assigns each player to either the crew team or Kemposter team.
HEAVEN
VS
Crew members must perform tasks around the spaceship.
They win by completing all the tasks or exiling all the Kemposters.
Kemposters beat up crew members and sow discord during the discussion phase get crew members exiled.
They win by reducing the number of crew members to equal to or less than the number of remaining Kemposters.
There are three Kemposters!
Guess who they are!

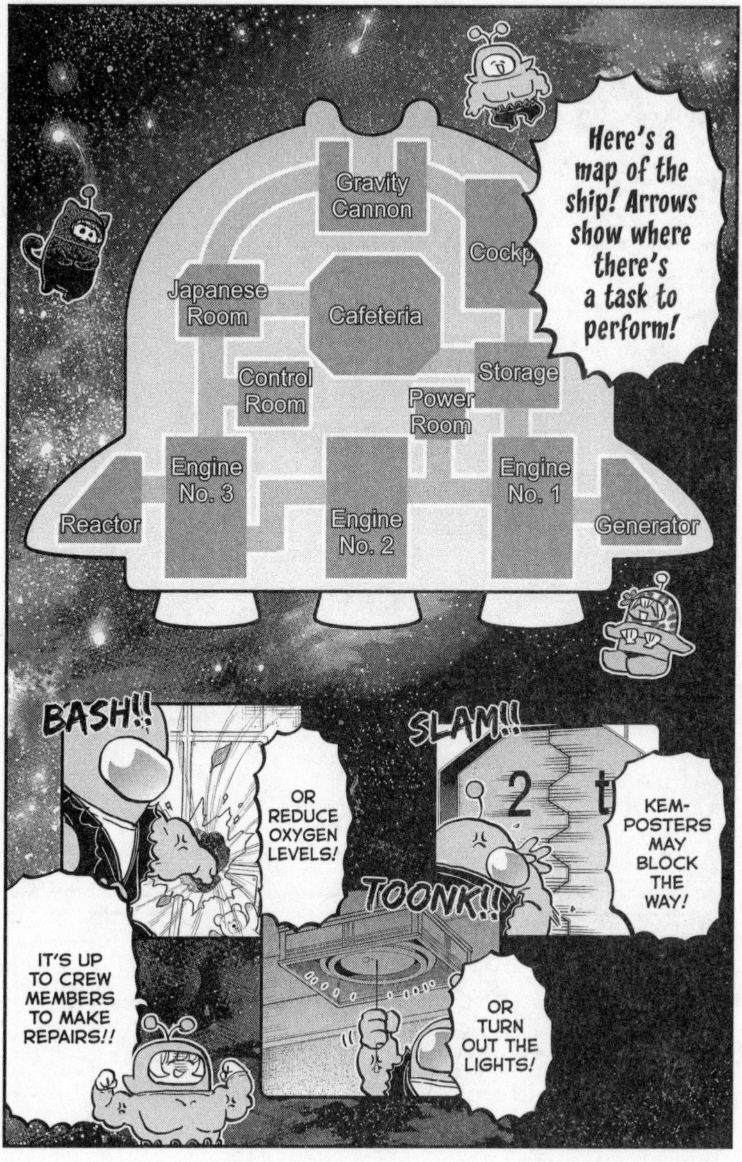
Here's a map of the ship! Arrows show where there's a task to perform!
Gravity Cannon
Cockp
Japanese Room
Cafeteria
Control Room
Storage
Power Room
Engine No. 3
Engine No. 1
Reactor
Engine No. 2
Generator
SLAM!!
2 t
KEM-POSTERS MAY BLOCK THE WAY!
BASH!!
OR REDUCE OXYGEN LEVELS!
TOONK!!
OR TURN OUT THE LIGHTS!
IT'S UP TO CREW MEMBERS TO MAKE REPAIRS!!

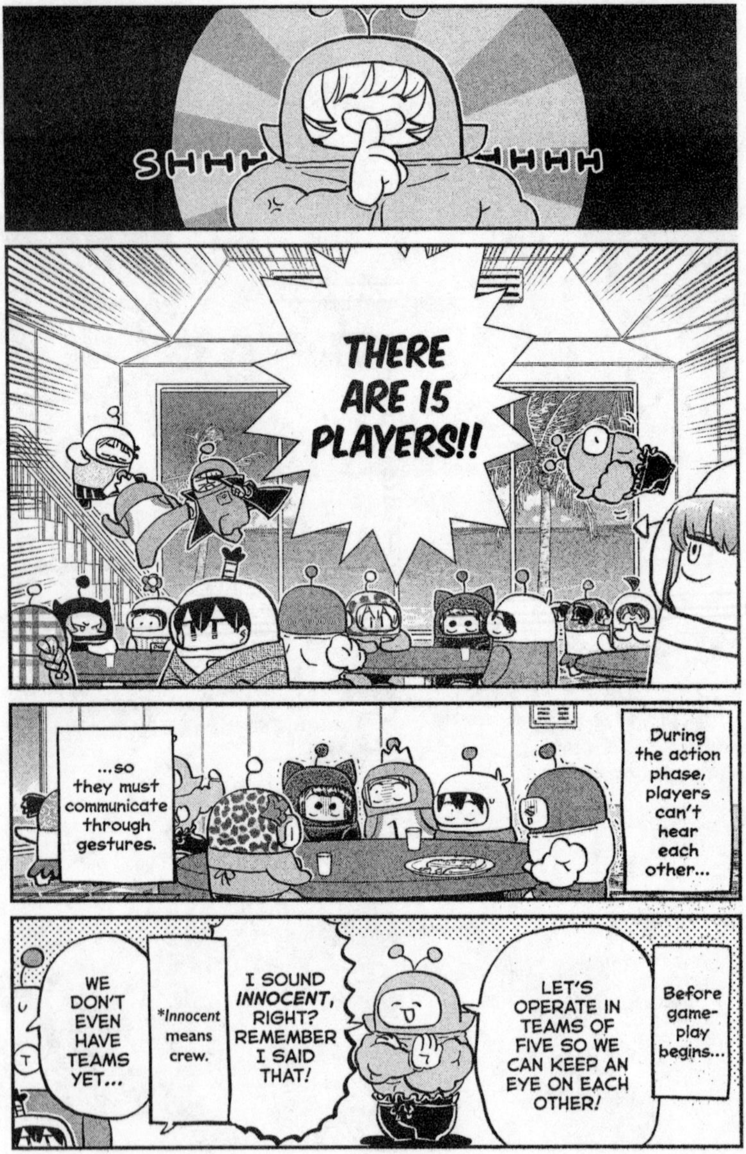
SHHH HHHH
THERE ARE 15 PLAYERS!!
During the action phase, players can't hear each other...
...so they must communicate through gestures.
Before game-play begins...
LET'S OPERATE IN TEAMS OF FIVE SO WE CAN KEEP AN EYE ON EACH OTHER!
I SOUND *INNOCENT*, RIGHT? REMEMBER I SAID THAT!
*Innocent means crew.
WE DON'T EVEN HAVE TEAMS YET...

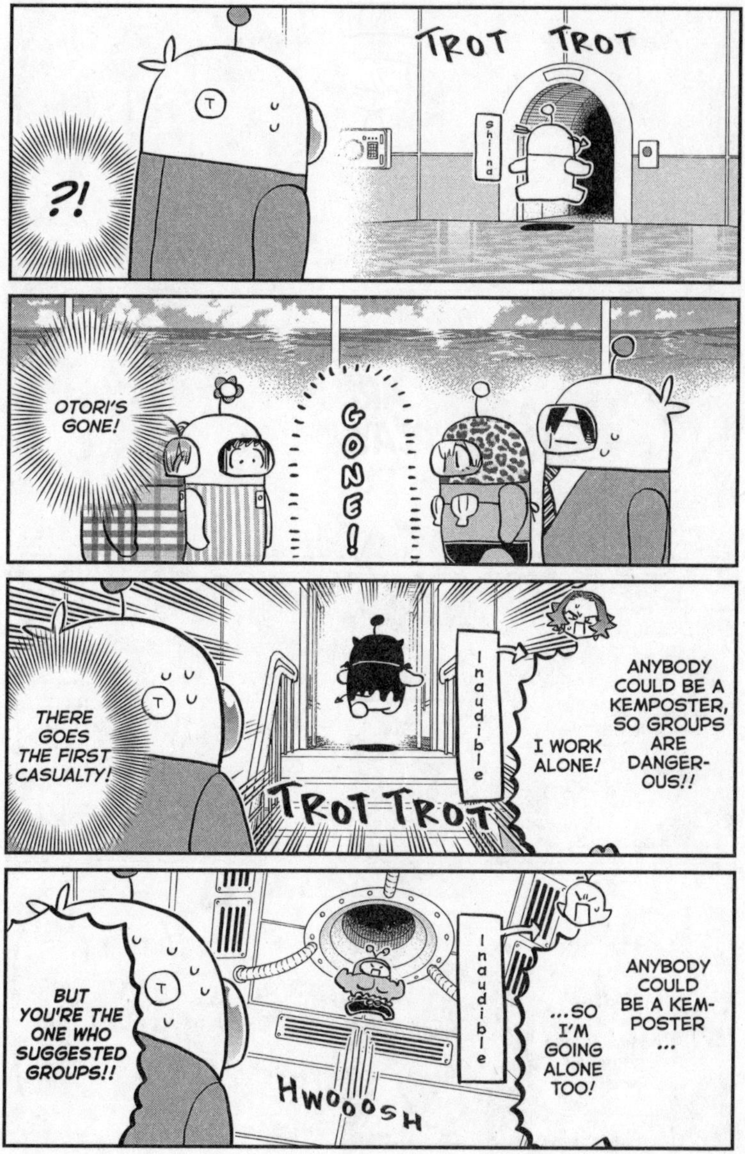
TROT TROT
Shiina
?!
GONE!
OTORI'S GONE!
ANYBODY COULD BE A KEMPOSTER, SO GROUPS ARE DANGEROUS!!
I WORK ALONE!
Inaudible
TROT TROT
THERE GOES THE FIRST CASUALTY!
ANYBODY COULD BE A KEMPOSTER...
...SO I'M GOING ALONE TOO!
Inaudible
HWOOOSH
BUT YOU'RE THE ONE WHO SUGGESTED GROUPS!!

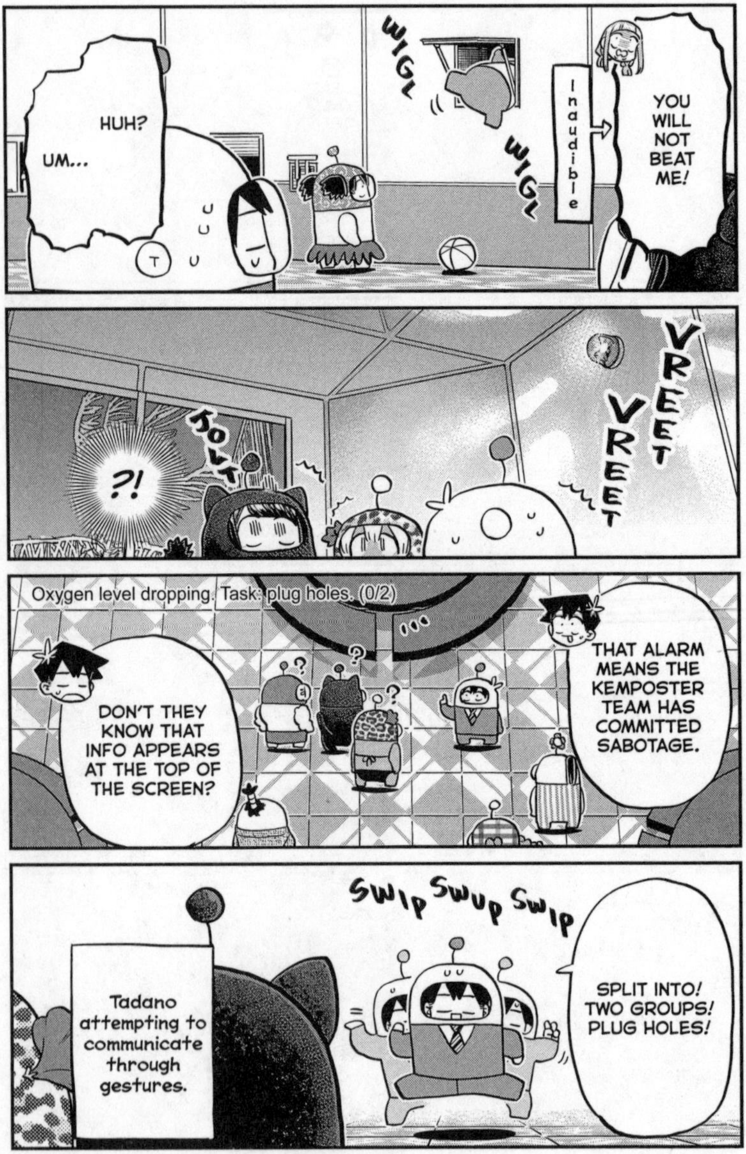
YOU WILL NOT BEAT ME!
Inaudible
WIGL
WIGL
HUH?
UM...
VREET
VREET
JOLT
?!
Oxygen level dropping. Task: plug holes. (0/2)
THAT ALARM MEANS THE KEMPOSTER TEAM HAS COMMITTED SABOTAGE.
DON'T THEY KNOW THAT INFO APPEARS AT THE TOP OF THE SCREEN?
SWIP SWUP SWIP
SPLIT INTO! TWO GROUPS! PLUG HOLES!
Tadano attempting to communicate through gestures.

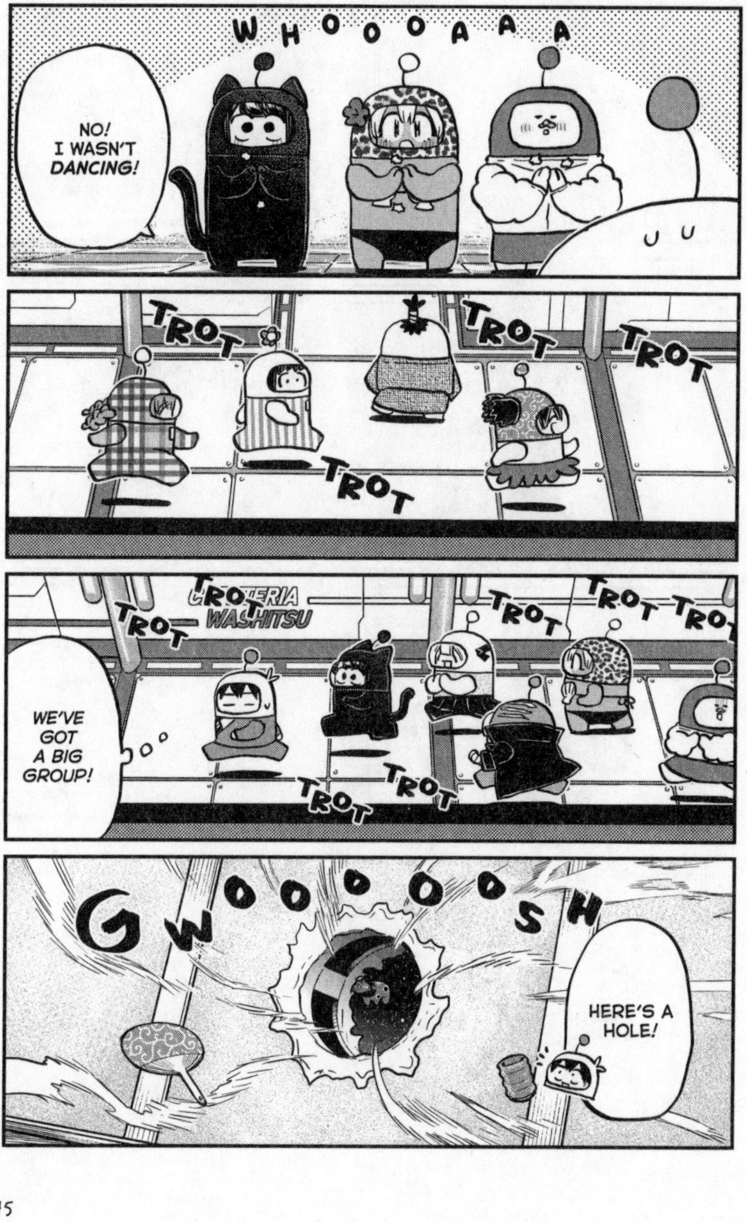
WHOOOAAA
NO! I WASN'T *DANCING!*
TROT
TROT
TROT
TROT
TROT
TROT
TROT
TROT
WASHITSU
WE'VE GOT A BIG GROUP!
TROT
TROT
GWOOOOOSH
HERE'S A HOLE!

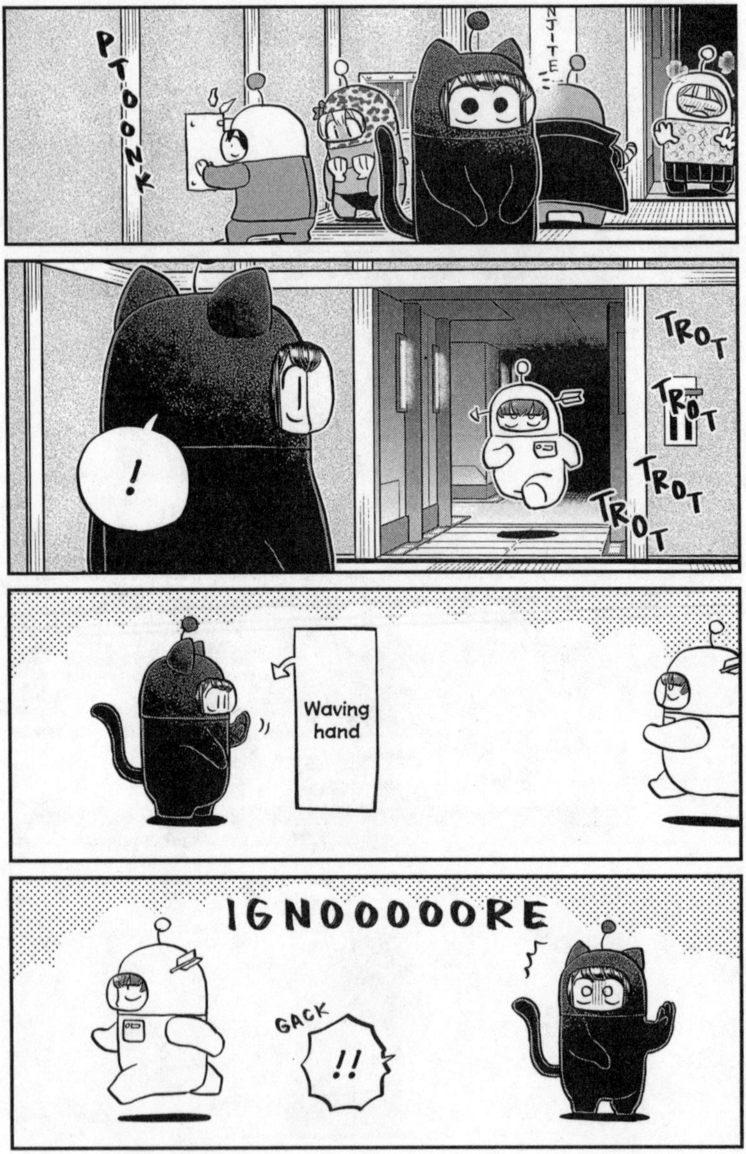
PTOONK
TROT
TROT
TROT
TROT
!
Waving hand
IGNOOOOORE
GACK
!!

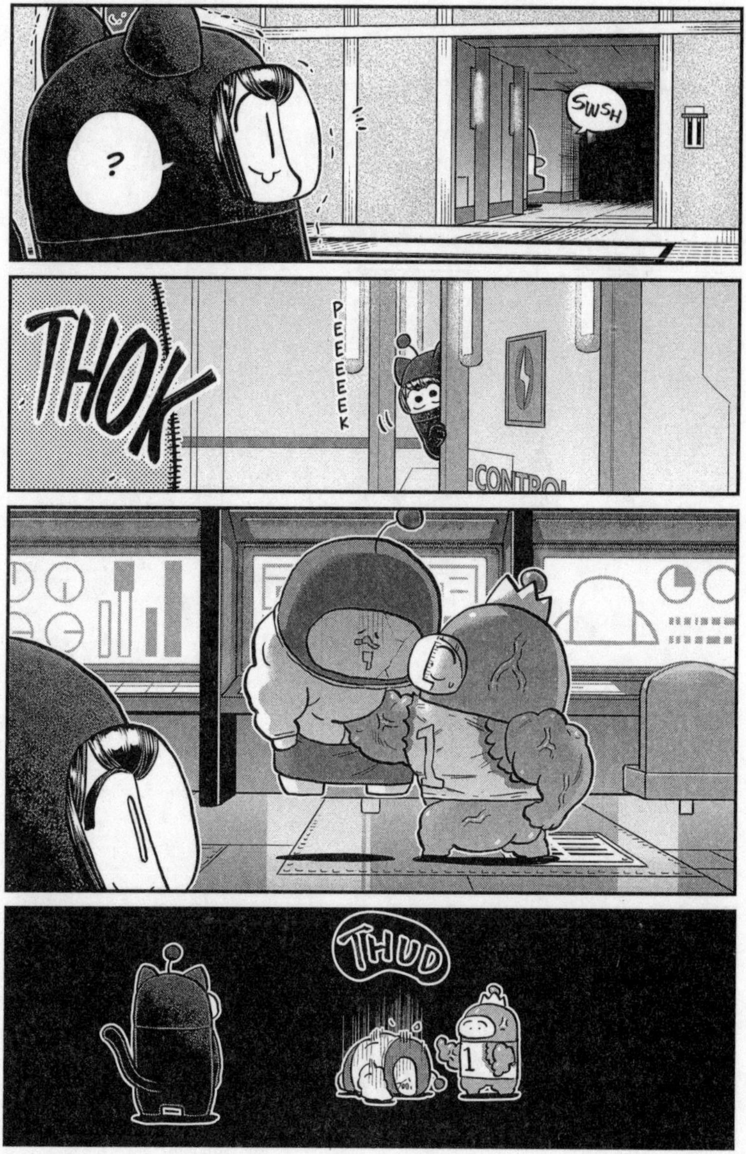
SWSH
?
PEEEEEK
THOK
CONTROL
THUD

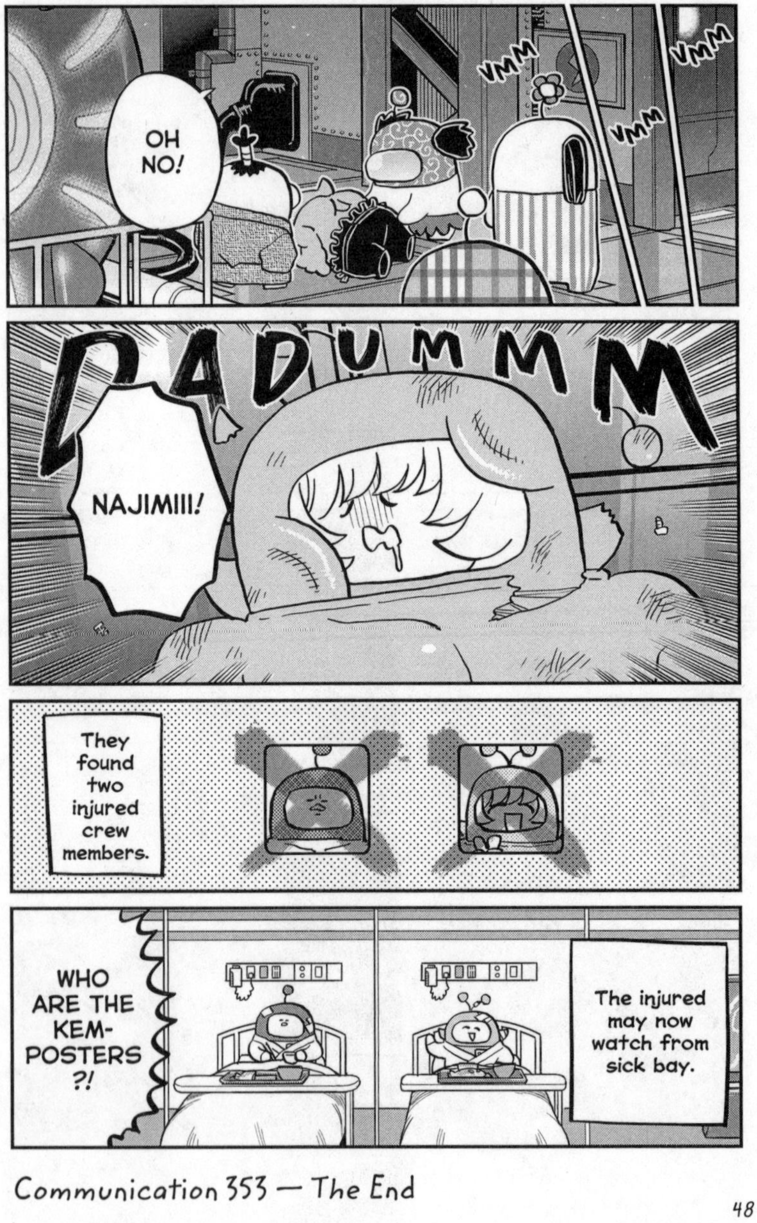
VMM
VMM
VMM
OH NO!
DADUMMM
NAJIMIII!
They found two injured crew members.
The injured may now watch from sick bay.
WHO ARE THE KEM-POSTERS?!

Communication 353 — The End

Komi Can't Communicate

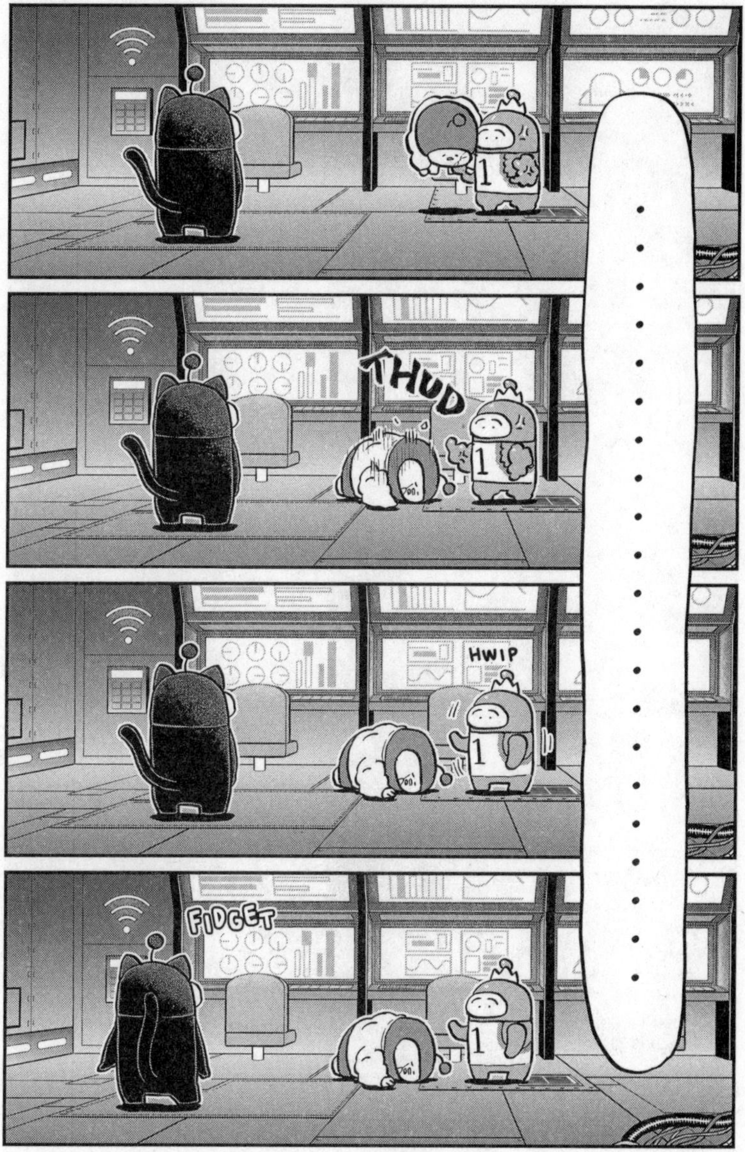

....
THUD
HWIP
FIDGET

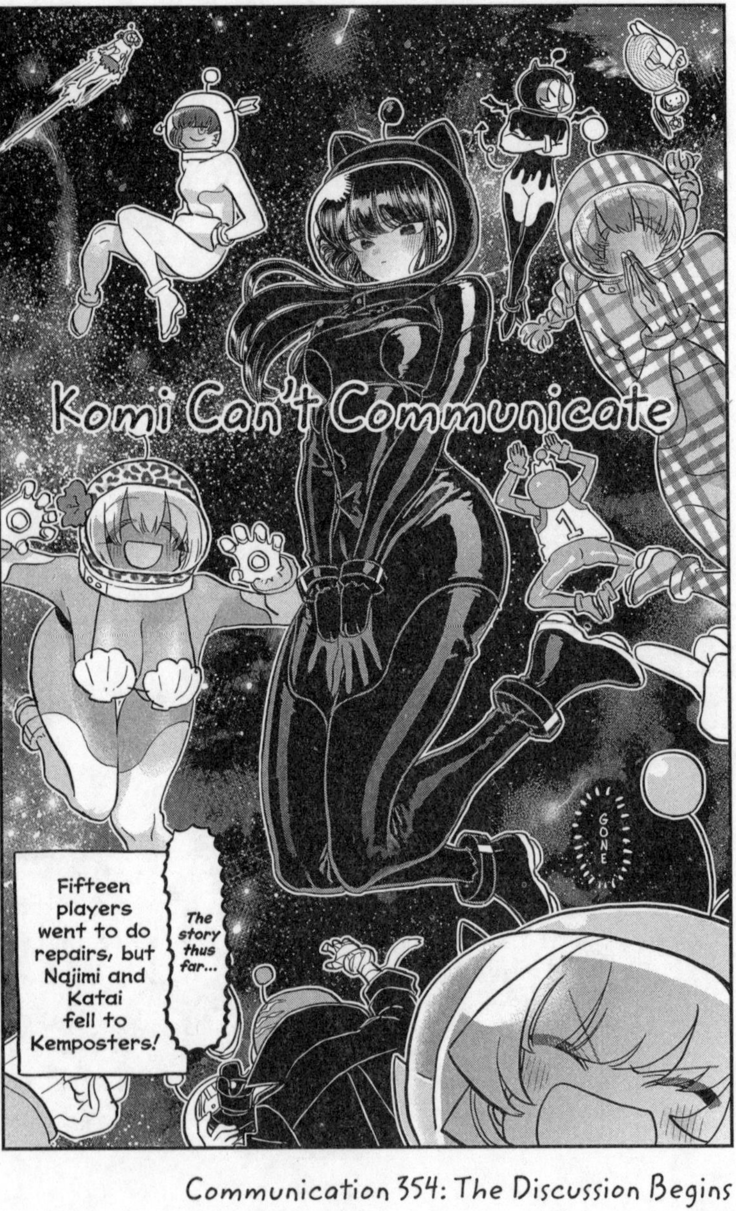
Komi Can't Communicate
GONE
The story thus far...
Fifteen players went to do repairs, but Najimi and Katai fell to Kemposters!

Communication 354: The Discussion Begins

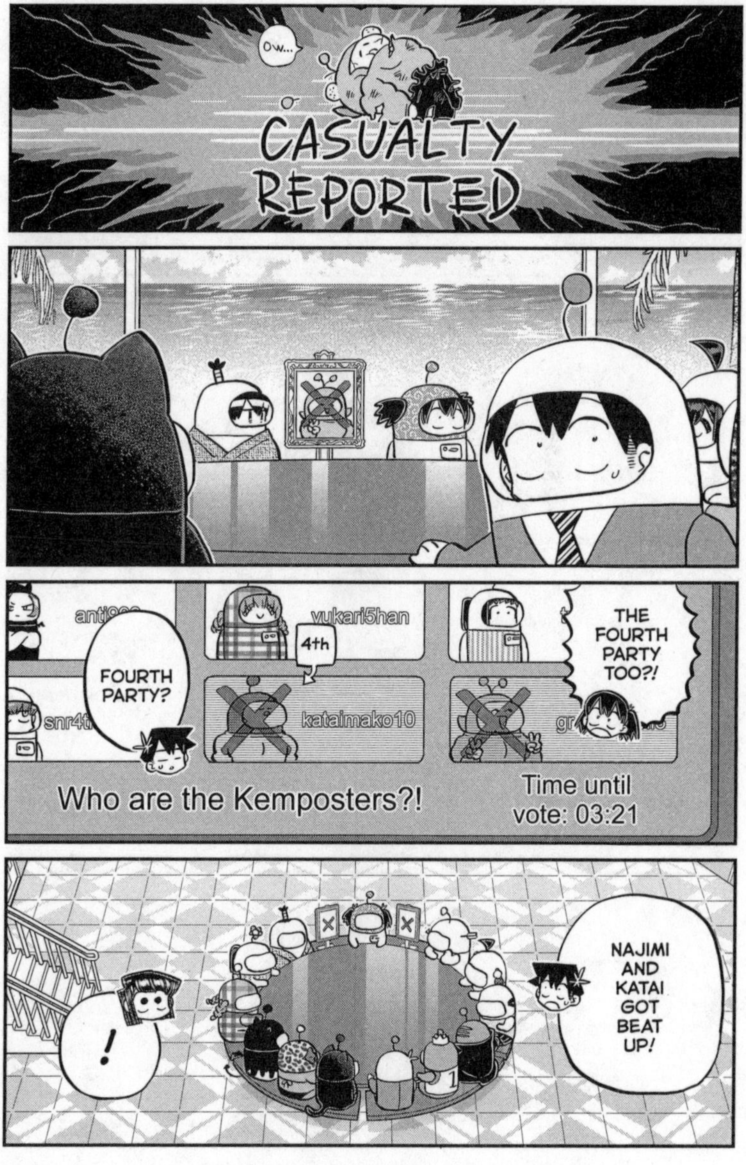
Ow...
CASUALTY REPORTED
THE FOURTH PARTY TOO?!
vukari5han
4th
FOURTH PARTY?
kataimako10
Time until vote: 03:21
Who are the Kemposters?!
NAJIMI AND KATAI GOT BEAT UP!
!

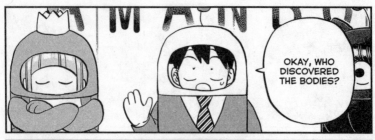

OKAY, WHO DISCOVERED THE BODIES?
I'M SHOSUKE! I FOUND AND REPORTED NAJIMI! (COOL VOICE)
FWIP
Looking toward Shosuke's room
?!
DO YOU *HAVE* TO DO THAT?
I WAS WITH KOMETANI, KOGOEN, AND TSUZURAFUJI! (COOL VOICE)
SO WE CAN'T BE GUILTY! (COOL VOICE)
UH-HUH.
What?!
*Agreed.
R-RIGHT...
WELL, WHAT ABOUT KATAI?
...
...
HMM...

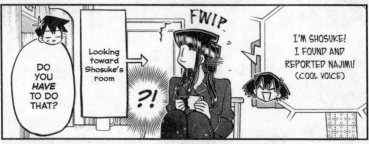

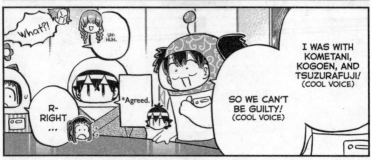

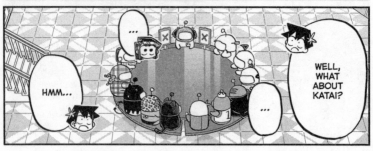

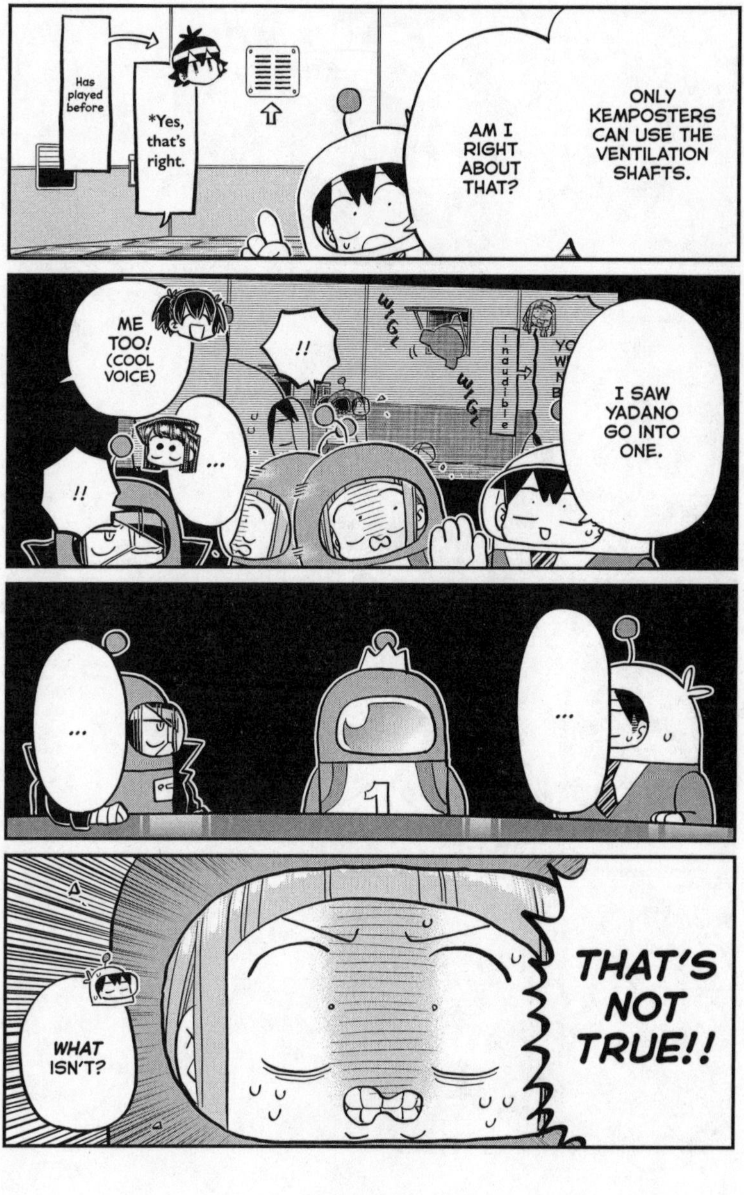
ONLY KEMPOSTERS CAN USE THE VENTILATION SHAFTS.
AM I RIGHT ABOUT THAT?
*Yes, that's right.
Has played before
I SAW YADANO GO INTO ONE.
Inaudible
WIGL
WIGL
!!
ME TOO! (COOL VOICE)
...
!!
...
...
THAT'S NOT TRUE!!
WHAT ISN'T?

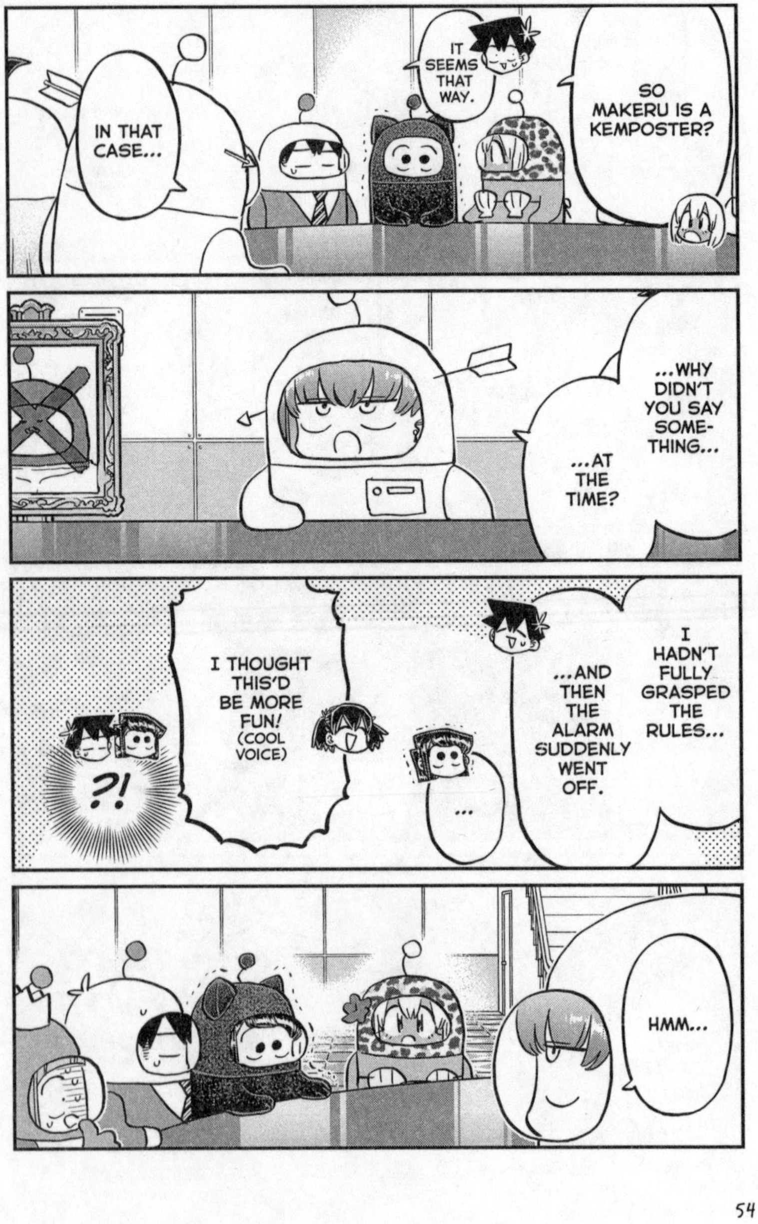

SO MAKERU IS A KEMPOSTER?
IT SEEMS THAT WAY.
IN THAT CASE...
...WHY DIDN'T YOU SAY SOME-THING...
...AT THE TIME?
I HADN'T FULLY GRASPED THE RULES...
...AND THEN THE ALARM SUDDENLY WENT OFF.
...
I THOUGHT THIS'D BE MORE FUN! (COOL VOICE)
?!
HMM...

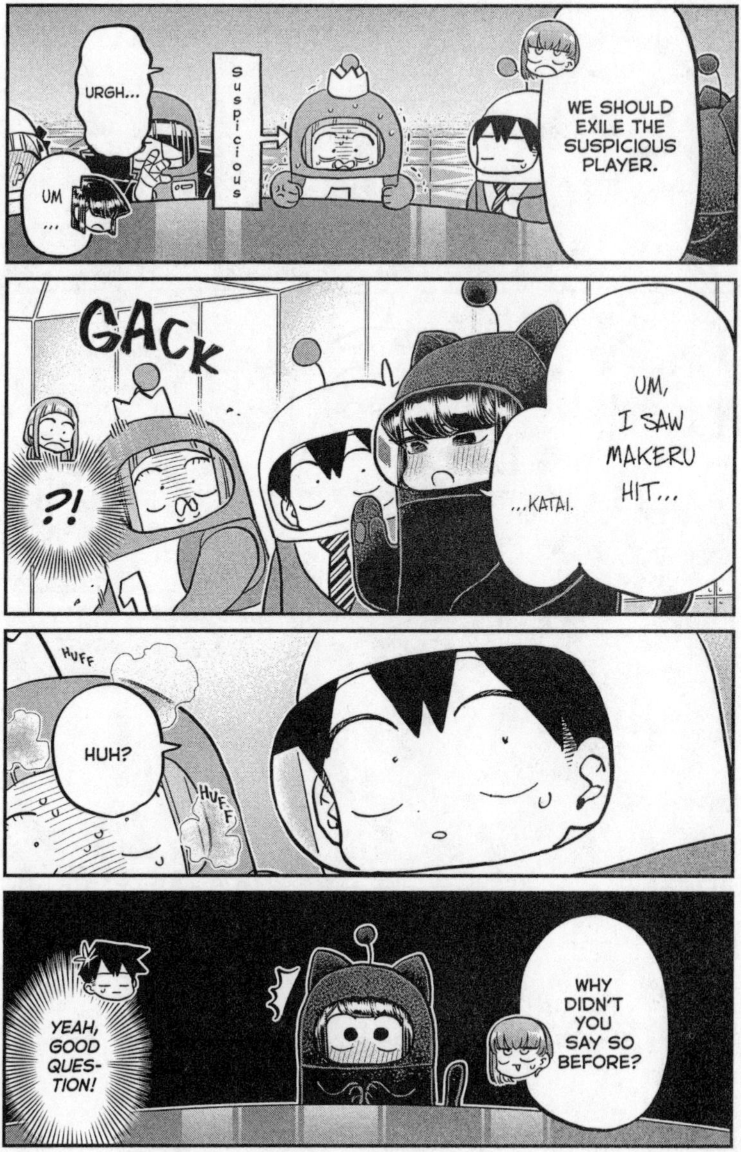
WE SHOULD EXILE THE SUSPICIOUS PLAYER.
Suspicious
URGH...
UM ...
UM, I SAW MAKERU HIT...
...KATAI.
GACK
?!
HUFF
HUFF
HUH?
WHY DIDN'T YOU SAY SO BEFORE?
YEAH, GOOD QUES-TION!

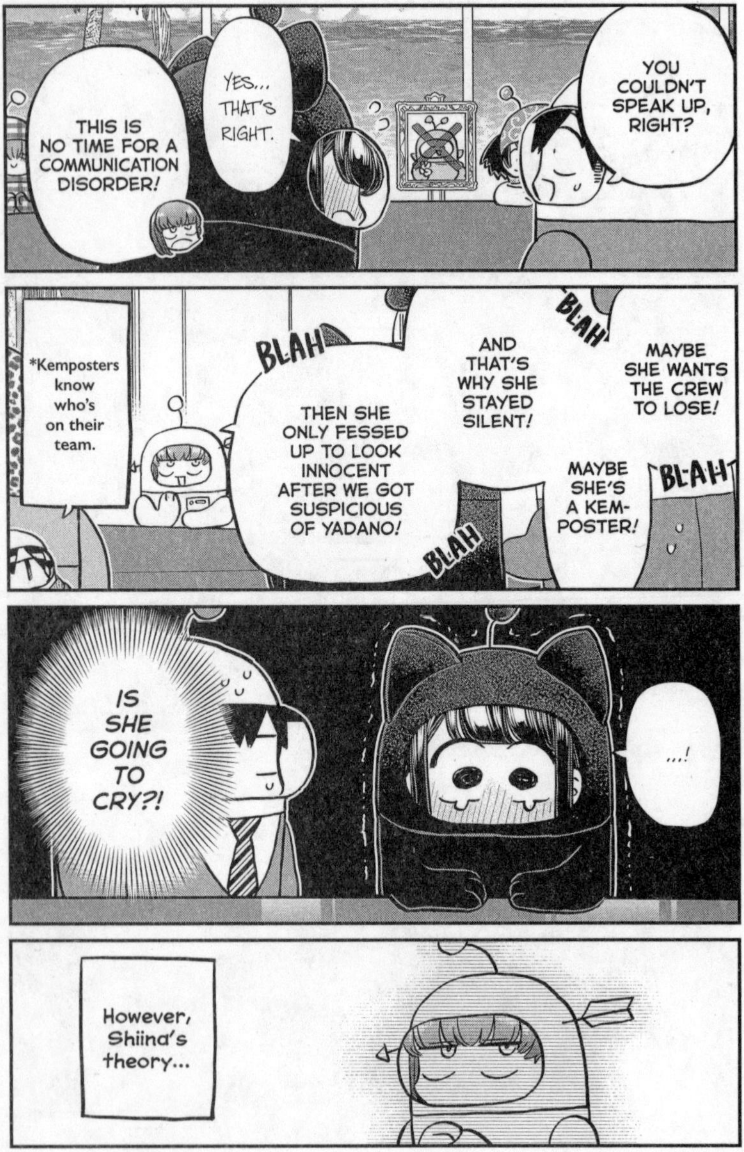
YOU COULDN'T SPEAK UP, RIGHT?
YES... THAT'S RIGHT.
THIS IS NO TIME FOR A COMMUNICATION DISORDER!
BLAH
MAYBE SHE WANTS THE CREW TO LOSE!
BL·A·H
MAYBE SHE'S A KEM-POSTER!
AND THAT'S WHY SHE STAYED SILENT!
BLAH
BLAH
THEN SHE ONLY FESSED UP TO LOOK INNOCENT AFTER WE GOT SUSPICIOUS OF YADANO!
*Kemposters know who's on their team.
...!
IS SHE GOING TO CRY?!
However, Shiina's theory...

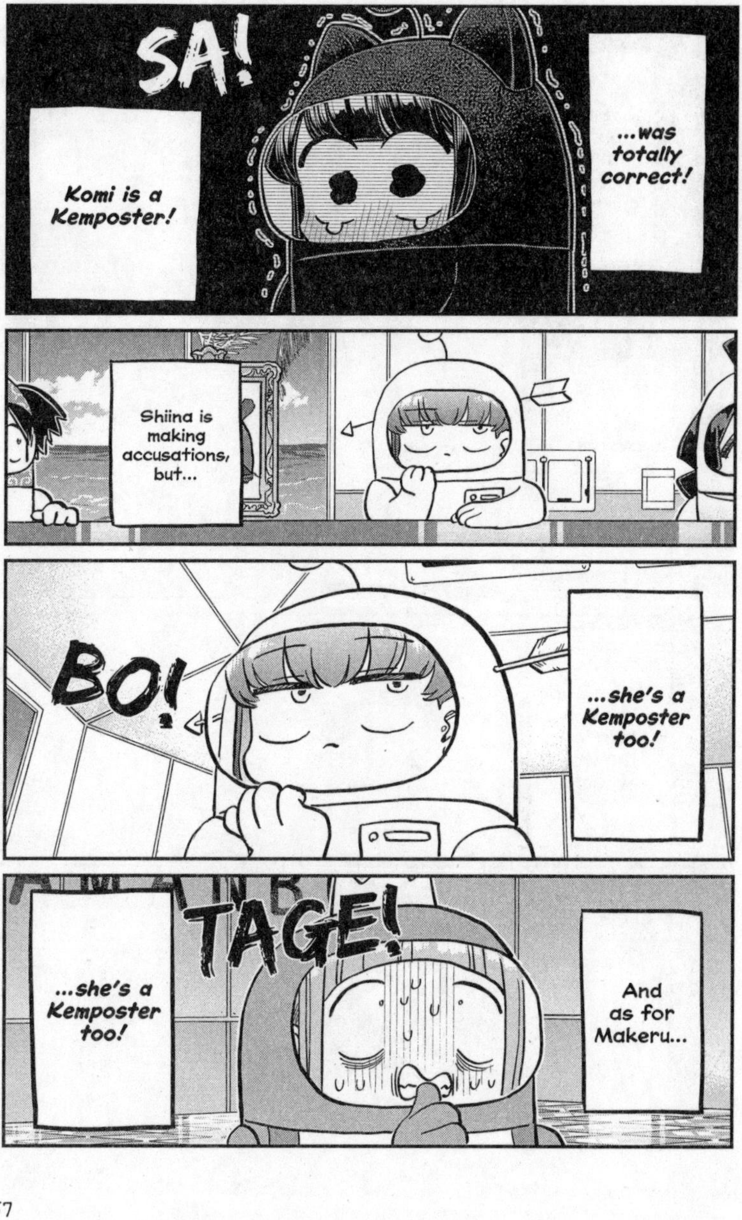
...was totally correct!
SA!
Komi is a Kemposter!
Shiina is making accusations, but...
...she's a Kemposter too!
BO!
And as for Makeru...
TAGE!
...she's a Kemposter too!

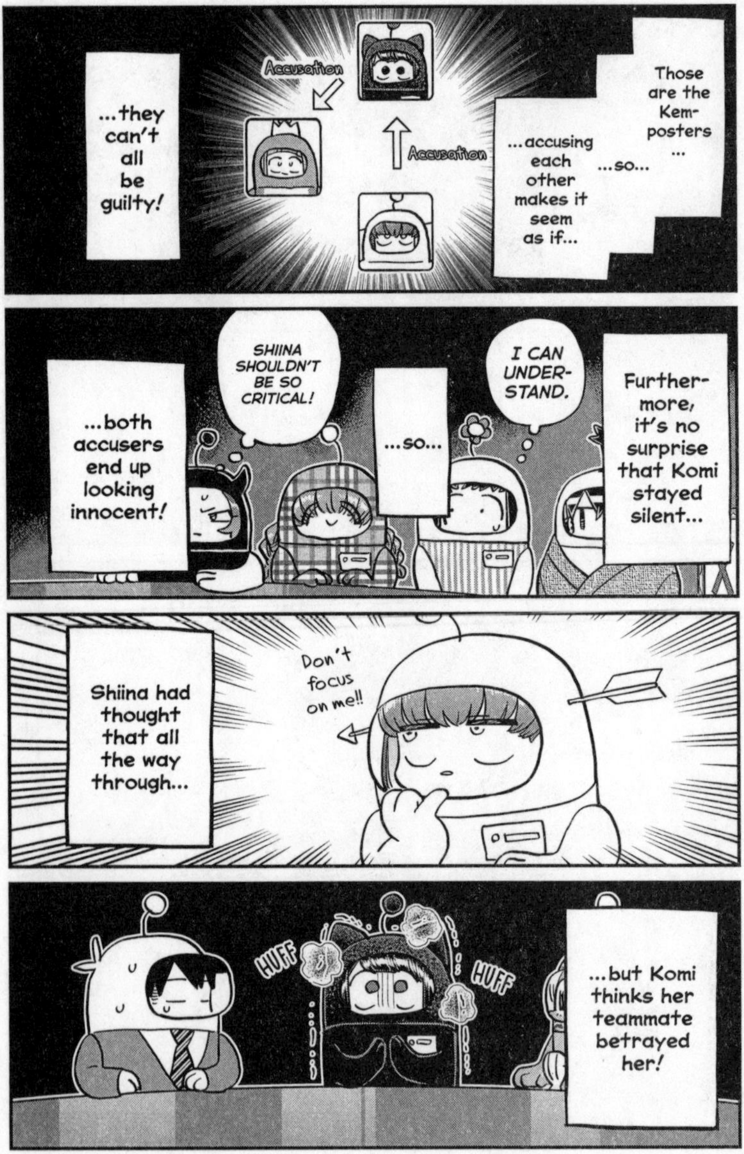
Those are the Kem-posters ...
...so...
...accusing each other makes it seem as if...
Accusation
Accusation
...they can't all be guilty!
Further-more, it's no surprise that Komi stayed silent...
I CAN UNDER-STAND.
...so...
SHIINA SHOULDN'T BE SO CRITICAL!
...both accusers end up looking innocent!
Don't focus on me!!
Shiina had thought that all the way through...
...but Komi thinks her teammate betrayed her!
HUFF
HUFF

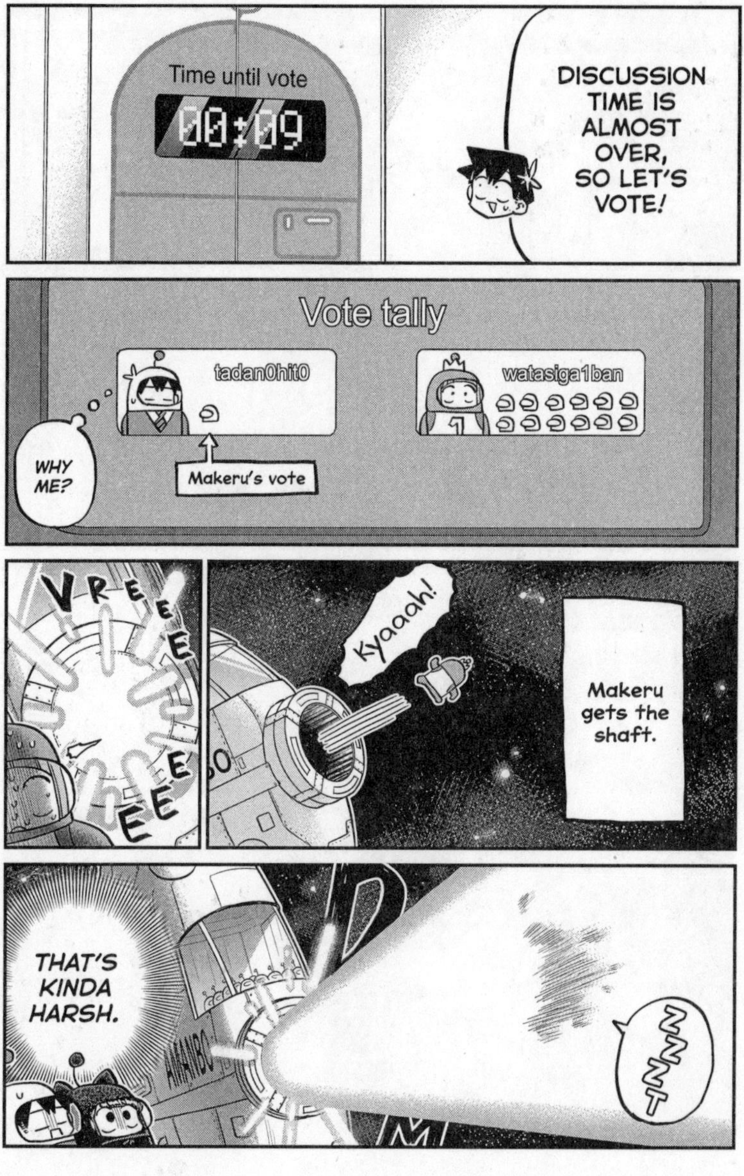
DISCUSSION TIME IS ALMOST OVER, SO LET'S VOTE!
Time until vote
00:09
Vote tally
watasiga1ban
tadan0hit0
Makeru's vote
WHY ME?
Makeru gets the shaft.
Kyaaah!
VREEEEEEE
ZZZT
THAT'S KINDA HARSH.

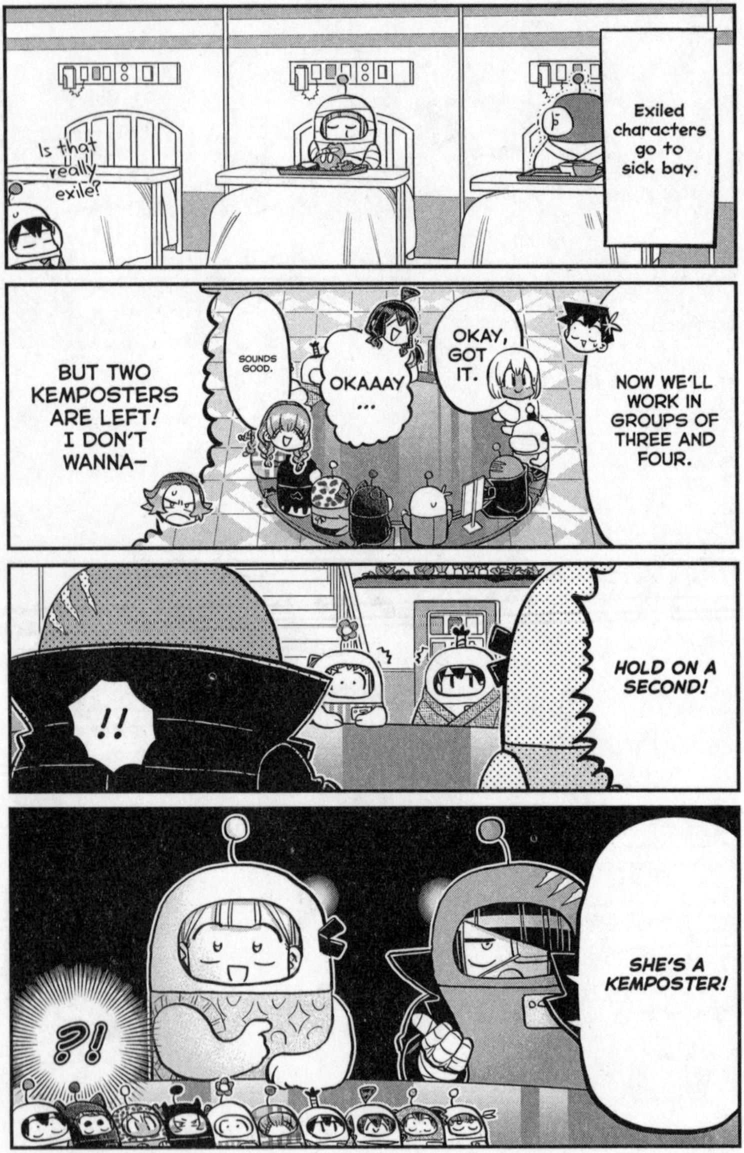
Exiled characters go to sick bay.
Is that really exile?
NOW WE'LL WORK IN GROUPS OF THREE AND FOUR.
OKAY, GOT IT.
OKAAAY ...
SOUNDS GOOD.
BUT TWO KEMPOSTERS ARE LEFT! I DON'T WANNA–
HOLD ON A SECOND!
!!
SHE'S A KEMPOSTER!
?!

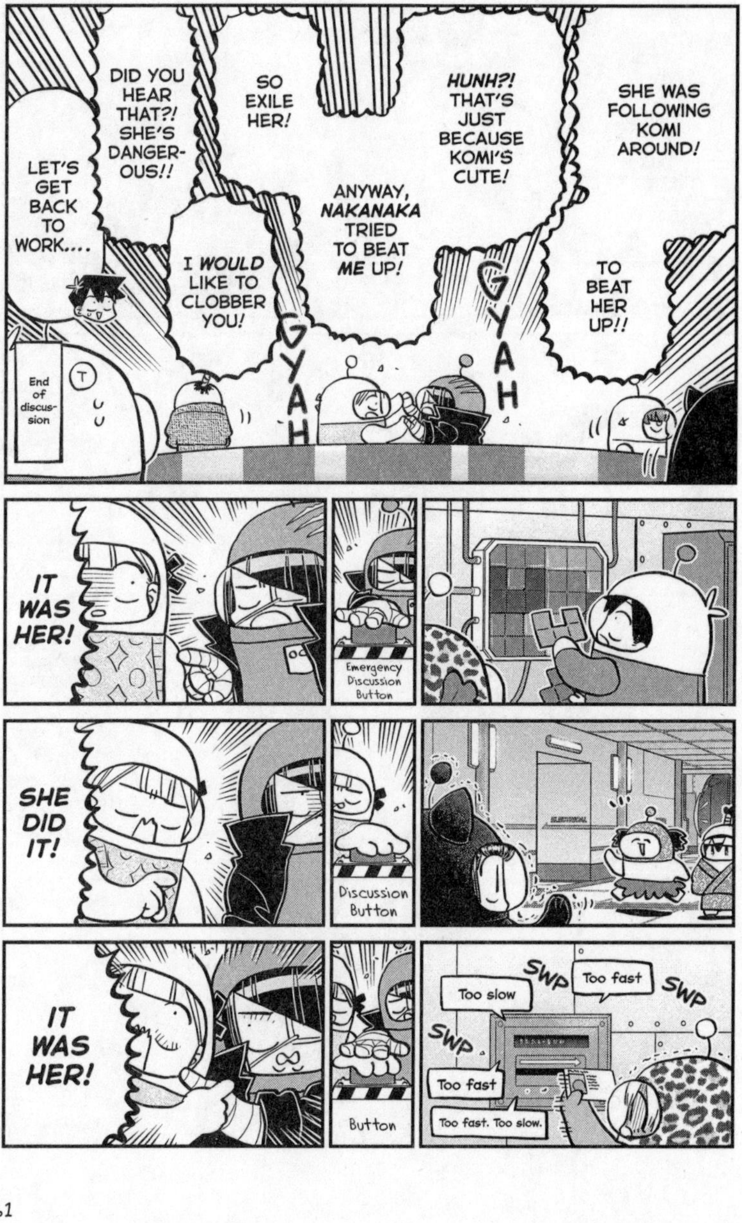
SHE WAS FOLLOWING KOMI AROUND!
TO BEAT HER UP!!
HUNH?! THAT'S JUST BECAUSE KOMI'S CUTE!
GYAH
ANYWAY, NAKANAKA TRIED TO BEAT ME UP!
SO EXILE HER!
GYAH
I WOULD LIKE TO CLOBBER YOU!
DID YOU HEAR THAT?! SHE'S DANGEROUS!!
LET'S GET BACK TO WORK....
End of discussion
Emergency Discussion Button
IT WAS HER!
Discussion Button
SHE DID IT!
SWP
Too fast
SWP
Too slow
SWP
Too fast
Too fast. Too slow.
Button
IT WAS HER!

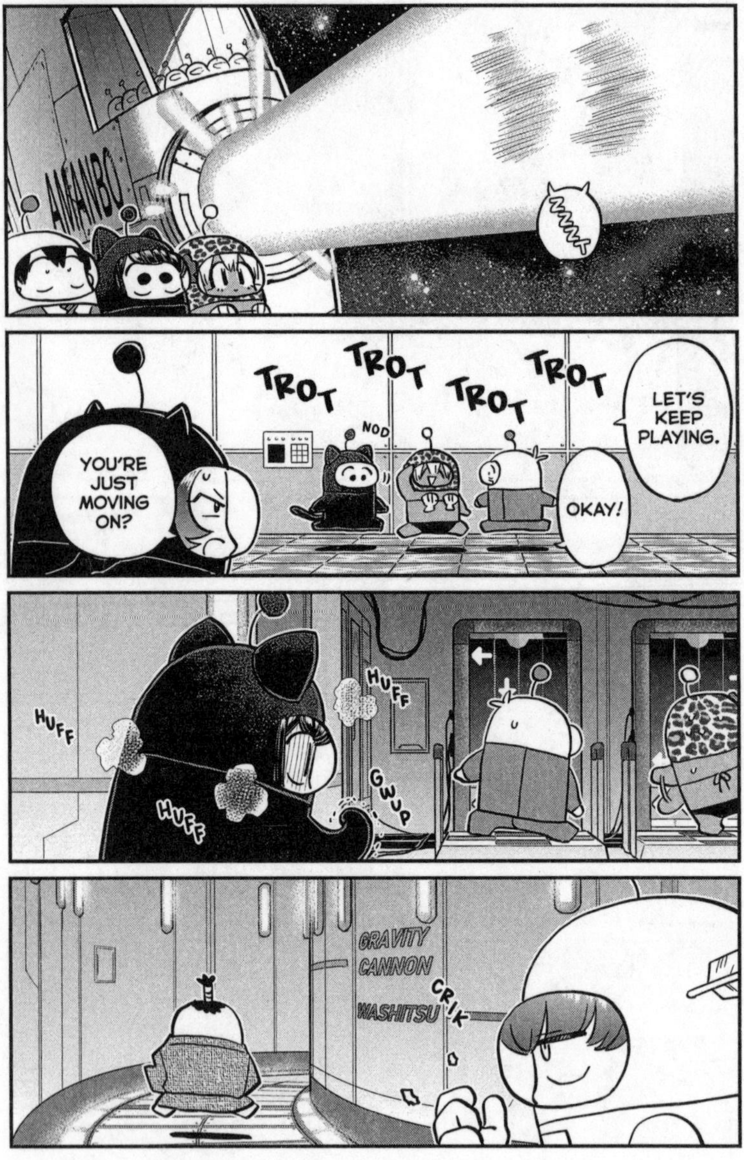
ZZZZT
AMANBO
LET'S KEEP PLAYING.
OKAY!
TROT
TROT
TROT
TROT
NOD
YOU'RE JUST MOVING ON?
HUFF
GWUP
HUFF
HUFF
HUFF
CRIK
GRAVITY CANNON
WASHITSU

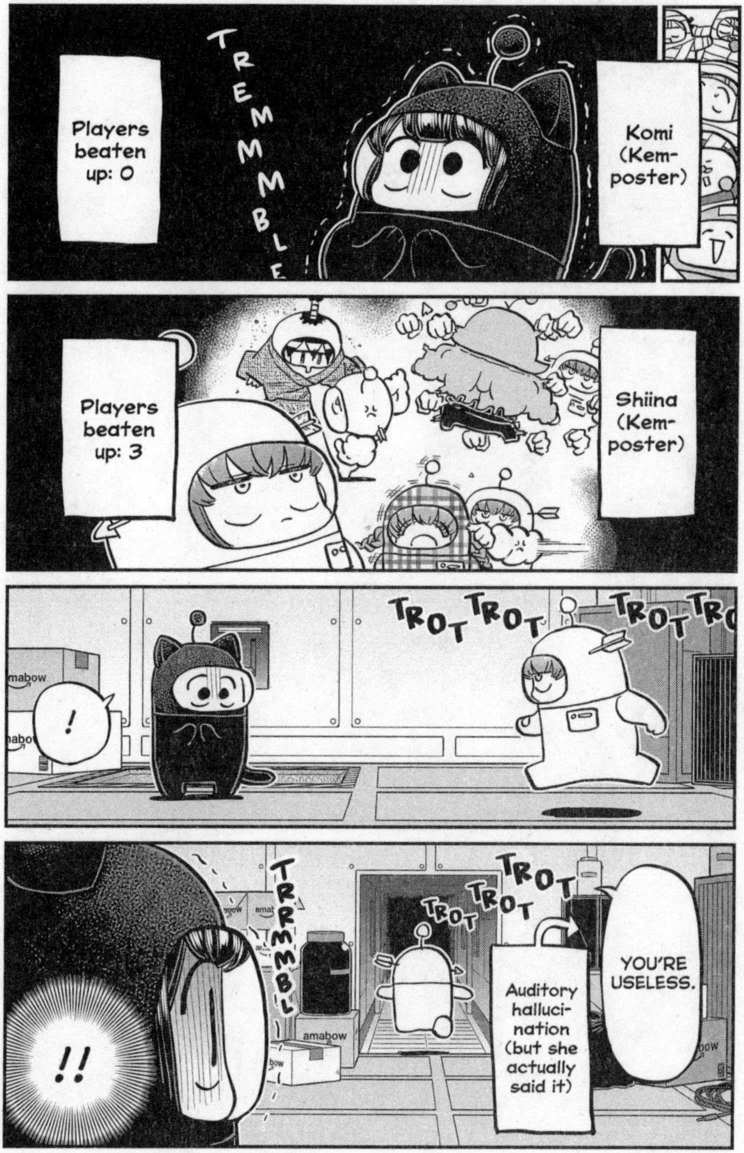
Komi (Kem-poster)
TREMMBLE
Players beaten up: 0
Shiina (Kem-poster)
Players beaten up: 3
TROT TRO
TROT TROT
!
YOU'RE USELESS.
TROT
TROT
TROT TROT
Auditory halluci-nation (but she actually said it)
TRRMMBL
!!

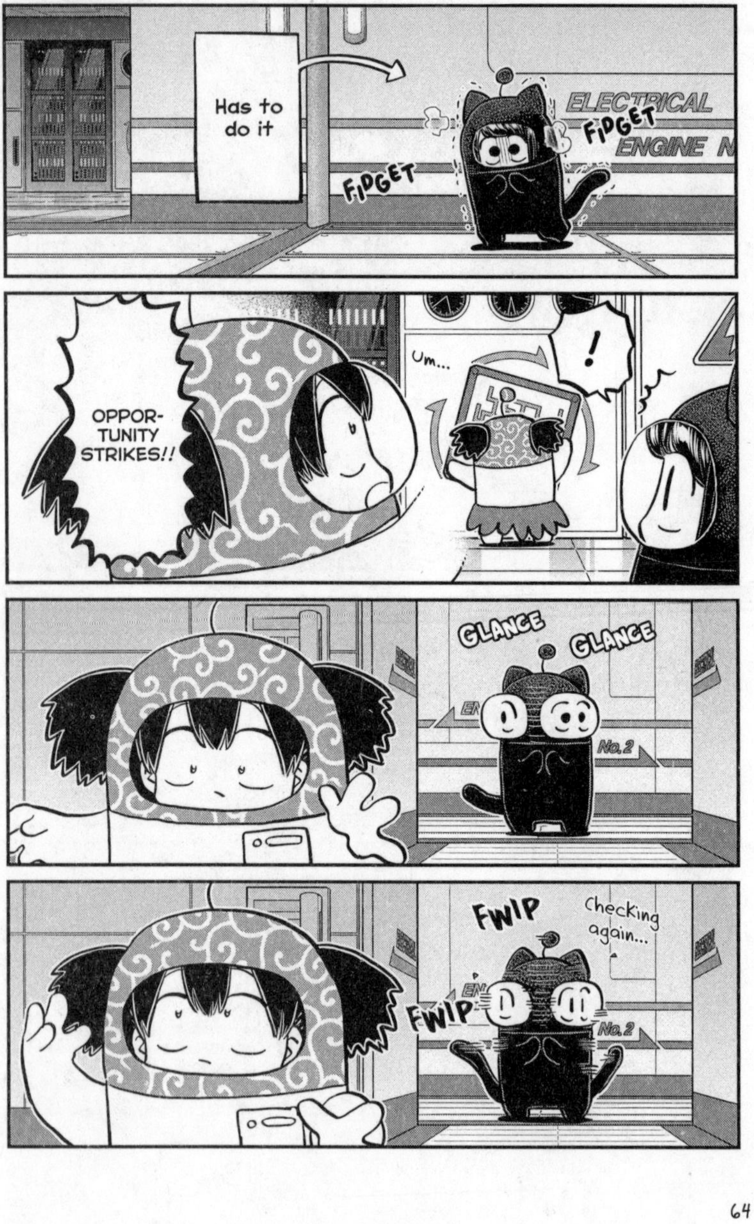
ELECTRICAL
FIDGET
ENGINE N
Has to do it
FIDGET
!
Um...
OPPOR-TUNITY STRIKES!!
GLANCE
GLANCE
No.2
Checking again...
FWIP
No.2
FWIP

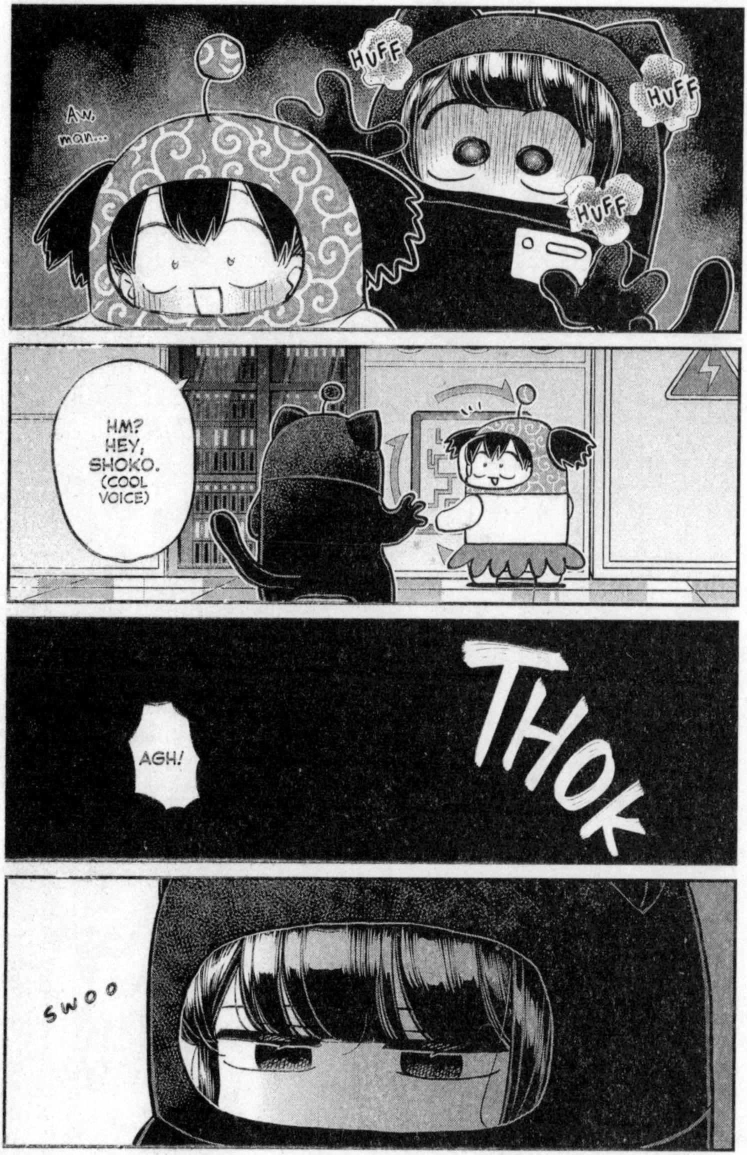
HUFF
HUFF
HUFF
Aw, man...
HM? HEY, SHOKO. (COOL VOICE)
THOK
AGH!
SWOO

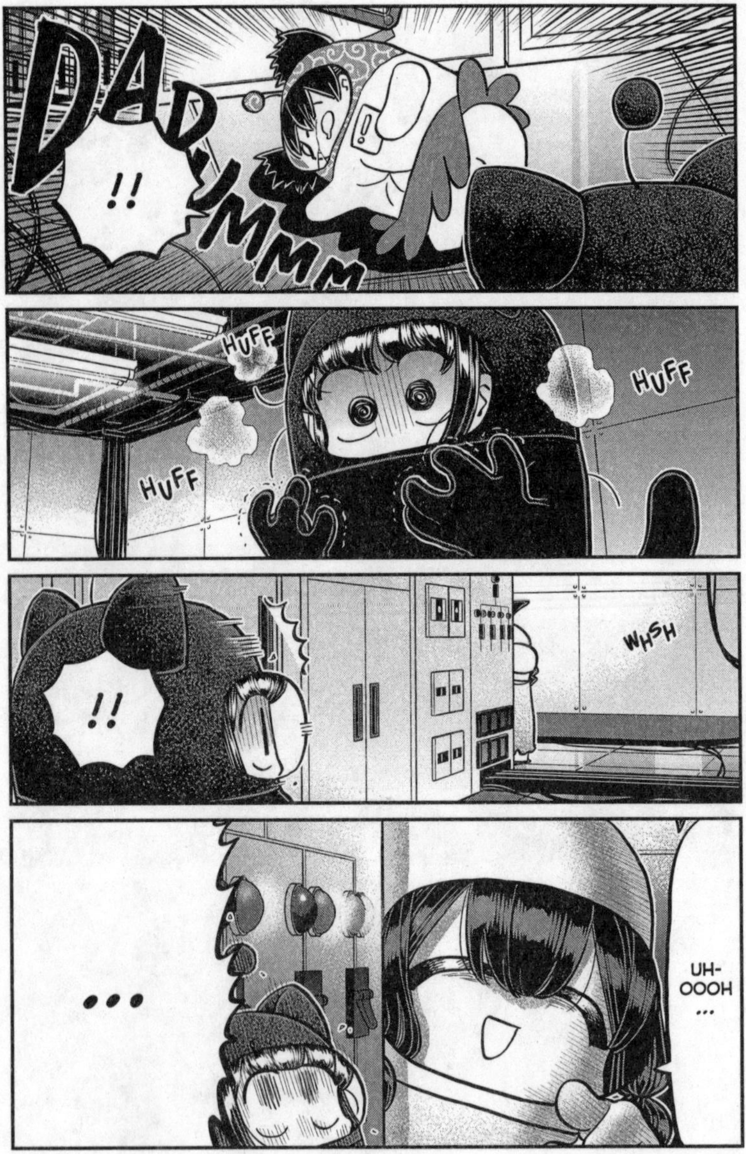
DADUMMMM
!!
HUFF
HUFF
HUFF
!!
WHSH
UH-OOOH...
...

Communication 354 — The End

Komi Can't Communicate

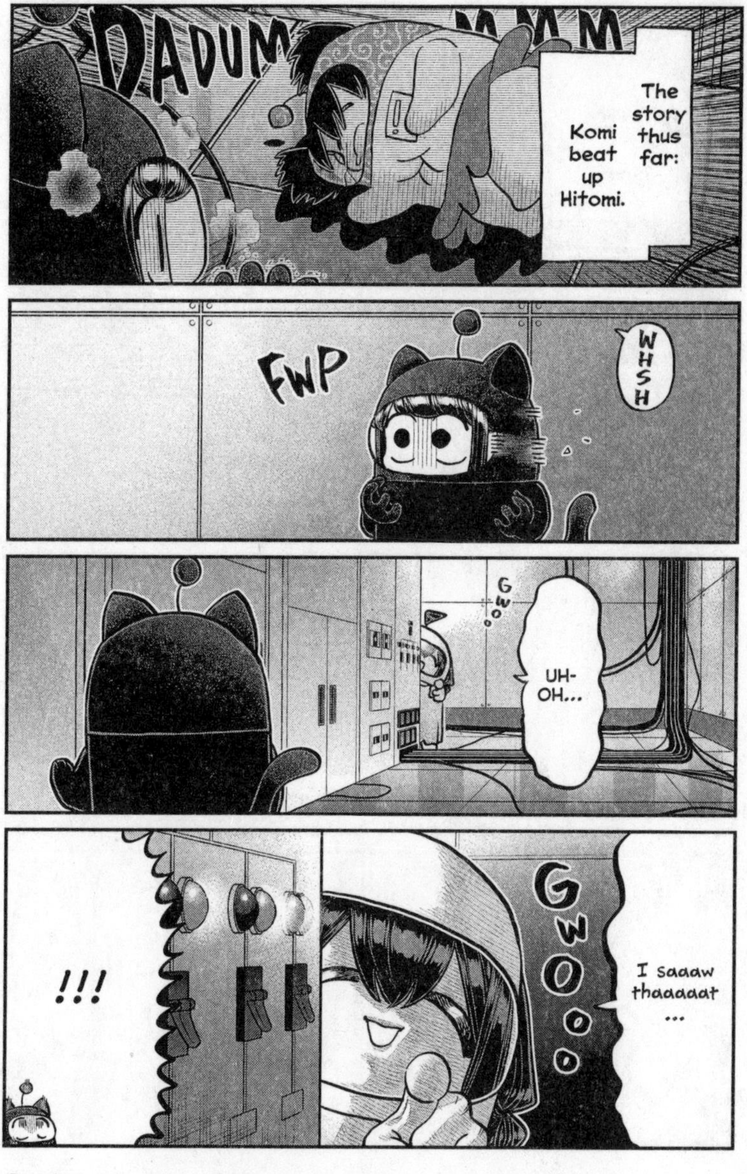
The story thus far:
Komi beat up Hitomi.
DADUM MMM
WHSH
FWP
UH-OH...
GWO
I saaaw thaaaaat...
GWOOO
!!!

Communication 355: Kemposters

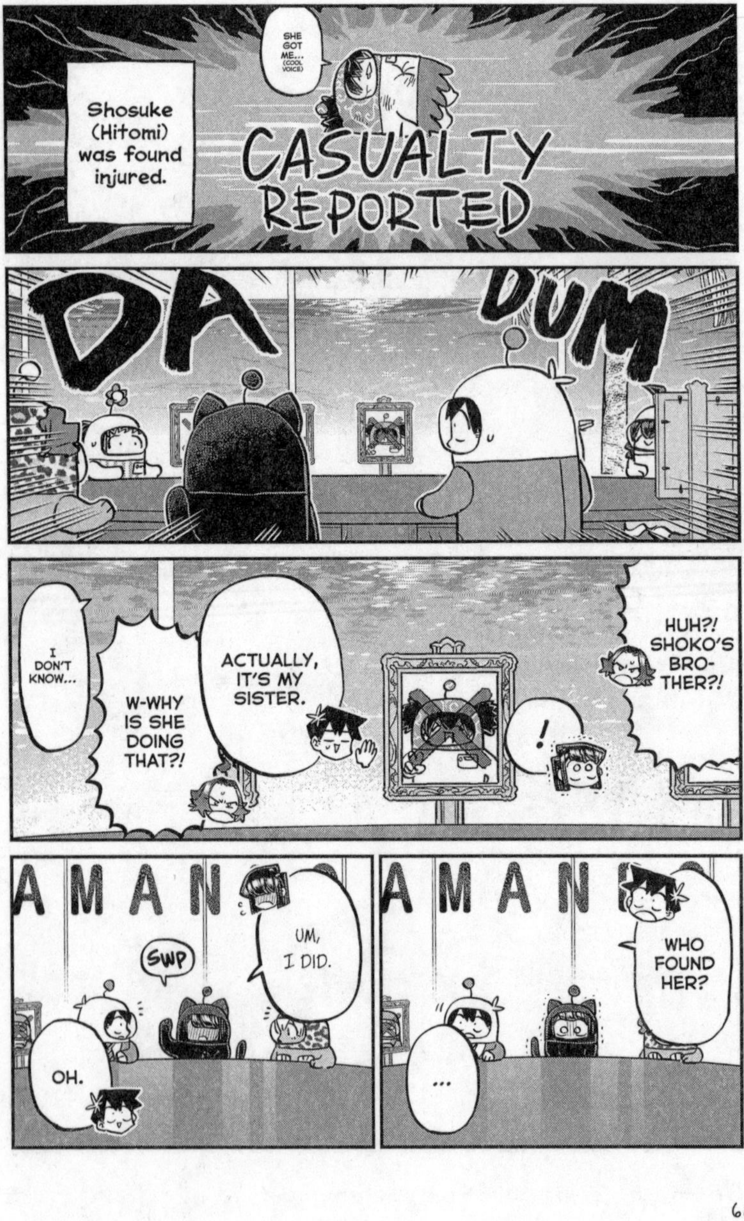
SHE GOT ME... (COOL VOICE)
CASUALTY REPORTED
Shosuke (Hitomi) was found injured.
DA DUM
HUH?! SHOKO'S BRO-THER?!
!
ACTUALLY, IT'S MY SISTER.
W-WHY IS SHE DOING THAT?!
I DON'T KNOW...
AMAN
WHO FOUND HER?
...
AMAN
UM, I DID.
SWP
OH.

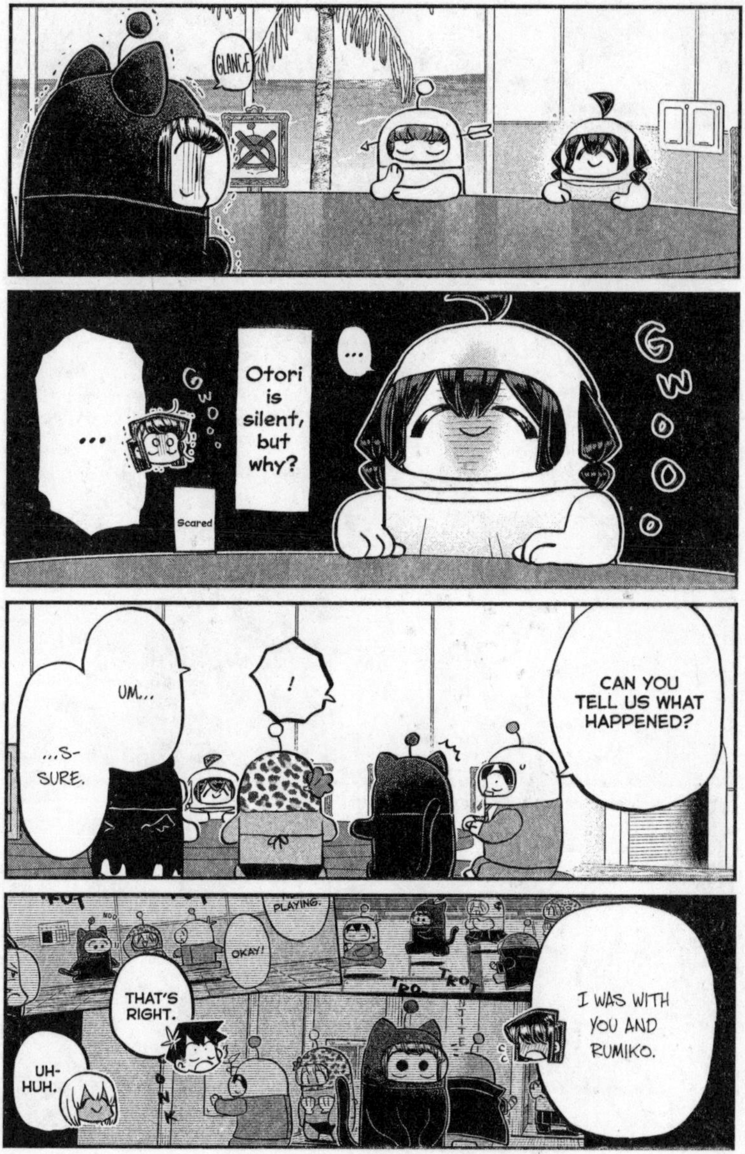
GLANCE
...
Otori is silent, but why?
Scared
...
CAN YOU TELL US WHAT HAPPENED?
!
UM...
...S-SURE.
I WAS WITH YOU AND RUMIKO.
OKAY!
THAT'S RIGHT.
UH-HUH.

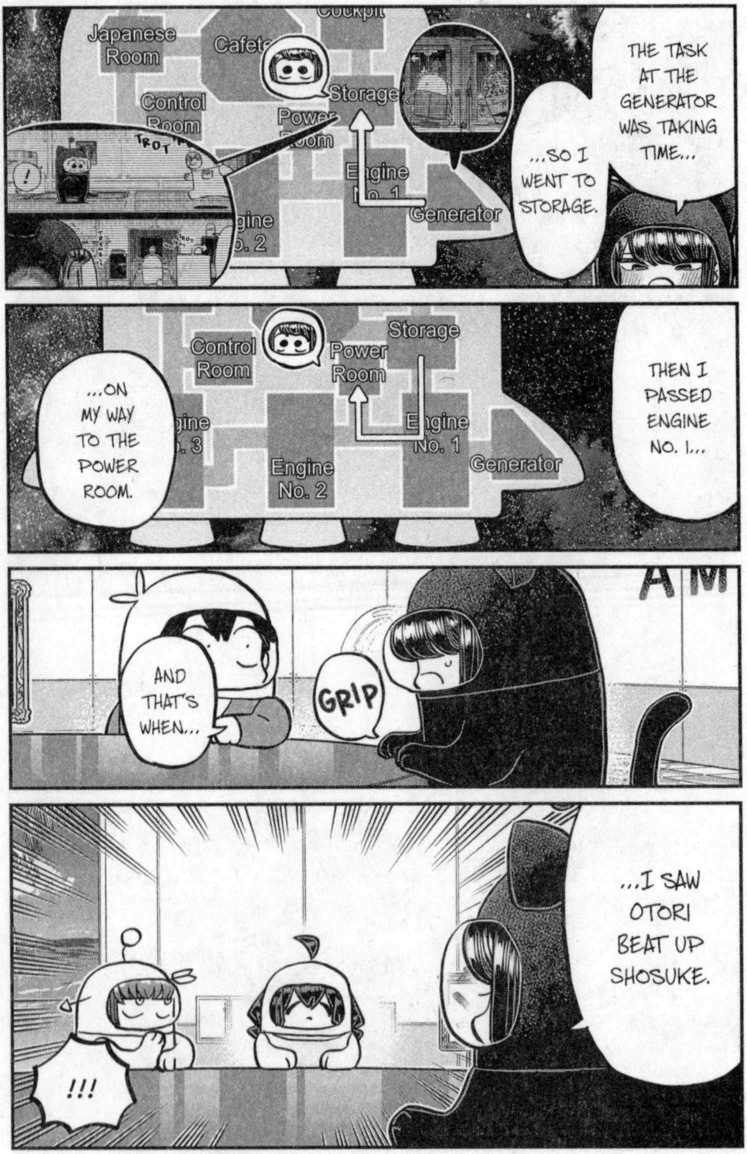
THE TASK AT THE GENERATOR WAS TAKING TIME...
...SO I WENT TO STORAGE.
Storage
Generator
Power Room
Control Room
Japanese Room
TROT
THEN I PASSED ENGINE NO. 1...
Storage
Power Room
Engine No. 1
Generator
Engine No. 2
Control Room
...ON MY WAY TO THE POWER ROOM.
GRIP
AND THAT'S WHEN...
...I SAW OTORI BEAT UP SHOSUKE.
!!!

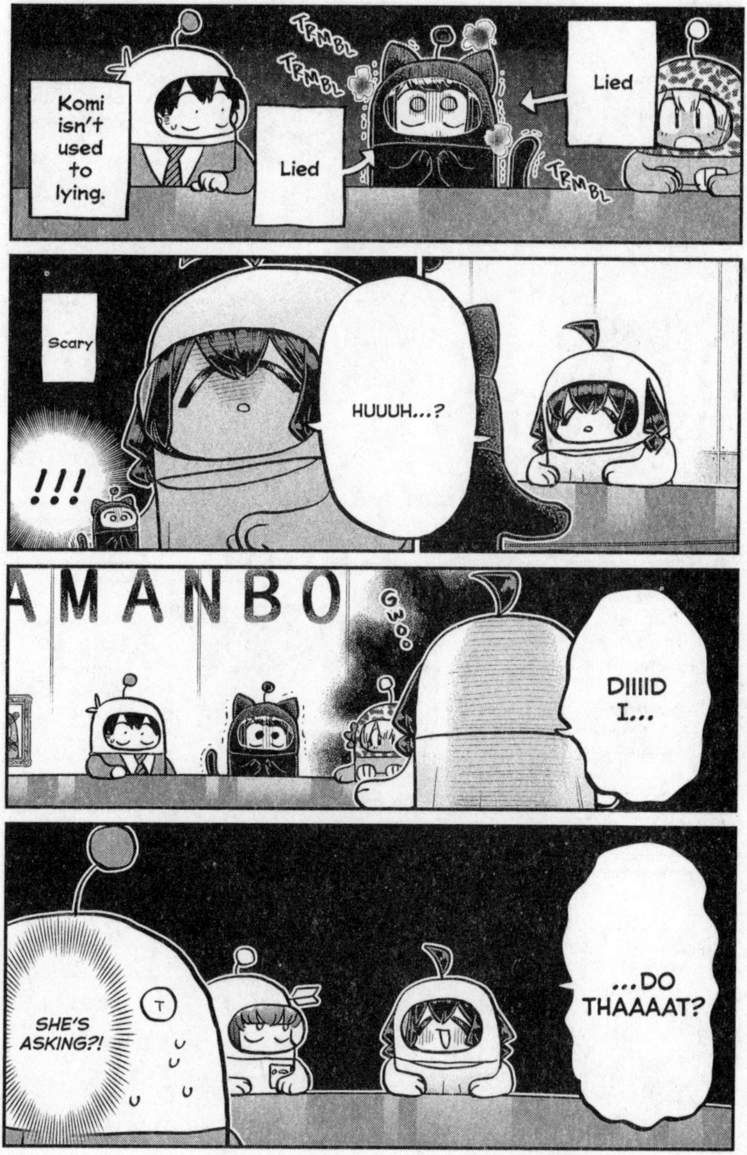
Lied
TRMBL
TRMBL
Lied
Komi isn't used to lying.
TRMBL
HUUUH...?
Scary
!!!
DIIIID I...
GWOO
AMANBO
...DO THAAAAT?
T
SHE'S ASKING?!

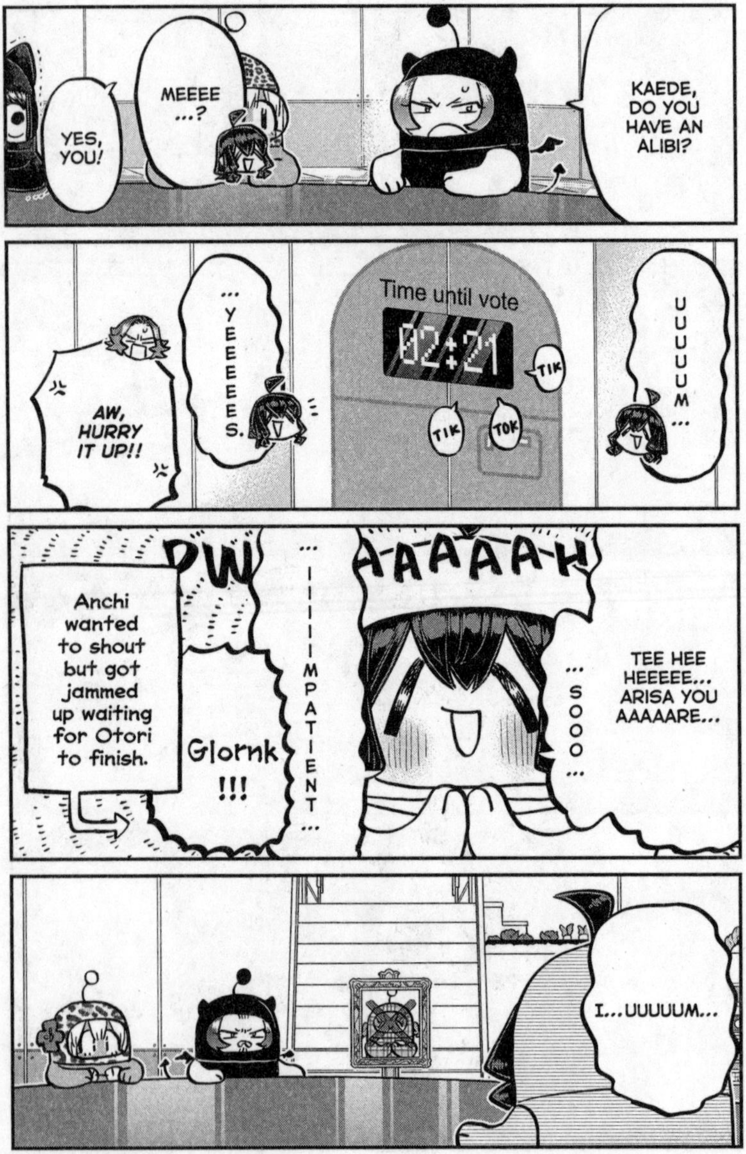
KAEDE, DO YOU HAVE AN ALIBI?
MEEEE...?
YES, YOU!
UUUUUM...
TIK
Time until vote
02:21
TOK
TIK
...YEEEEEES.
AW, HURRY IT UP!!
TEE HEE HEEEEE... ARISA YOU AAAAARE...
...SOOO...
AAAAAH
...I-I-IMPATIENT...
DW
Glornk!!!
Anchi wanted to shout but got jammed up waiting for Otori to finish.
I...UUUUUM...

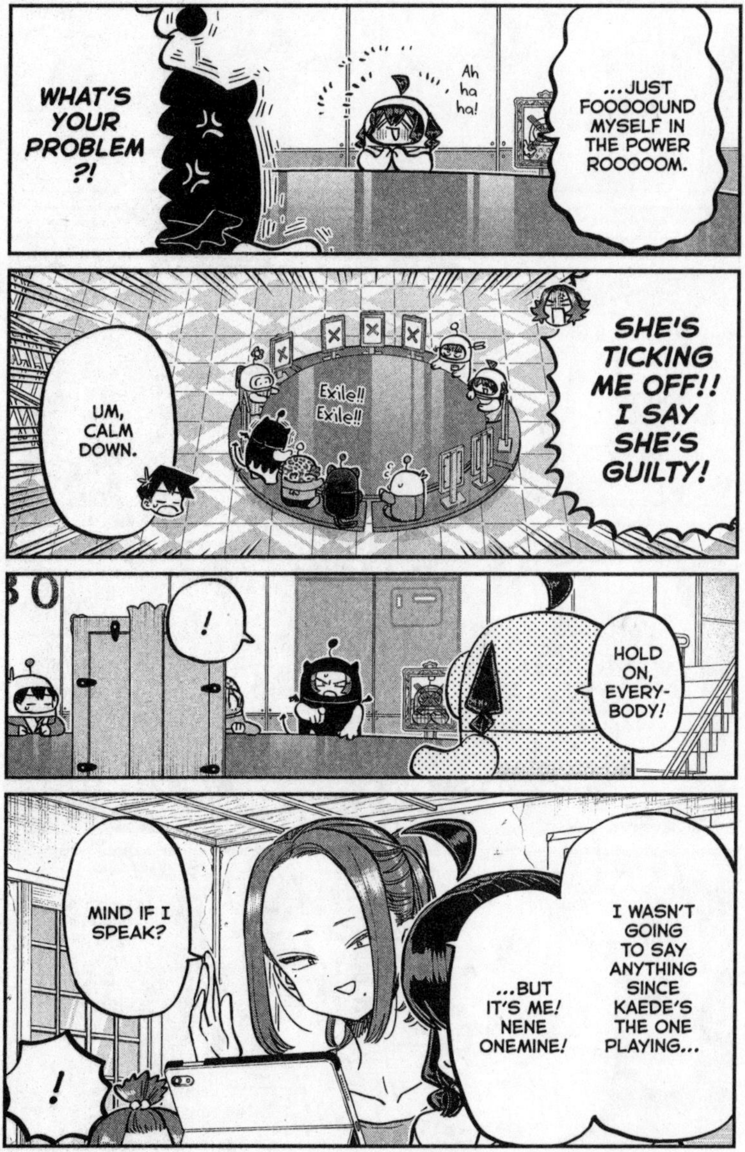
...JUST FOOOOOUND MYSELF IN THE POWER ROOOOOM.
Ah ha ha!
WHAT'S YOUR PROBLEM ?!
SHE'S TICKING ME OFF!! I SAY SHE'S GUILTY!
Exile!! Exile!!
UM, CALM DOWN.
HOLD ON, EVERY-BODY!
!
I WASN'T GOING TO SAY ANYTHING SINCE KAEDE'S THE ONE PLAYING...
...BUT IT'S ME! NENE ONEMINE!
MIND IF I SPEAK?
!

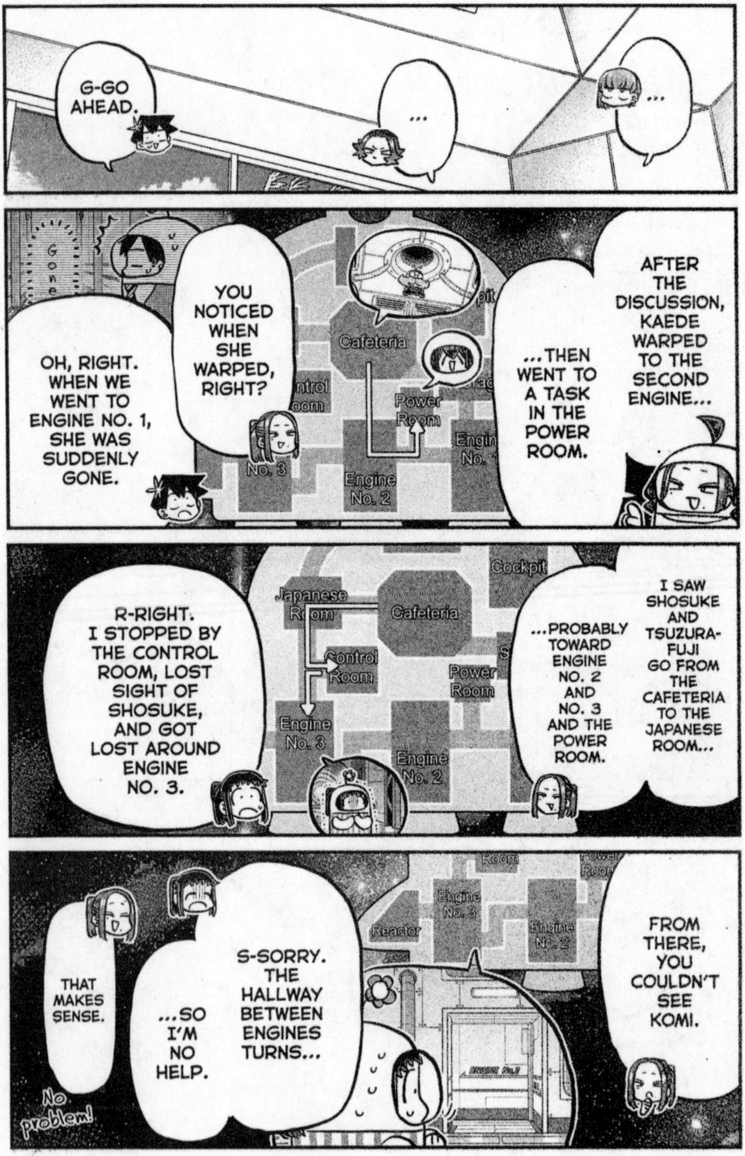
...
...
G-GO AHEAD.
AFTER THE DISCUSSION, KAEDE WARPED TO THE SECOND ENGINE...
...THEN WENT TO A TASK IN THE POWER ROOM.
Cafeteria
Power Room
Engine No. 2
YOU NOTICED WHEN SHE WARPED, RIGHT?
Gone
OH, RIGHT. WHEN WE WENT TO ENGINE NO. 1, SHE WAS SUDDENLY GONE.
I SAW SHOSUKE AND TSUZURA-FUJI GO FROM THE CAFETERIA TO THE JAPANESE ROOM...
...PROBABLY TOWARD ENGINE NO. 2 AND NO. 3 AND THE POWER ROOM.
Cockpit
Japanese Room
Cafeteria
Control Room
Power Room
Engine No. 3
Engine No. 2
R-RIGHT. I STOPPED BY THE CONTROL ROOM, LOST SIGHT OF SHOSUKE, AND GOT LOST AROUND ENGINE NO. 3.
FROM THERE, YOU COULDN'T SEE KOMI.
Engine No. 3
Reactor
Engine No. 2
S-SORRY. THE HALLWAY BETWEEN ENGINES TURNS...
...SO I'M NO HELP.
THAT MAKES SENSE.
No problem!

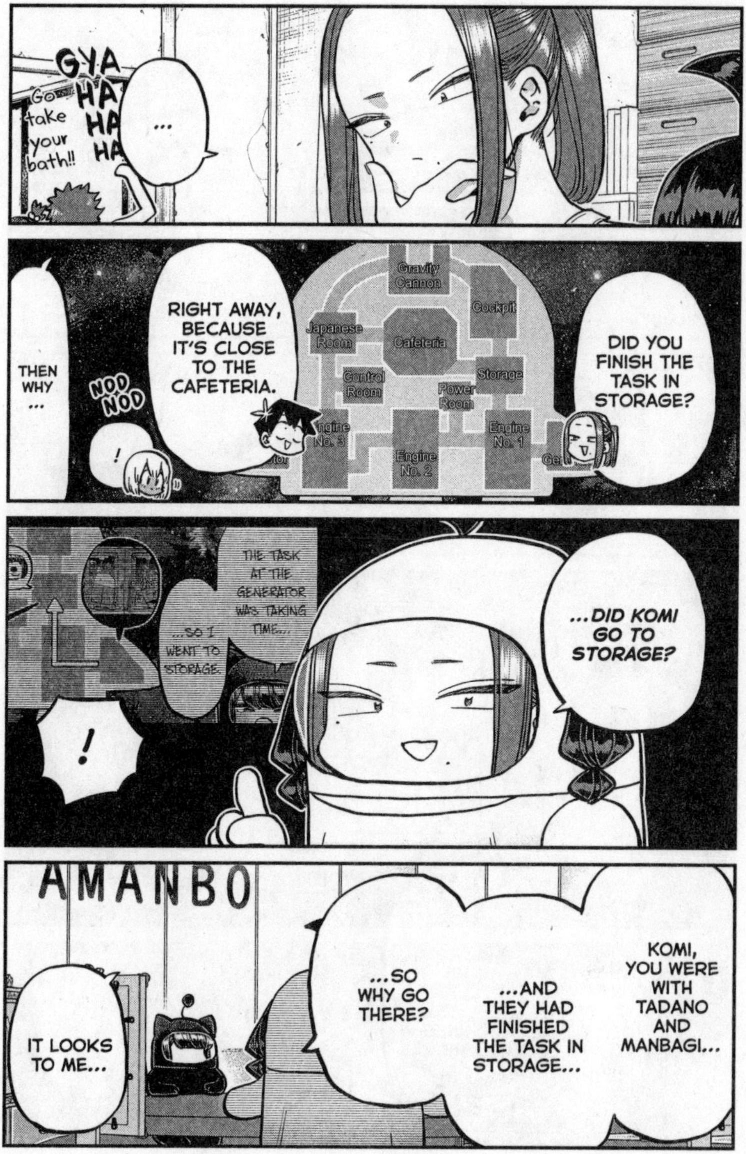
...
GYA HA HA HA HA
Go take your bath!!
DID YOU FINISH THE TASK IN STORAGE?
Gravity Cannon
Cockpit
Japanese Room
Cafeteria
Storage
Control Room
Power Room
Engine No. 1
Engine No. 2
RIGHT AWAY, BECAUSE IT'S CLOSE TO THE CAFETERIA.
NOD NOD
!
THEN WHY ...
...DID KOMI GO TO STORAGE?
THE TASK AT THE GENERATOR WAS TAKING TIME...
...SO I WENT TO STORAGE.
!
KOMI, YOU WERE WITH TADANO AND MANBAGI...
...AND THEY HAD FINISHED THE TASK IN STORAGE...
...SO WHY GO THERE?
AMANBO
IT LOOKS TO ME...

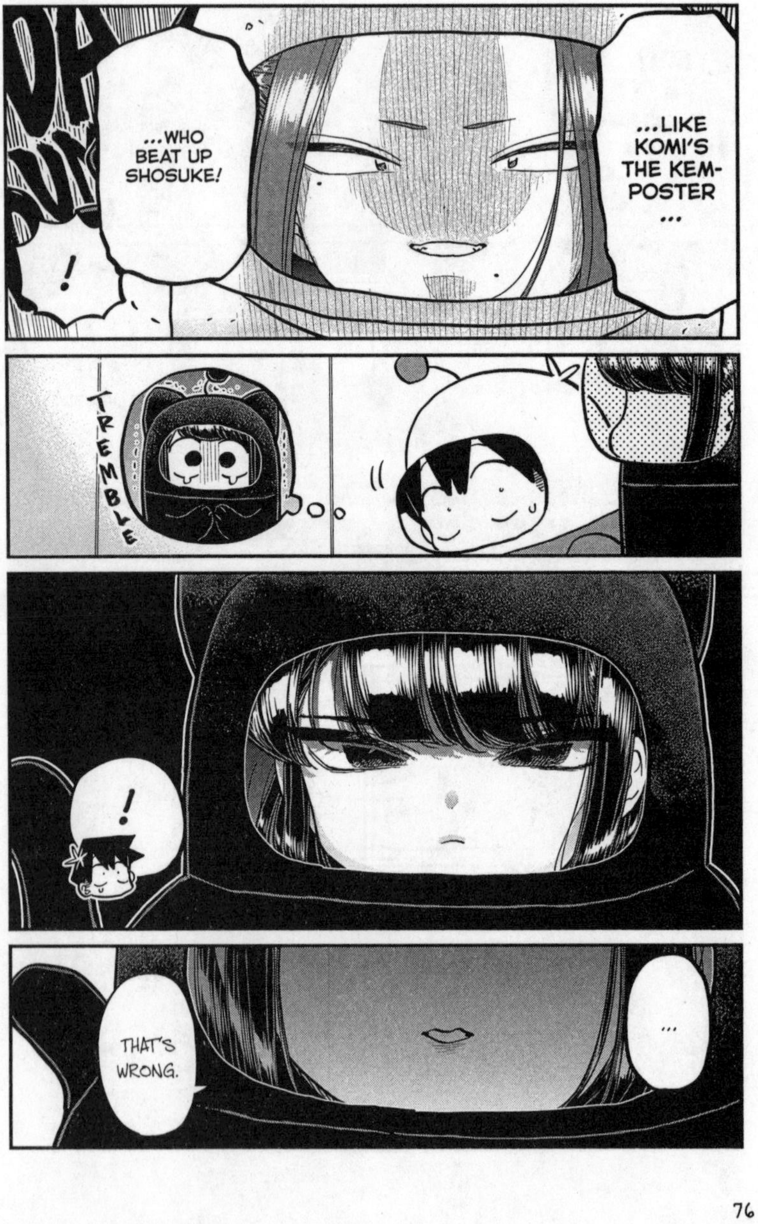
...LIKE KOMI'S THE KEM-POSTER ...
...WHO BEAT UP SHOSUKE!
!
TREMBLE
!
...
THAT'S WRONG.

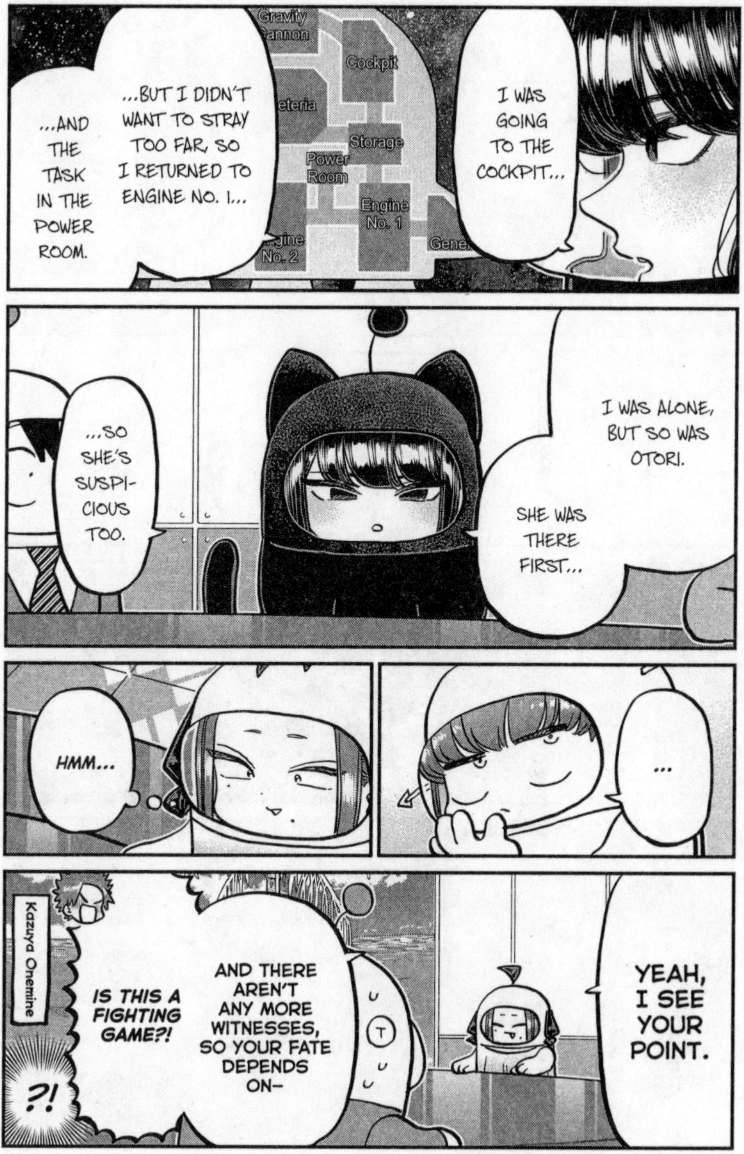
I WAS GOING TO THE COCKPIT...
...BUT I DIDN'T WANT TO STRAY TOO FAR, SO I RETURNED TO ENGINE NO. 1...
...AND THE TASK IN THE POWER ROOM.
Gravity Cannon
Cockpit
Storage
Power Room
Engine No. 1
I WAS ALONE, BUT SO WAS OTORI.
SHE WAS THERE FIRST...
...SO SHE'S SUSPICIOUS TOO.
...
HMM...
YEAH, I SEE YOUR POINT.
AND THERE AREN'T ANY MORE WITNESSES, SO YOUR FATE DEPENDS ON–
IS THIS A FIGHTING GAME?!
?!
Kazuya Onemine

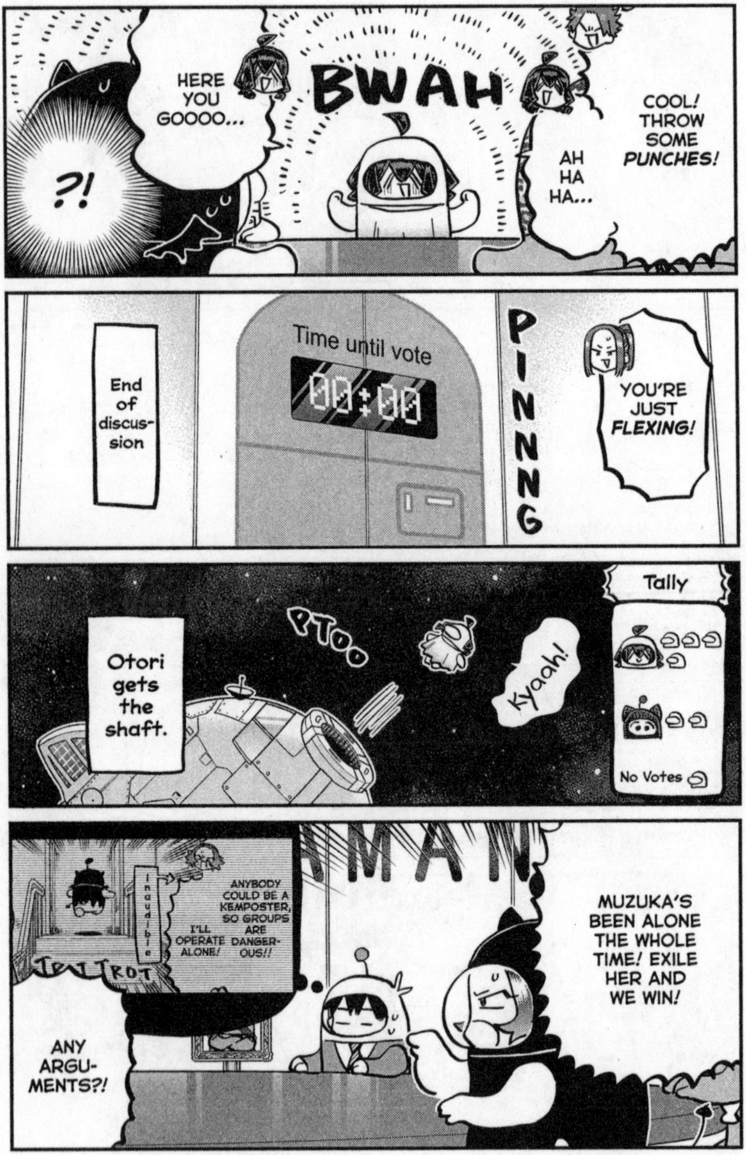
COOL! THROW SOME PUNCHES!
AH HA HA...
BWAH
HERE YOU GOOOO...
?!
YOU'RE JUST FLEXING!
PINNNG
Time until vote
00:00
End of discus-sion
Tally
No Votes
Kyaah!
PTOO
Otori gets the shaft.
MUZUKA'S BEEN ALONE THE WHOLE TIME! EXILE HER AND WE WIN!
ANYBODY COULD BE A KEMPOSTER, SO GROUPS ARE DANGER-OUS!!
I'LL OPERATE ALONE!
Inaudible
TROT TROT
ANY ARGU-MENTS?!

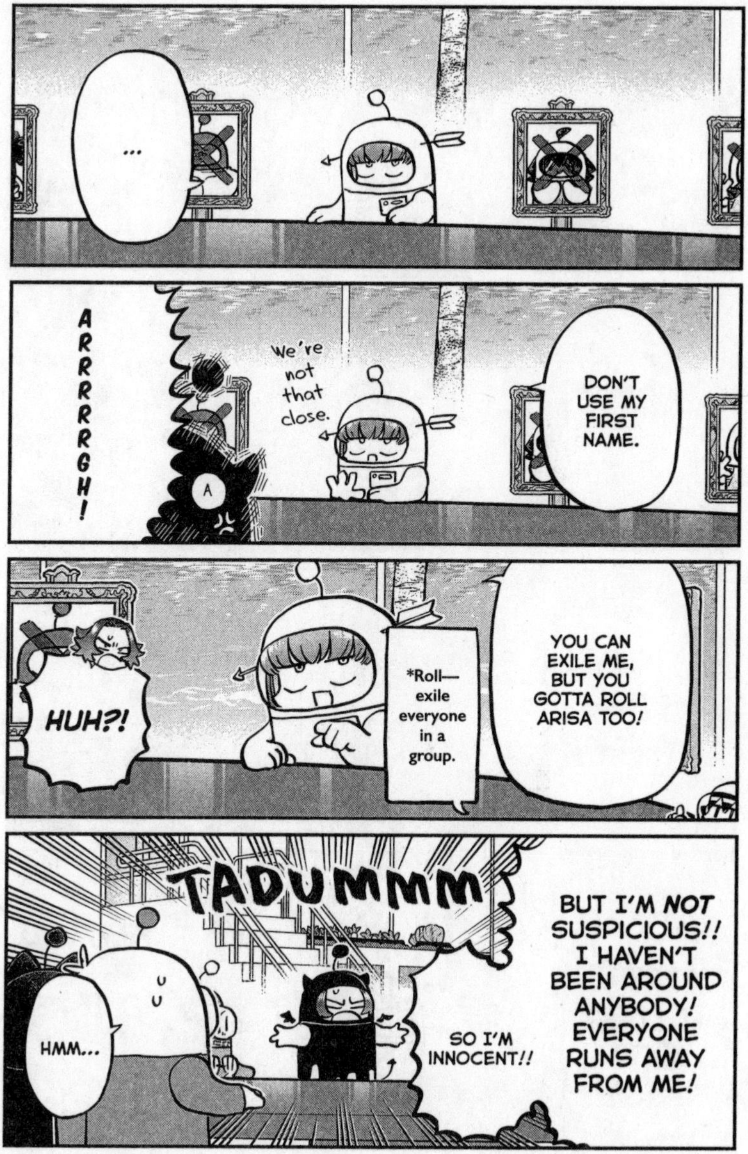
...
DON'T USE MY FIRST NAME.
We're not that close.
ARRRRRRGH!
A
YOU CAN EXILE ME, BUT YOU GOTTA ROLL ARISA TOO!
*Roll—exile everyone in a group.
HUH?!
BUT I'M *NOT* SUSPICIOUS!! I HAVEN'T BEEN AROUND ANYBODY! EVERYONE RUNS AWAY FROM ME!
TADUMMM
SO I'M INNOCENT!!
HMM...

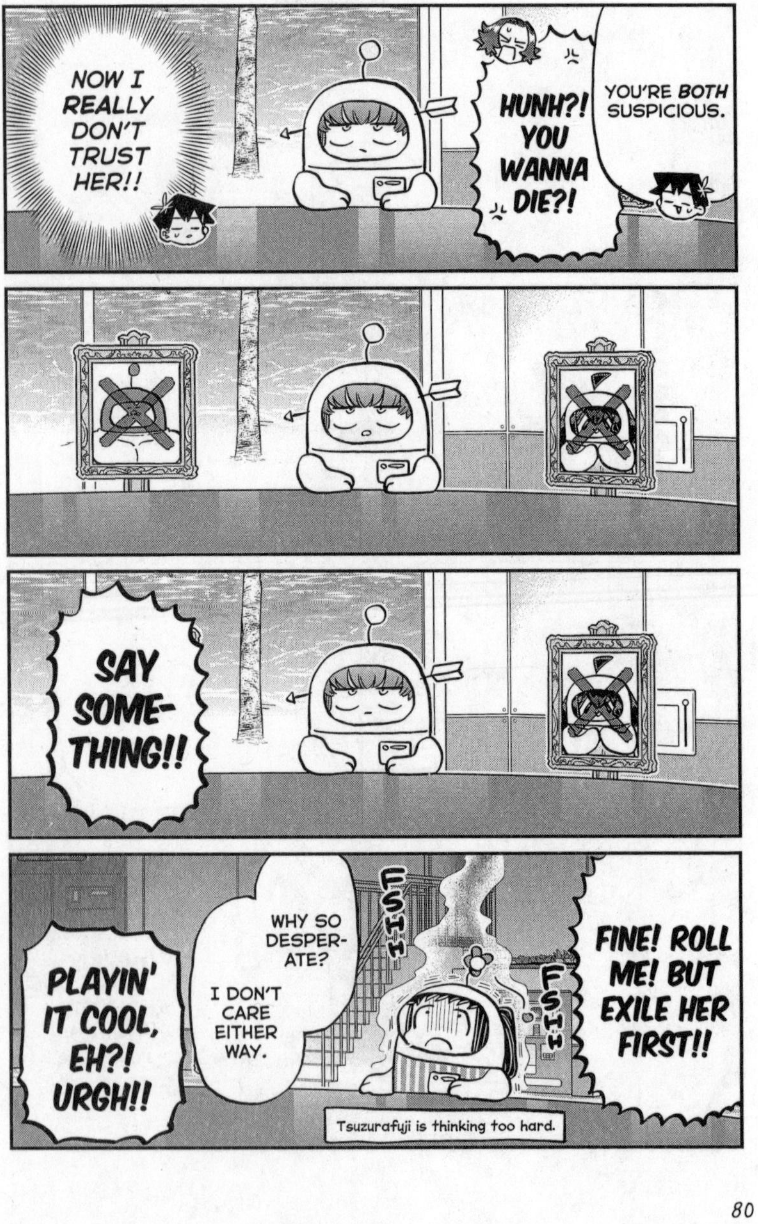
YOU'RE BOTH SUSPICIOUS.
HUNH?! YOU WANNA DIE?!
NOW I REALLY DON'T TRUST HER!!
SAY SOME-THING!!
FINE! ROLL ME! BUT EXILE HER FIRST!!
FSHH
FSHH
WHY SO DESPER-ATE?
I DON'T CARE EITHER WAY.
PLAYIN' IT COOL, EH?! URGH!!
Tsuzurafuji is thinking too hard.

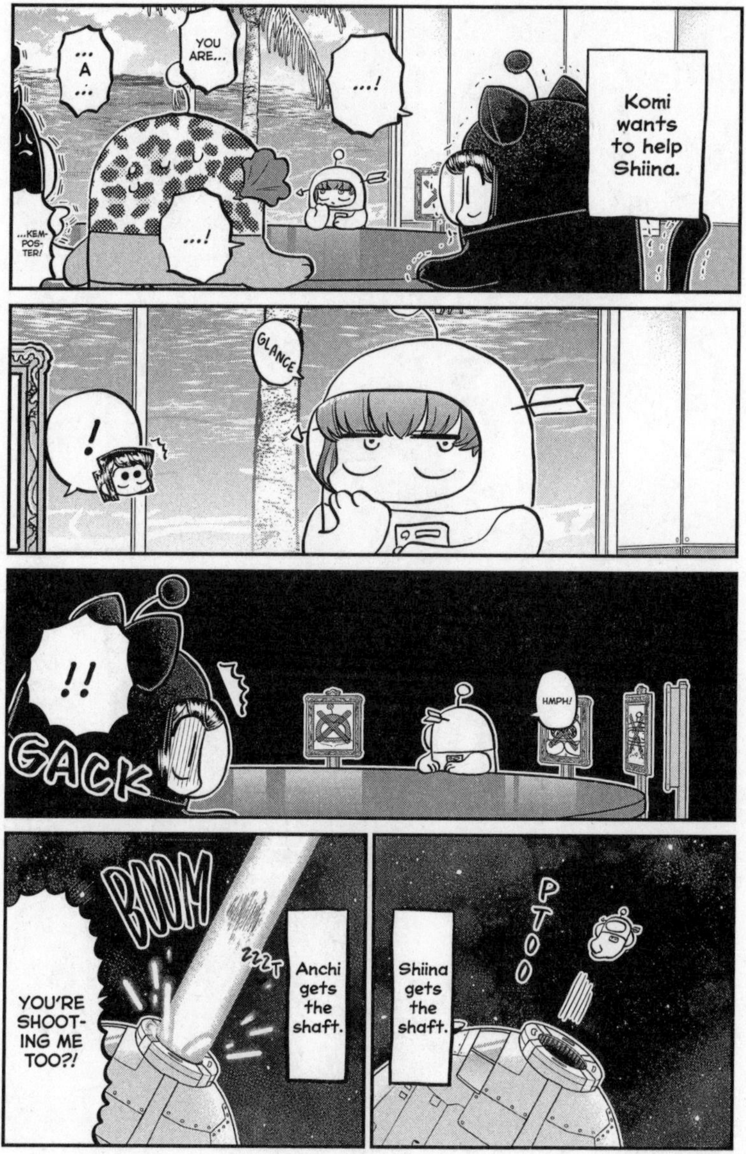
Komi wants to help Shiina.
...!
YOU ARE...
...A...
...!
...KEM-POSTER!
GLANCE
!
HMPH!
!!
GACK
PTOO
Shiina gets the shaft.
BOOM
Anchi gets the shaft.
ZZZT
YOU'RE SHOOT-ING ME TOO?!

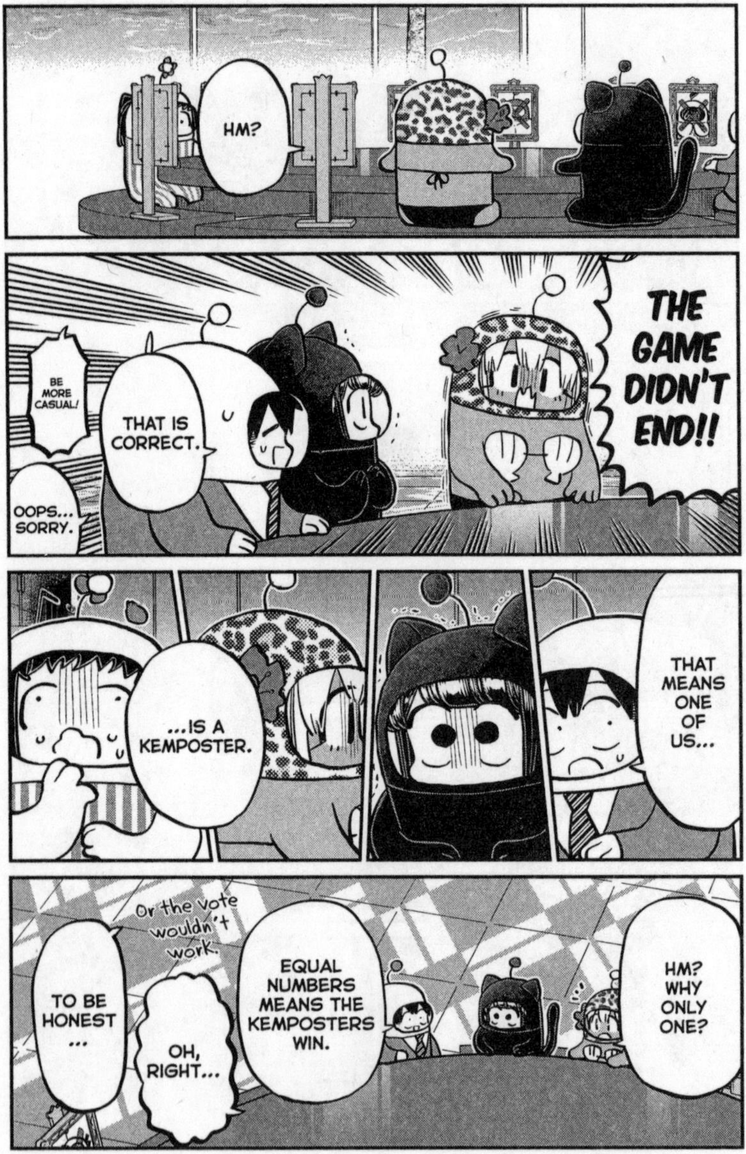
HM?
THE GAME DIDN'T END!!
THAT IS CORRECT.
BE MORE CASUAL!
OOPS... SORRY.
THAT MEANS ONE OF US...
...IS A KEMPOSTER.
HM? WHY ONLY ONE?
EQUAL NUMBERS MEANS THE KEMPOSTERS WIN.
Or the vote wouldn't work.
OH, RIGHT...
TO BE HONEST ...

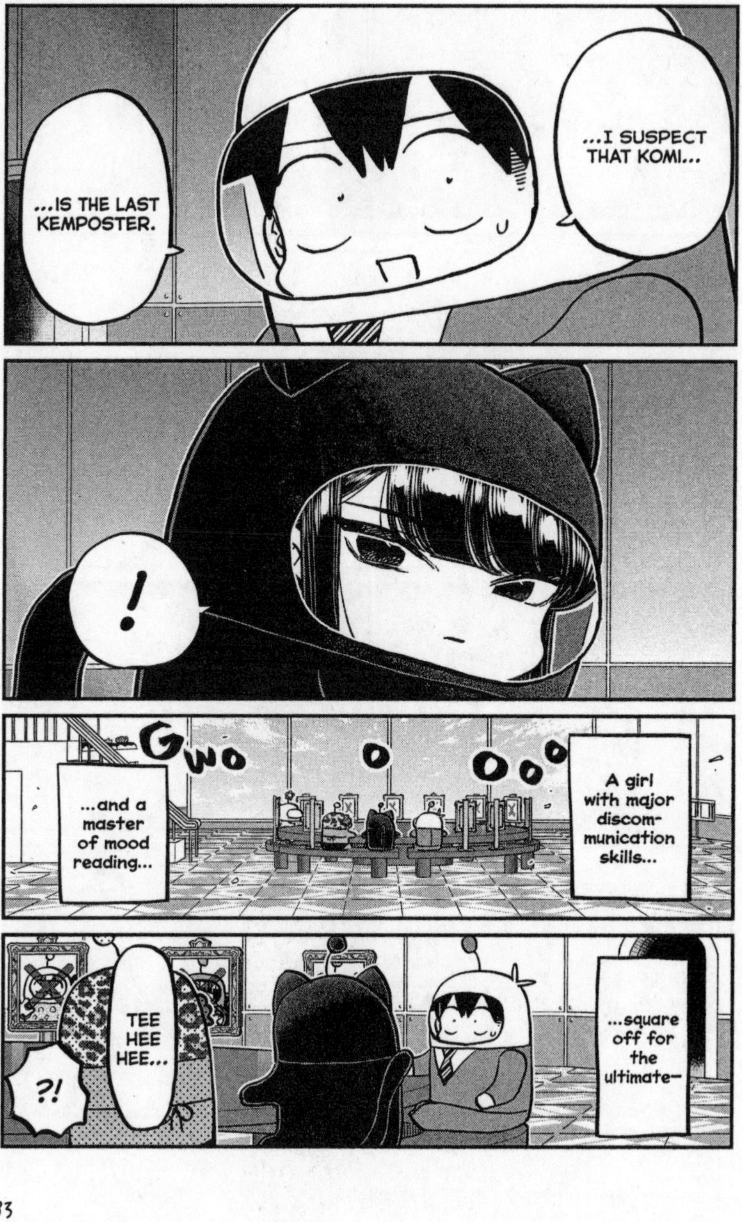
...I SUSPECT THAT KOMI...
...IS THE LAST KEMPOSTER.
!
A girl with major discom- munication skills...
GWO O OOO
...and a master of mood reading...
...square off for the ultimate—
TEE HEE HEE...
?!

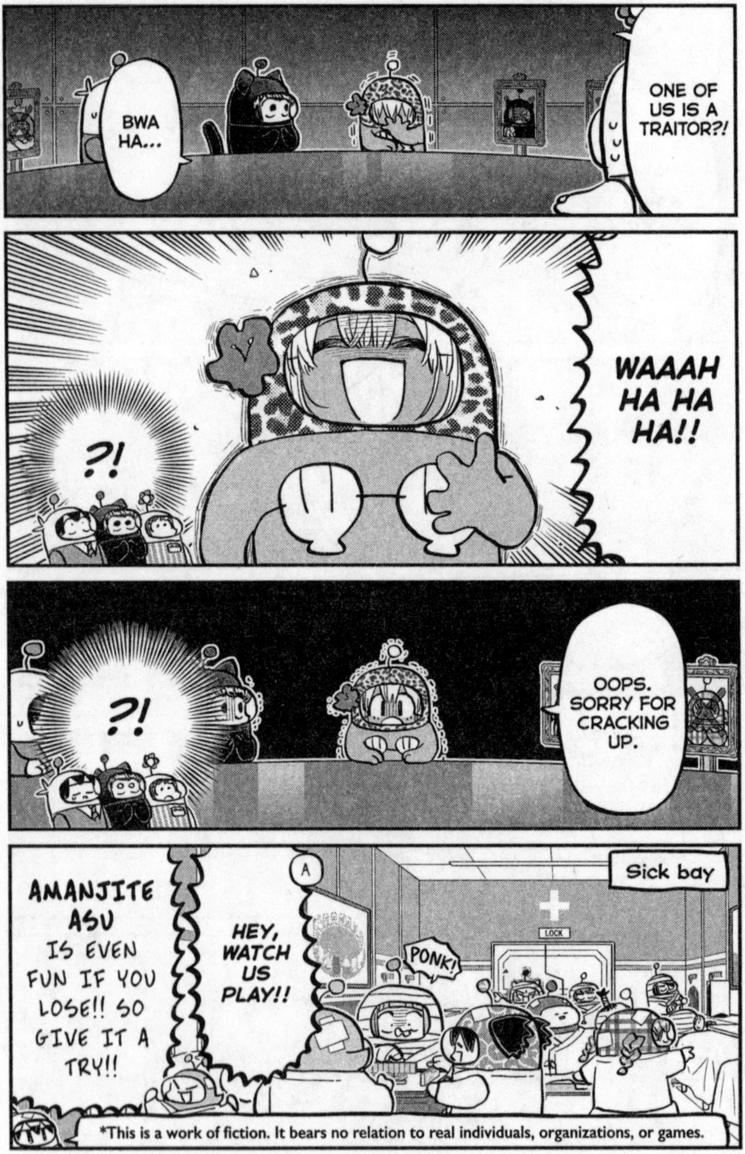
ONE OF US IS A TRAITOR?!
BWA HA...
WAAAH HA HA HA!!
?!
OOPS. SORRY FOR CRACKING UP.
?!
Sick bay
LOCK
PONK!
A
HEY, WATCH US PLAY!!
AMANJITE ASU IS EVEN FUN IF YOU LOSE!! SO GIVE IT A TRY!!
*This is a work of fiction. It bears no relation to real individuals, organizations, or games.

Communication 355 — The End

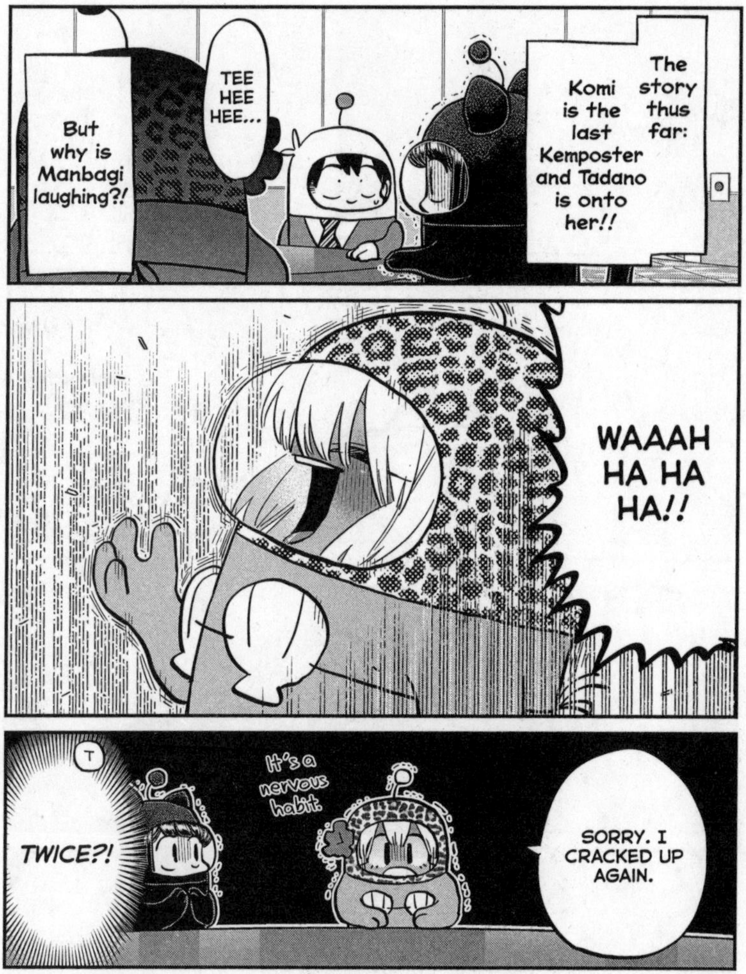
The story thus far: Komi is the last Kemposter and Tadano is onto her!!
TEE HEE HEE...
But why is Manbagi laughing?!
WAAAH HA HA HA!!
SORRY. I CRACKED UP AGAIN.
It's a nervous habit.
TWICE?!

Komi Can't Communicate

Communication 356: Amanjite Asu

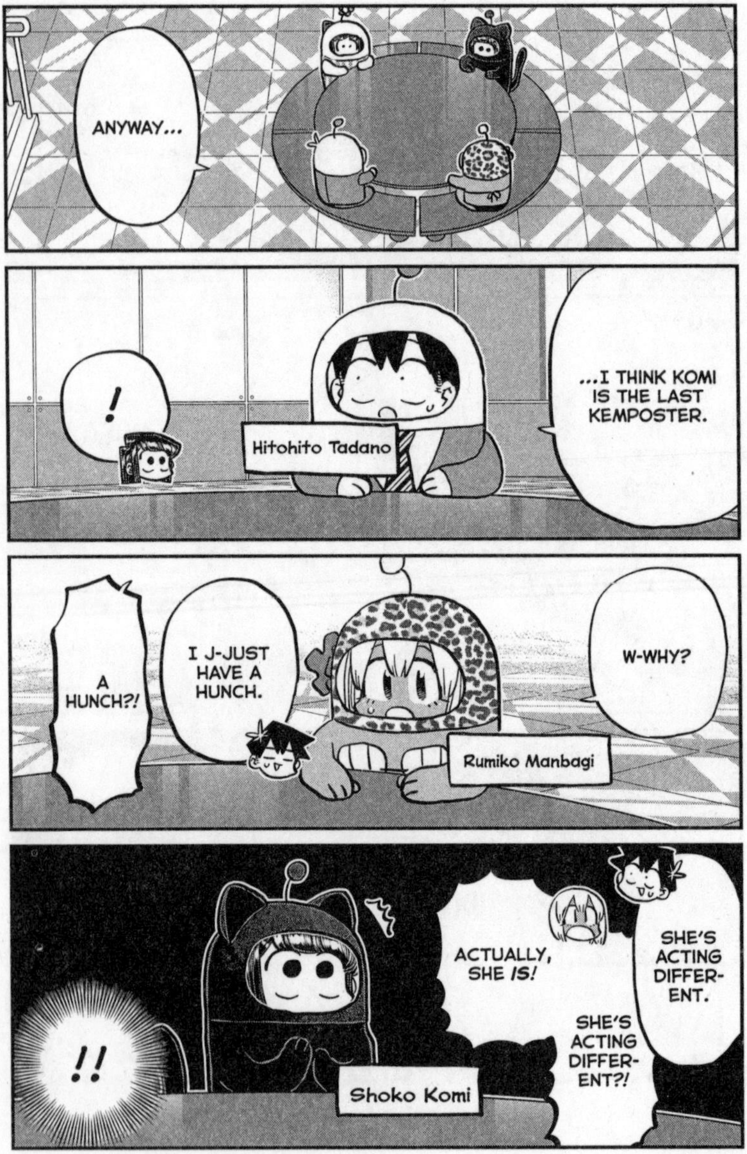
ANYWAY...
...I THINK KOMI IS THE LAST KEMPOSTER.
Hitohito Tadano
!
W-WHY?
Rumiko Manbagi
I J-JUST HAVE A HUNCH.
A HUNCH?!
SHE'S ACTING DIFFER-ENT.
SHE'S ACTING DIFFER-ENT?!
ACTUALLY, SHE *IS*!
Shoko Komi
!!

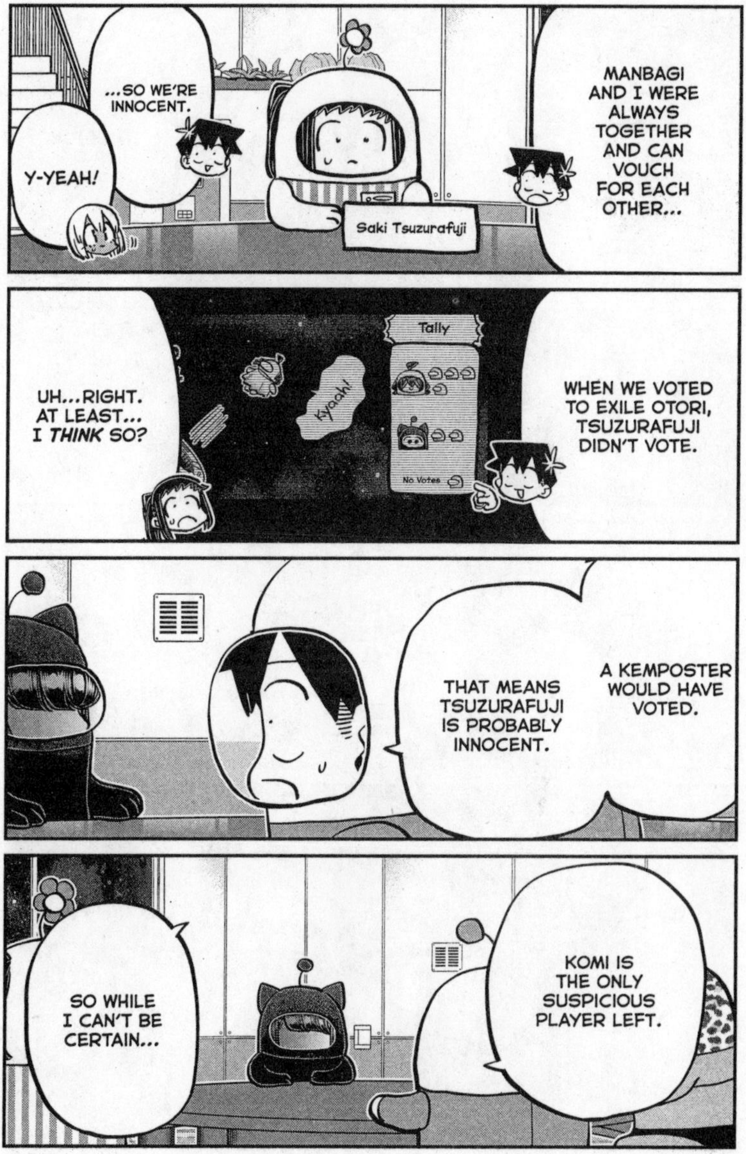
MANBAGI AND I WERE ALWAYS TOGETHER AND CAN VOUCH FOR EACH OTHER...
Saki Tsuzurafuji
...SO WE'RE INNOCENT.
Y-YEAH!
WHEN WE VOTED TO EXILE OTORI, TSUZURAFUJI DIDN'T VOTE.
Tally
No Votes
Kyaah!
UH...RIGHT. AT LEAST... I *THINK* SO?
A KEMPOSTER WOULD HAVE VOTED.
THAT MEANS TSUZURAFUJI IS PROBABLY INNOCENT.
KOMI IS THE ONLY SUSPICIOUS PLAYER LEFT.
SO WHILE I CAN'T BE CERTAIN...

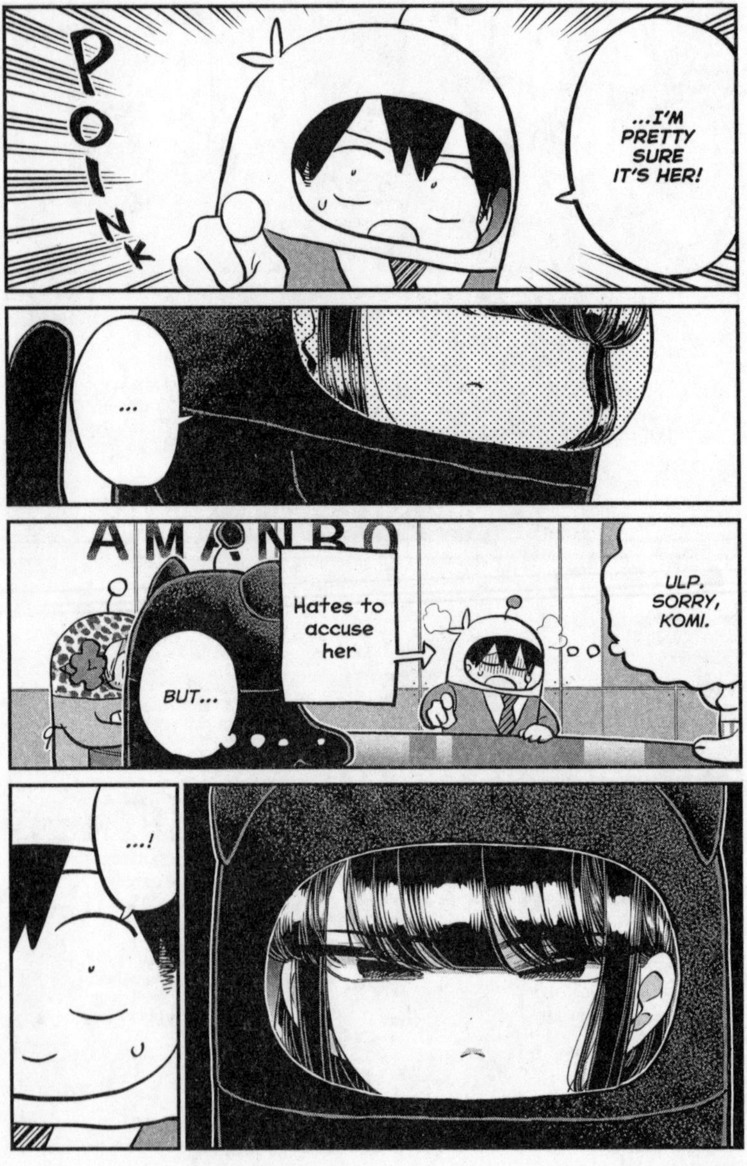
...I'M PRETTY SURE IT'S HER!
POINK
...
ULP. SORRY, KOMI.
Hates to accuse her
AMANBO
BUT...
...!

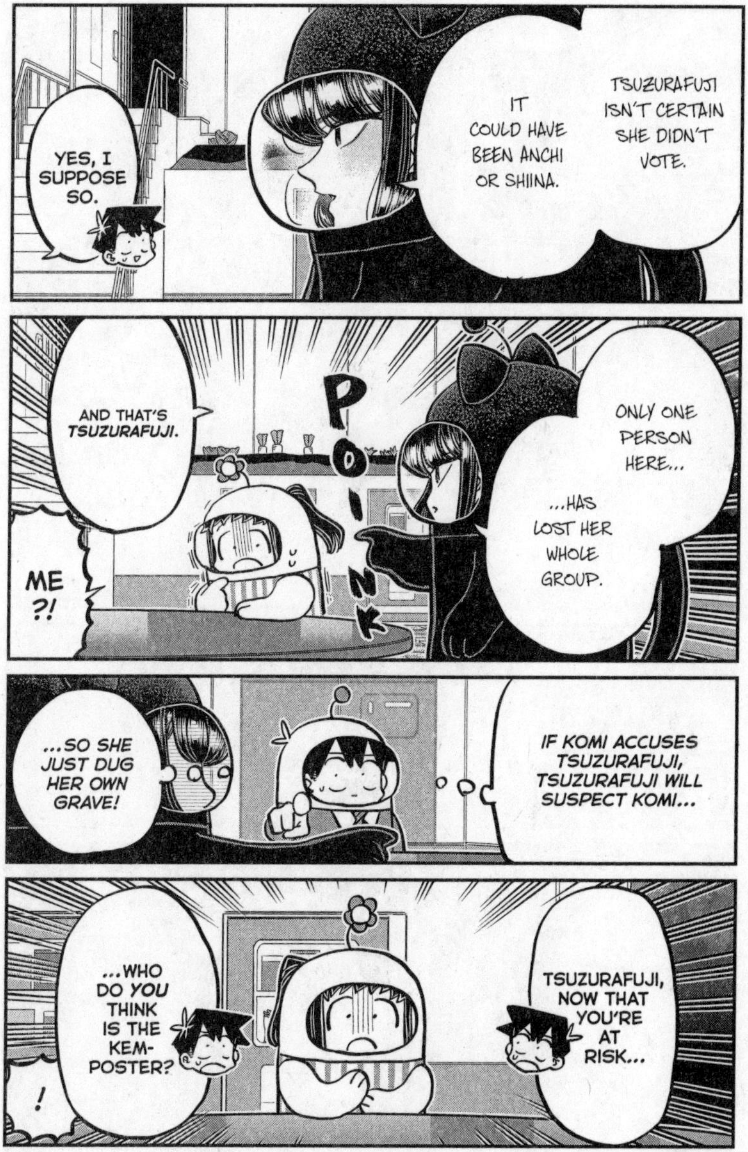
TSUZURAFUJI ISN'T CERTAIN SHE DIDN'T VOTE.
IT COULD HAVE BEEN ANCHI OR SHIINA.
YES, I SUPPOSE SO.
ONLY ONE PERSON HERE...
...HAS LOST HER WHOLE GROUP.
POINK
AND THAT'S *TSUZURAFUJI.*
ME?!
IF KOMI ACCUSES TSUZURAFUJI, TSUZURAFUJI WILL SUSPECT KOMI...
...SO SHE JUST DUG HER OWN GRAVE!
TSUZURAFUJI, NOW THAT YOU'RE AT RISK...
...WHO DO *YOU* THINK IS THE KEM-POSTER?
!

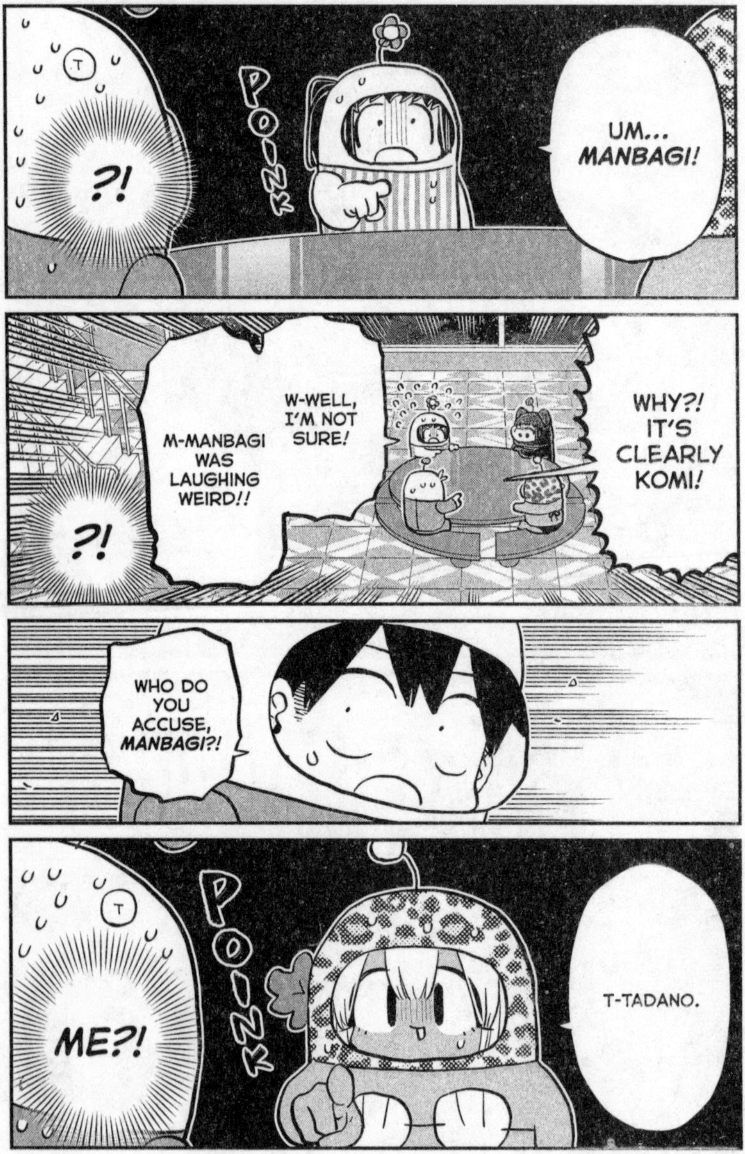
UM... MANBAGI!
POINK
T
?!
WHY?! IT'S CLEARLY KOMI!
W-WELL, I'M NOT SURE!
M-MANBAGI WAS LAUGHING WEIRD!!
?!
WHO DO YOU ACCUSE, MANBAGI?!
T-TADANO.
POINK
T
ME?!

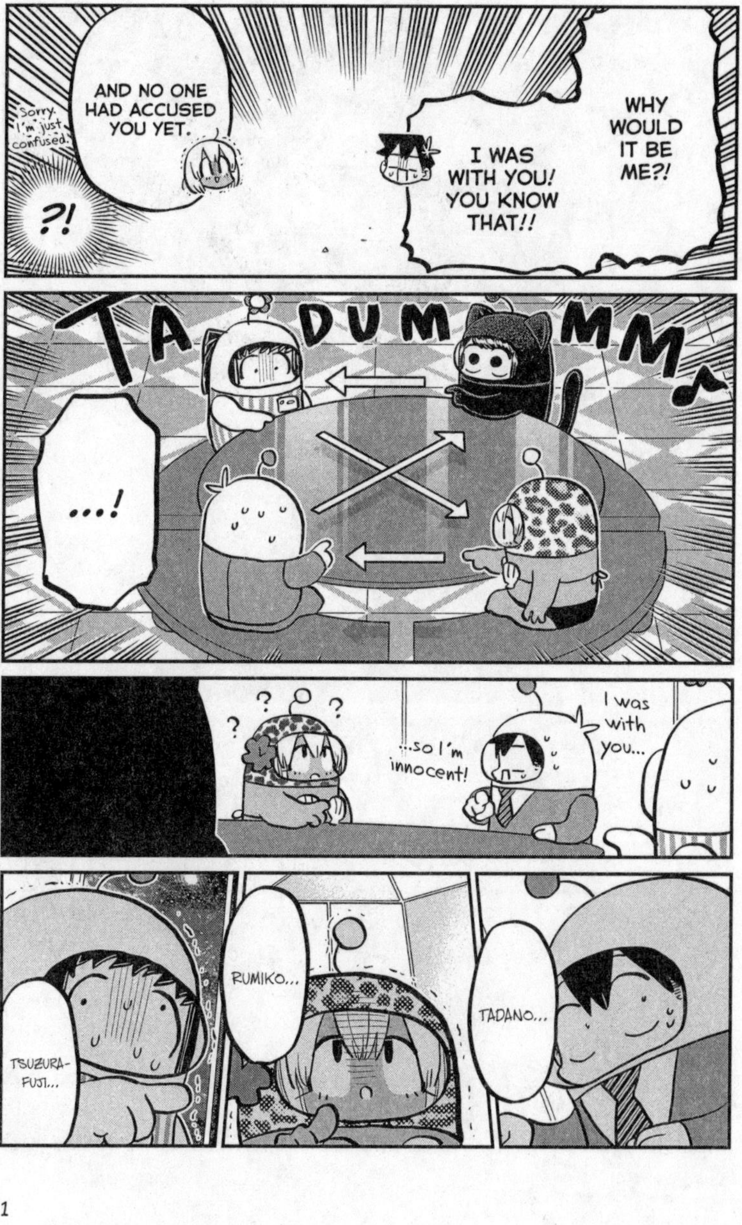
WHY WOULD IT BE ME?!
I WAS WITH YOU! YOU KNOW THAT!!
AND NO ONE HAD ACCUSED YOU YET.
?!
Sorry. I'm just confused.
TA DUMMM
...!
I was with you...
...so I'm innocent!
TADANO...
RUMIKO...
TSUZURA-FUJI...

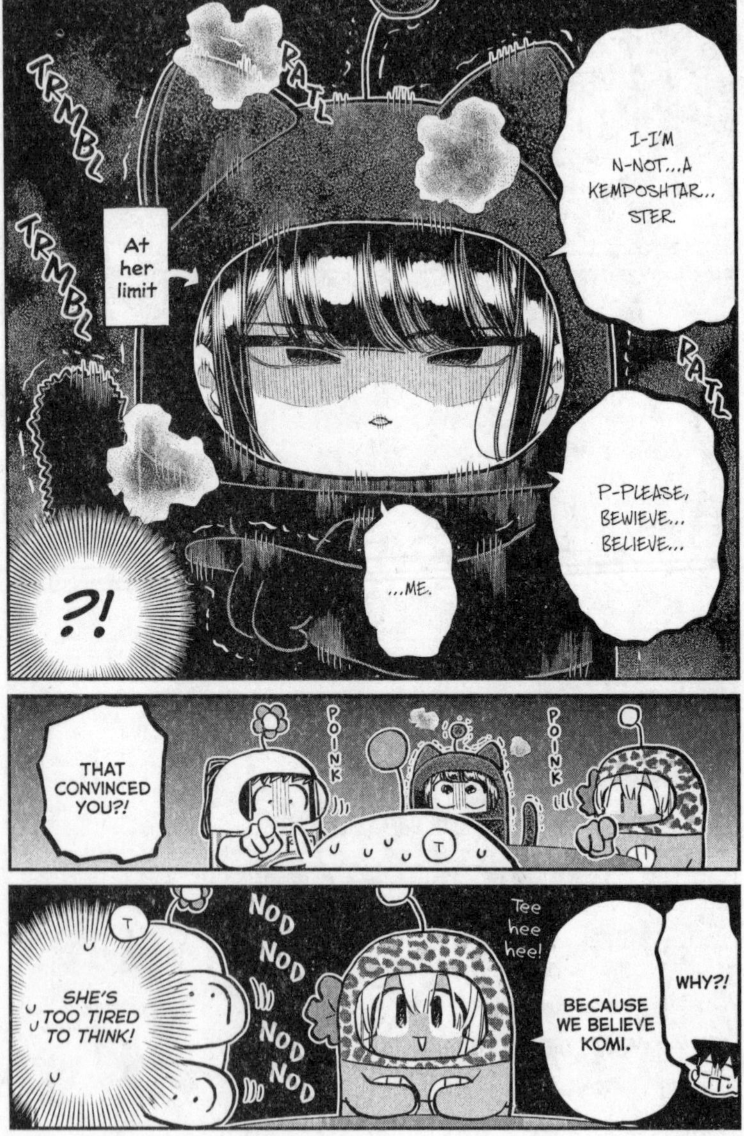
RATL
I-I'M N-NOT...A KEMPOSHTAR... STER.
RATL
TRMBL
At her limit
TRMBL
P-PLEASE, BEWIEVE... BELIEVE...
...ME.
?!
POINK
POINK
THAT CONVINCED YOU?!
WHY?!
BECAUSE WE BELIEVE KOMI.
Tee hee hee!
NOD NOD NOD NOD
SHE'S TOO TIRED TO THINK!

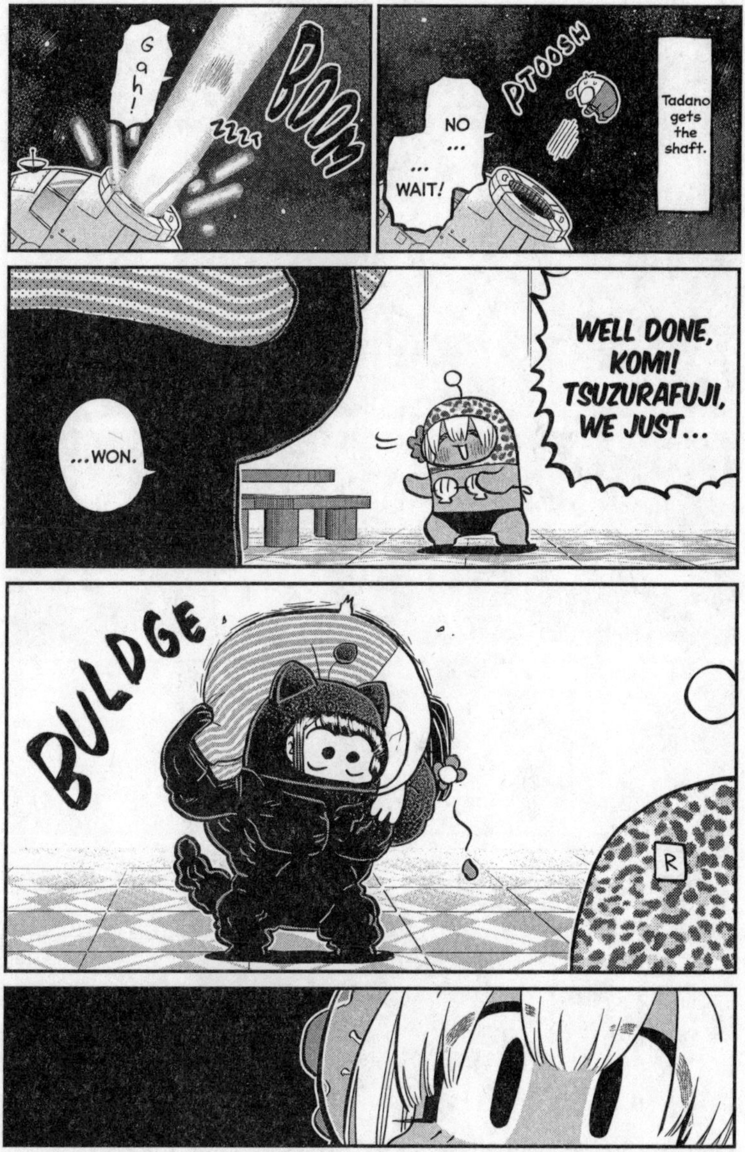
Tadano gets the shaft.
PTOOSH
NO ... ... WAIT!
Gah!
BOOM
WELL DONE, KOMI! TSUZURAFUJI, WE JUST...
...WON.
BULDGE
R

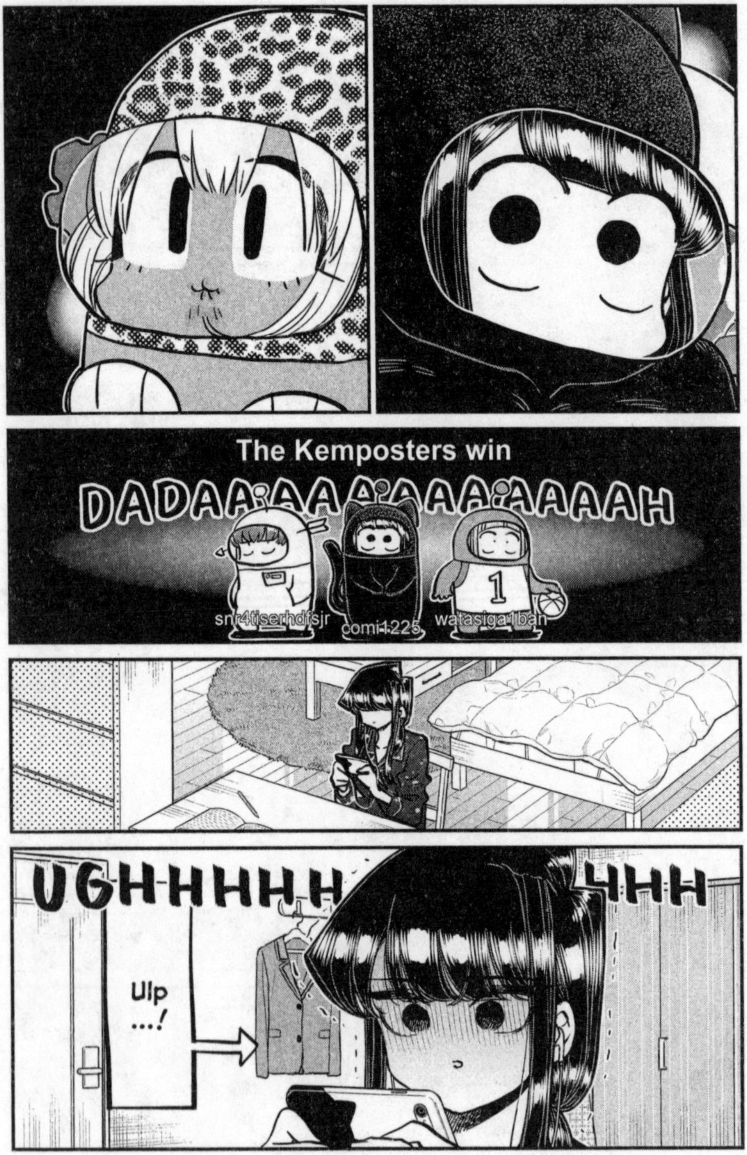
The Kemposters win
DADAAAAAAAAAAAAAH
snr4tiserhdfsjr
comi1225
watasiga1ban
UGHHHHHHHH
Ulp ...!

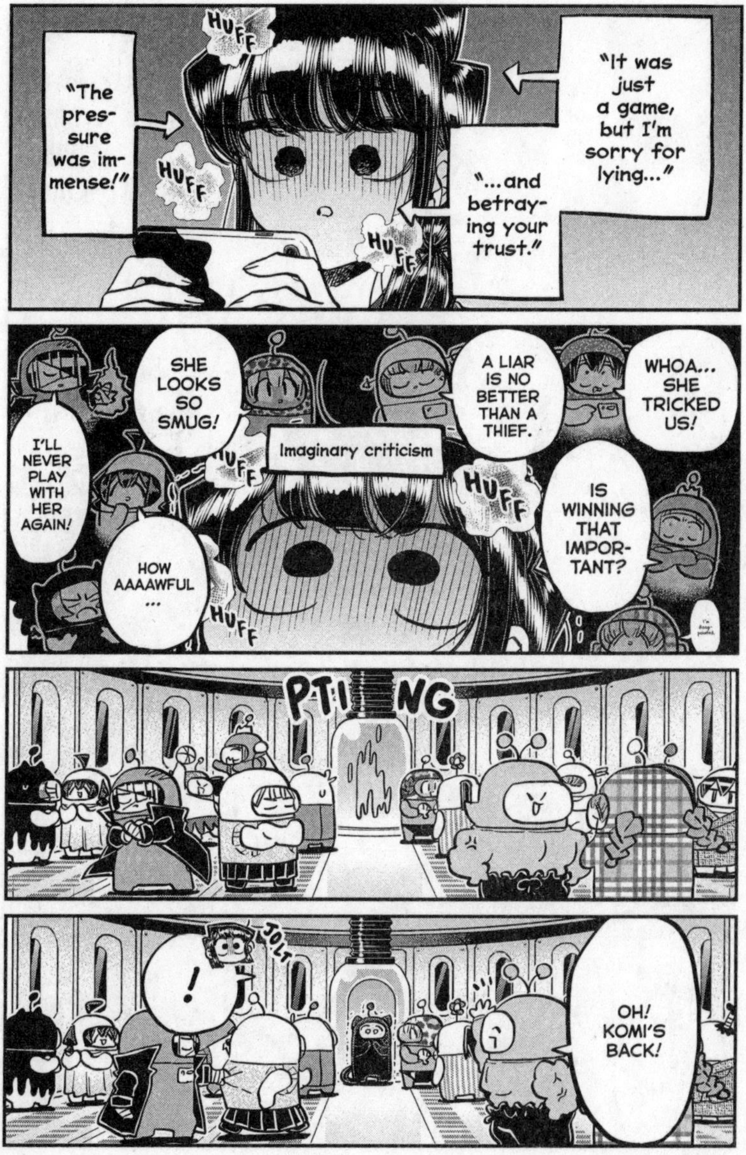
"It was just a game, but I'm sorry for lying..."
"...and betraying your trust."
HUFF
"The pressure was immense!"
HUFF
HUFF
WHOA... SHE TRICKED US!
A LIAR IS NO BETTER THAN A THIEF.
Imaginary criticism
SHE LOOKS SO SMUG!
HUFF
IS WINNING THAT IMPORTANT?
HUFF
I'LL NEVER PLAY WITH HER AGAIN!
HOW AAAAWFUL ...
HUFF
PTING
OH! KOMI'S BACK!
JOLT
!

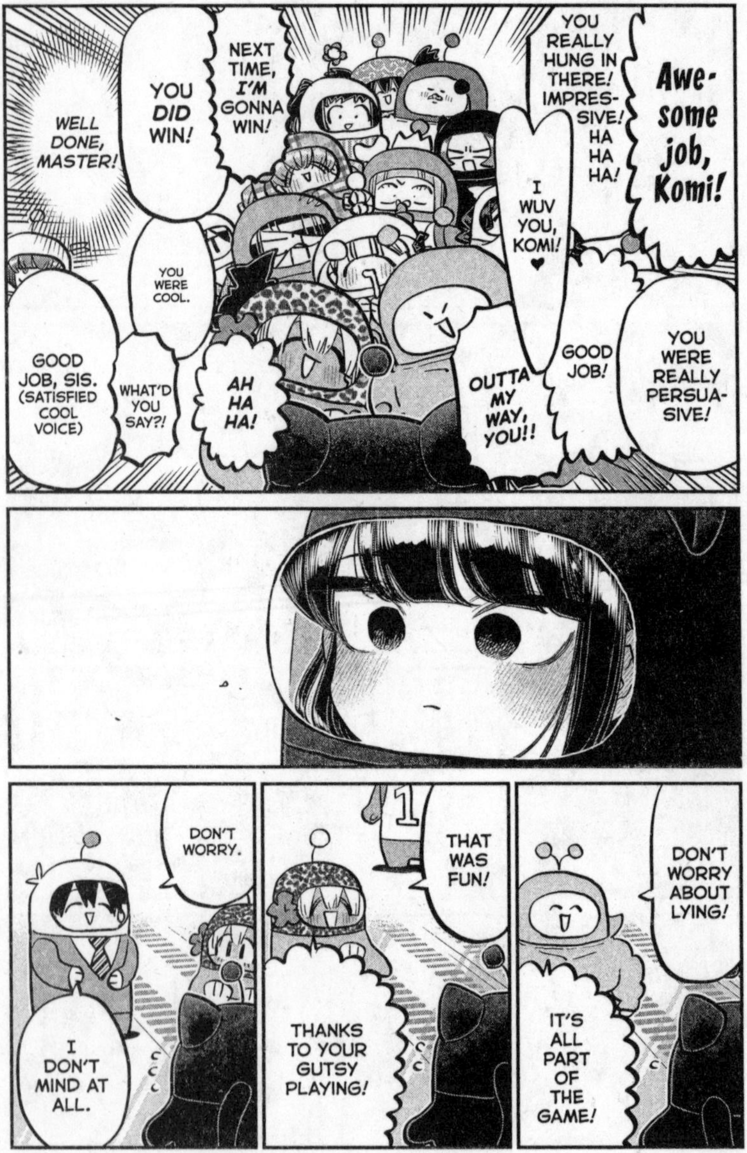
Awe-some job, Komi!
YOU REALLY HUNG IN THERE! IMPRES-SIVE! HA HA HA!
I WUV YOU, KOMI! ♥
NEXT TIME, I'M GONNA WIN!
YOU DID WIN!
WELL DONE, MASTER!
YOU WERE REALLY PERSUA-SIVE!
GOOD JOB!
OUTTA MY WAY, YOU!!
AH HA HA!
YOU WERE COOL.
WHAT'D YOU SAY?!
GOOD JOB, SIS. (SATISFIED COOL VOICE)
DON'T WORRY ABOUT LYING!
IT'S ALL PART OF THE GAME!
THAT WAS FUN!
THANKS TO YOUR GUTSY PLAYING!
DON'T WORRY.
I DON'T MIND AT ALL.

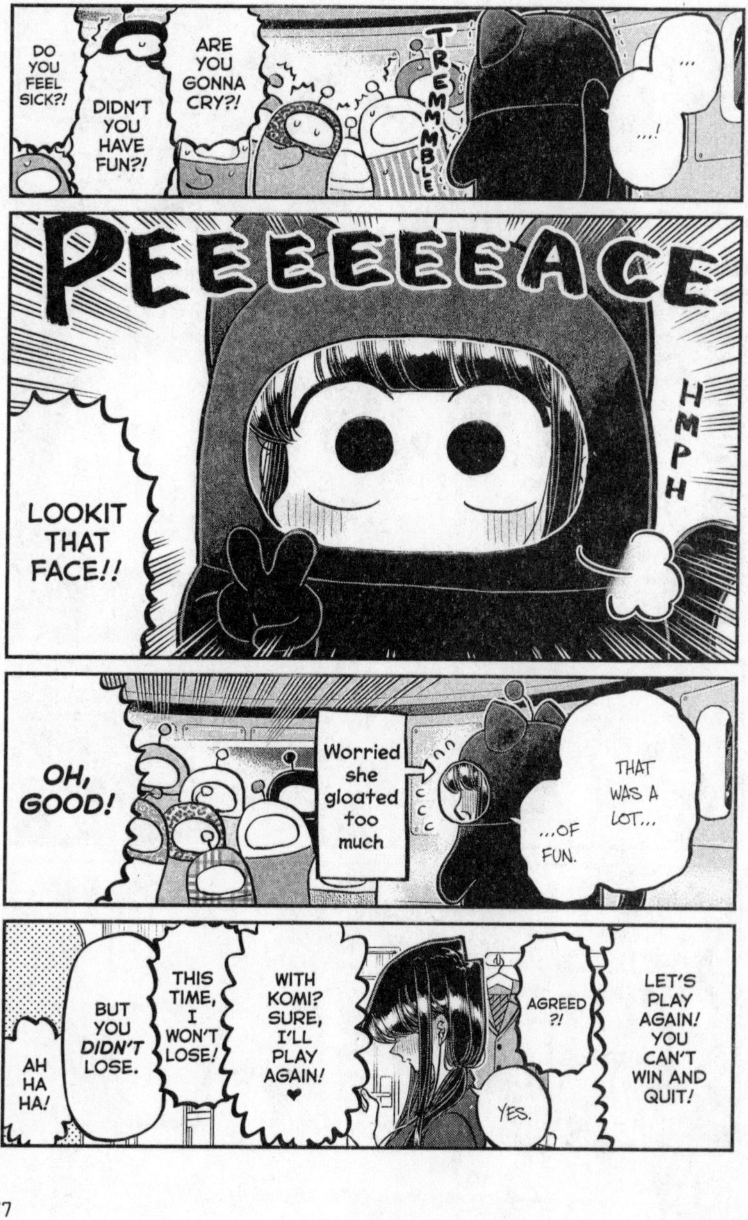
...
...!
TREMMMBLE
ARE YOU GONNA CRY?!
DIDN'T YOU HAVE FUN?!
DO YOU FEEL SICK?!
PEEEEEACE
HMPH
LOOKIT THAT FACE!!
THAT WAS A LOT...
...OF FUN.
Worried she gloated too much
OH, GOOD!
LET'S PLAY AGAIN! YOU CAN'T WIN AND QUIT!
YES.
AGREED?!
WITH KOMI? SURE, I'LL PLAY AGAIN! ❤
THIS TIME, I WON'T LOSE!
BUT YOU DIDN'T LOSE.
AH HA HA!

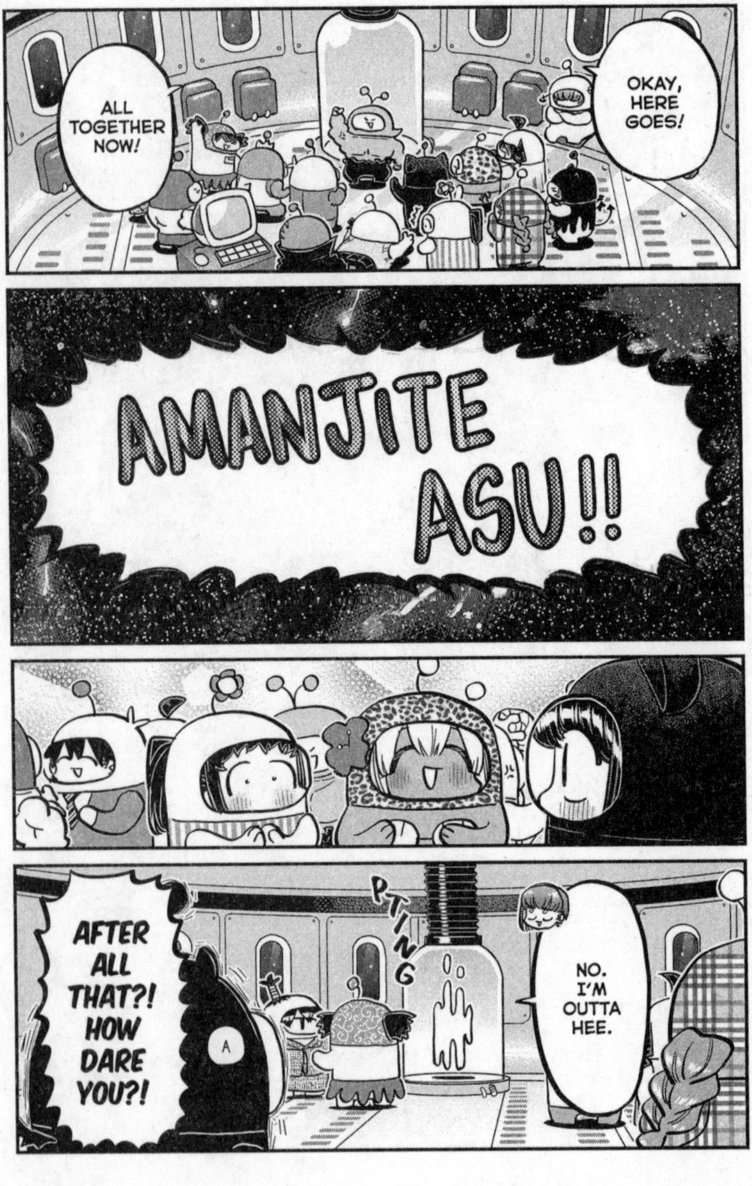
OKAY, HERE GOES!
ALL TOGETHER NOW!
AMANJITE ASU!!
NO. I'M OUTTA HEE.
PTING
AFTER ALL THAT?! HOW DARE YOU?!

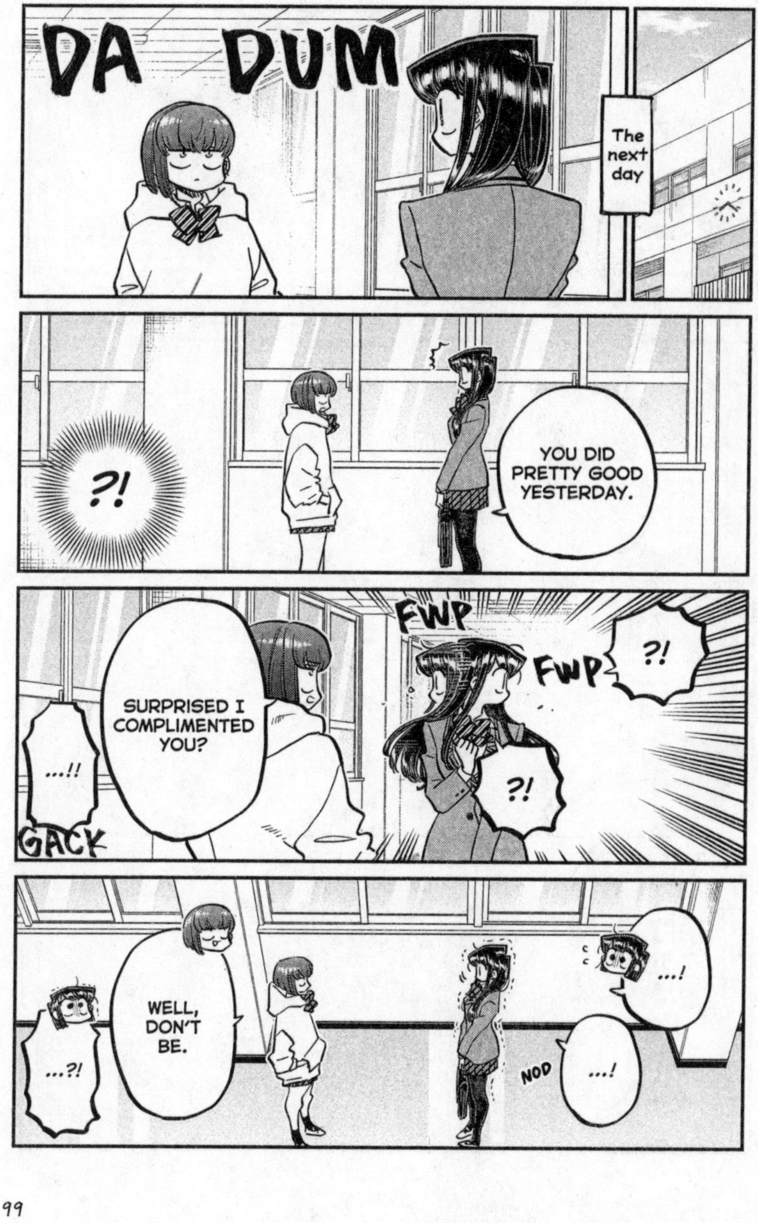
The next day
DA DUM
YOU DID PRETTY GOOD YESTERDAY.
?!
FWP
FWP
?!
?!
SURPRISED I COMPLIMENTED YOU?
...!!
GACK
...!
NOD
...!
WELL, DON'T BE.
...?!

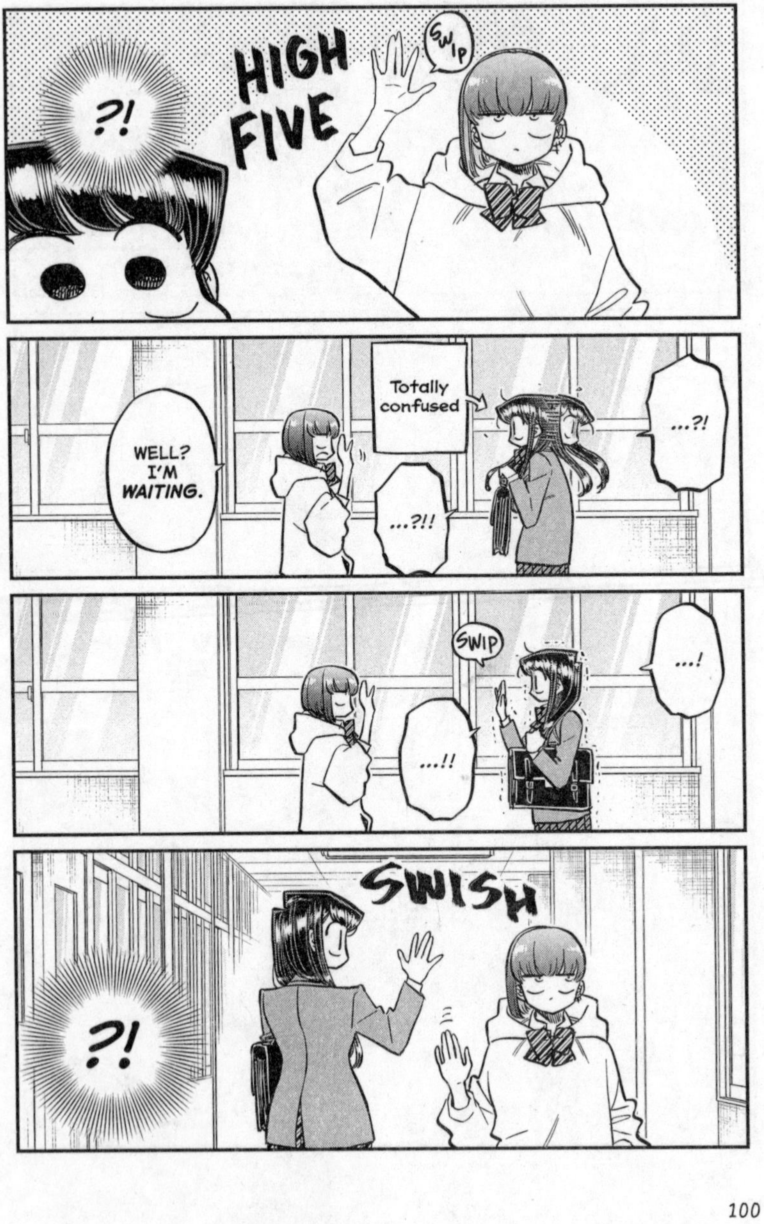
SWIP
HIGH FIVE
?!
...?!
Totally confused
...?!!
WELL? I'M WAITING.
...!
SWIP
...!!
SWISH
?!

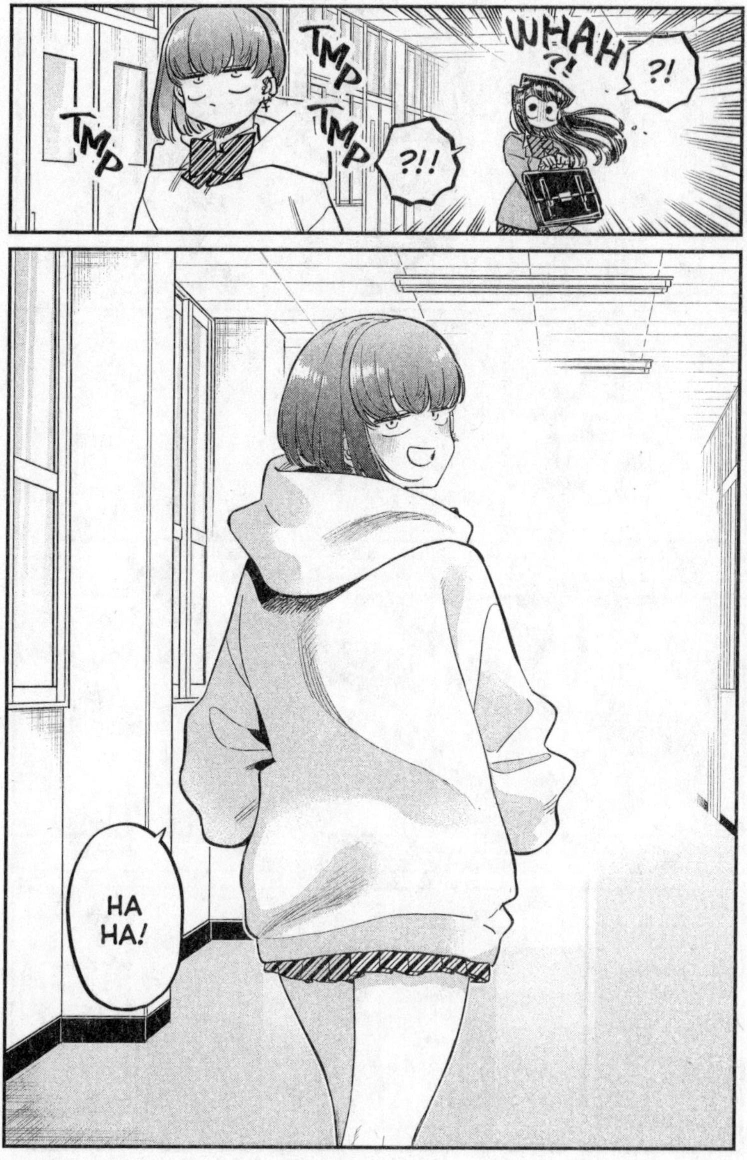
?!
WHAH ?!
?!!
TMP TMP
TMP
HA HA!

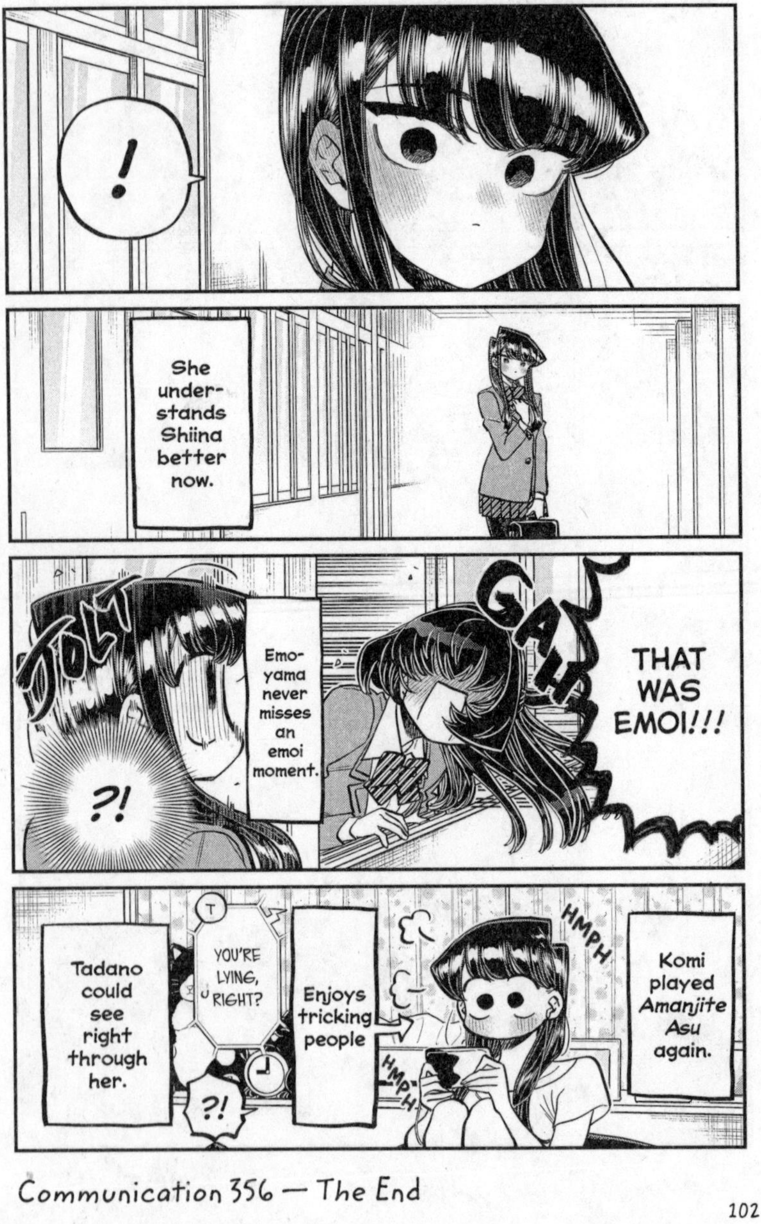
!
She understands Shiina better now.
THAT WAS EMOI!!!
GAH
Emo-yama never misses an emoi moment.
JOLT
?!
Komi played Amanjite Asu again.
HMPH
HMPH
Enjoys tricking people
T
YOU'RE LYING, RIGHT?
?!
Tadano could see right through her.

Communication 356 — The End

Komi Can't Communicate

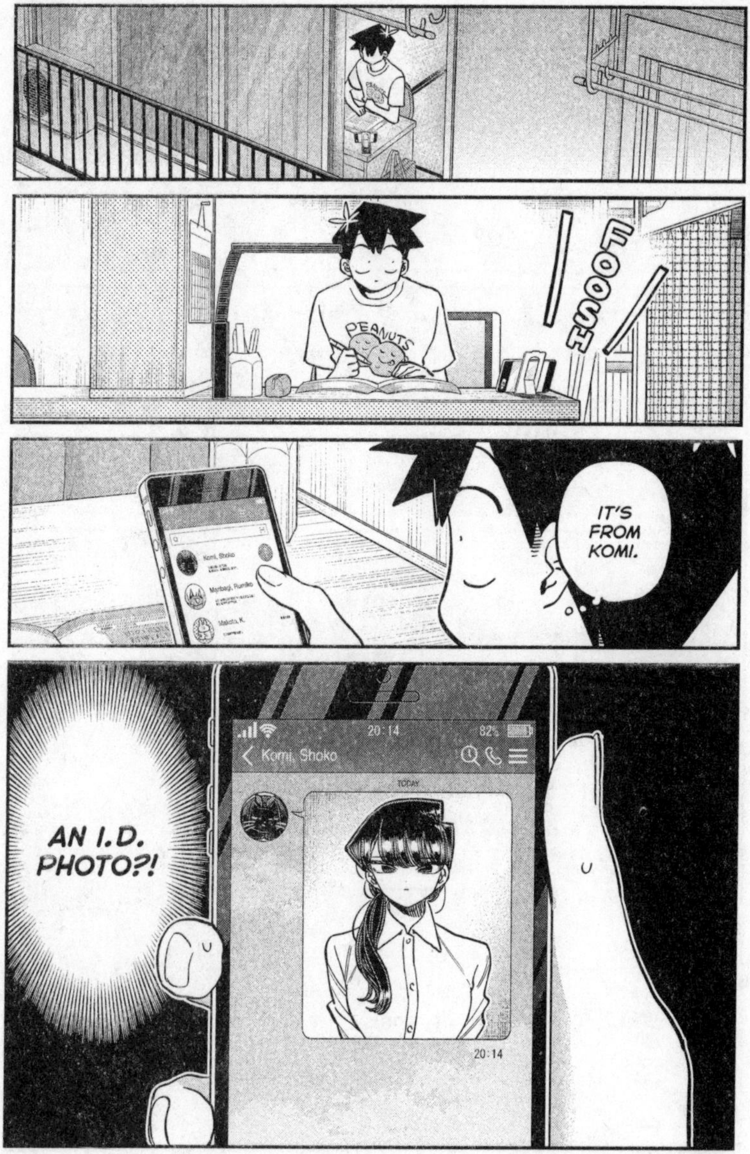
FOOSH
IT'S FROM KOMI.
Komi, Shoko
20:14
82%
TODAY
20:14
AN I.D. PHOTO?!

Communication 357: Selfie, Part 2

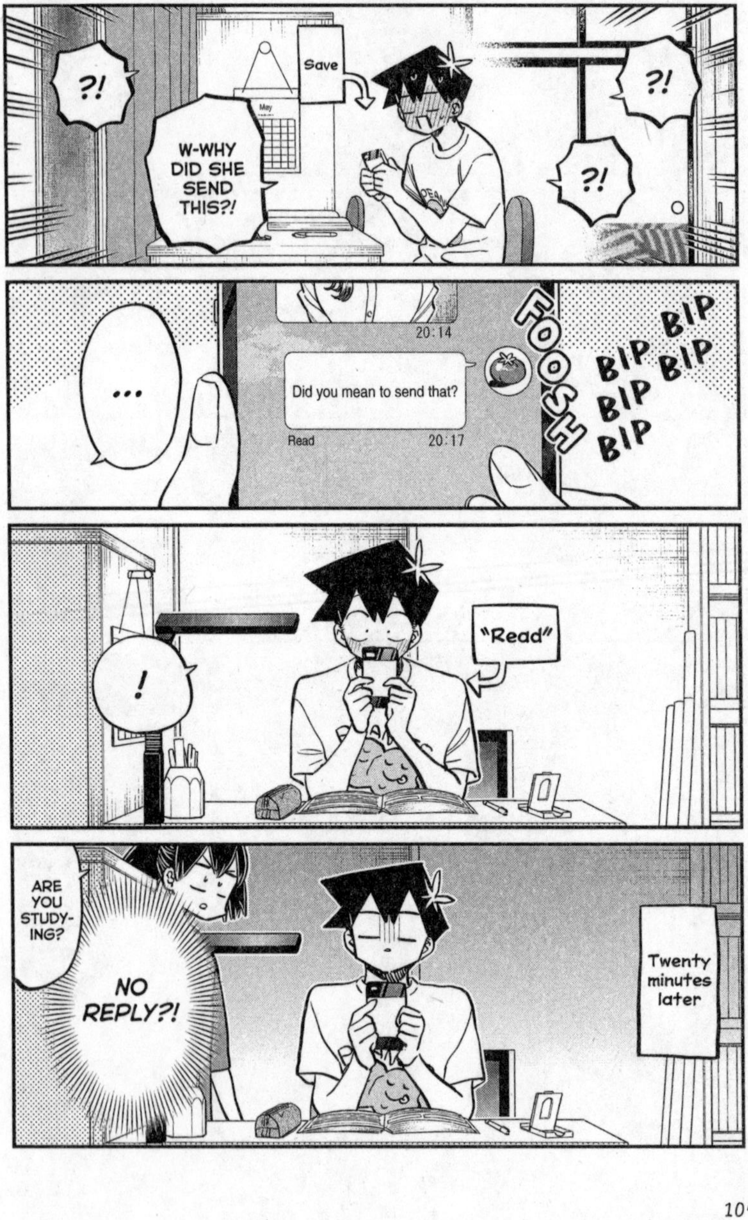
?!
Save
?!
?!
W-WHY DID SHE SEND THIS?!
BIP BIP BIP BIP BIP BIP
FOOSH
20:14
Did you mean to send that?
Read
20:17
...
"Read"
!
Twenty minutes later
ARE YOU STUDYING?
NO REPLY?!

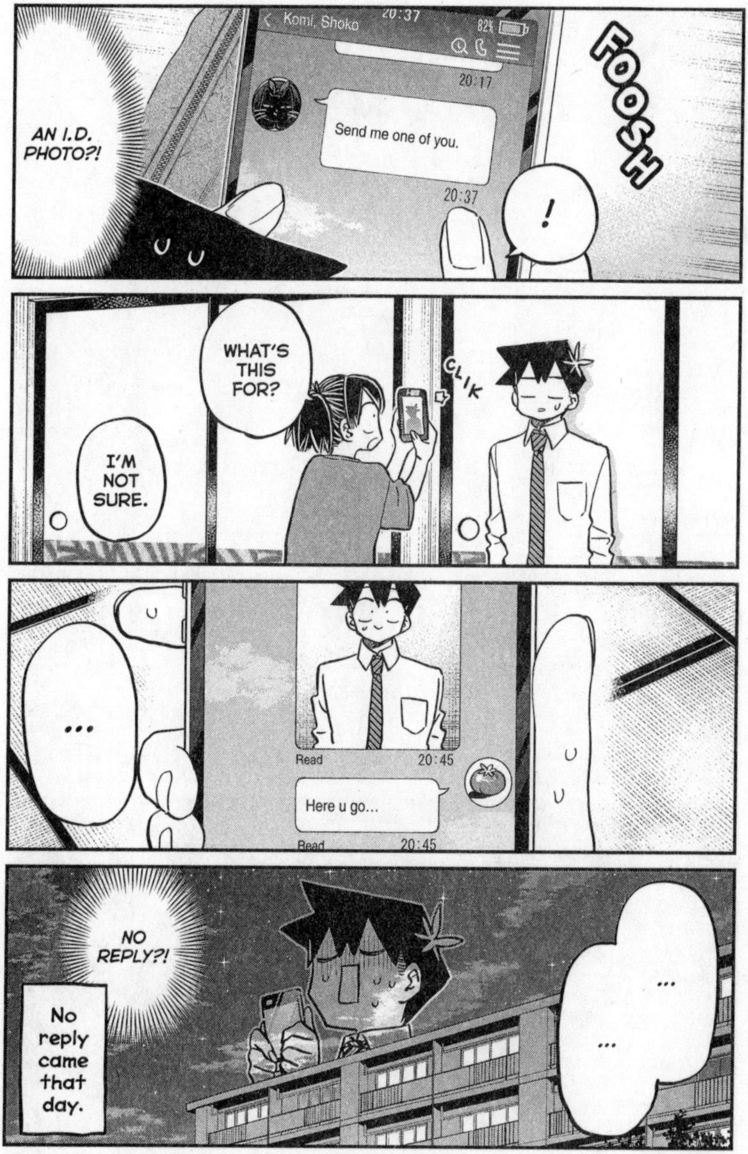
FOOSH
!
Komi, Shoko
20:37
82%
20:17
Send me one of you.
20:37
AN I.D. PHOTO?!
CLIK
WHAT'S THIS FOR?
I'M NOT SURE.
Read
20:45
Here u go...
Read
20:45
...
...
...
NO REPLY?!
No reply came that day.

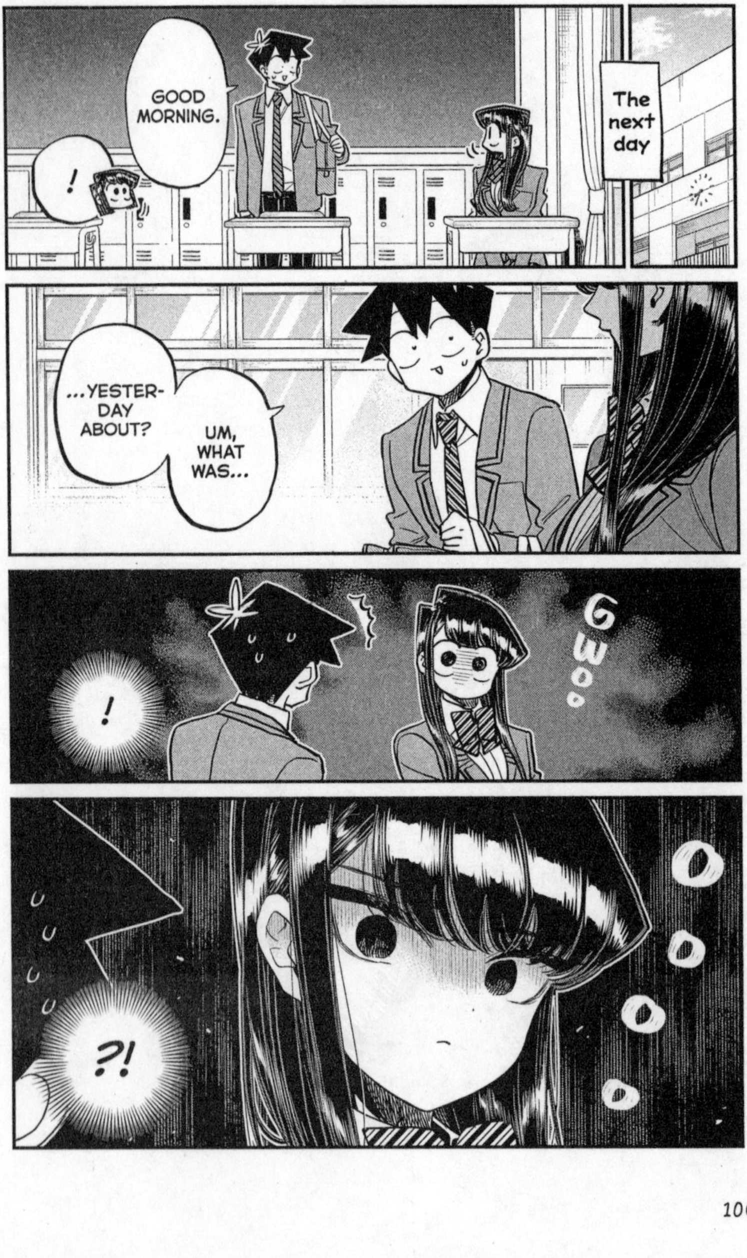
The next day
GOOD MORNING.
!
UM, WHAT WAS...
...YESTERDAY ABOUT?
GWOO
!
OOOO
?!

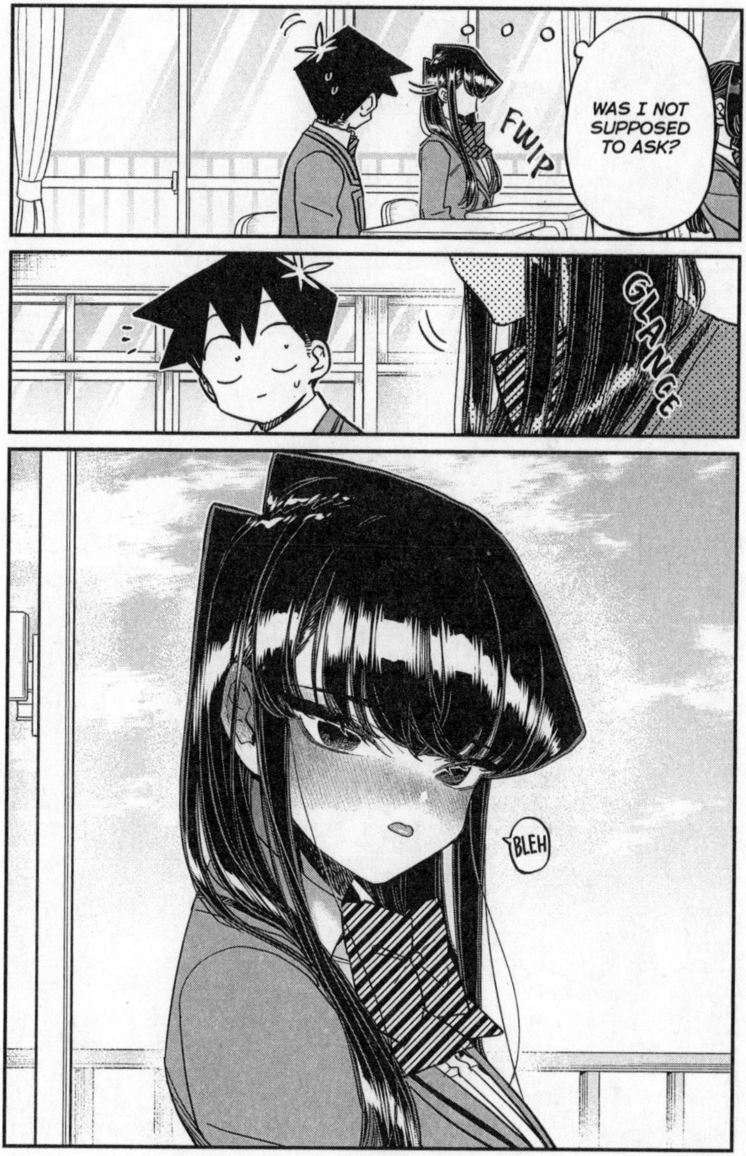
WAS I NOT SUPPOSED TO ASK?
FWIP
GLANCE
BLEH

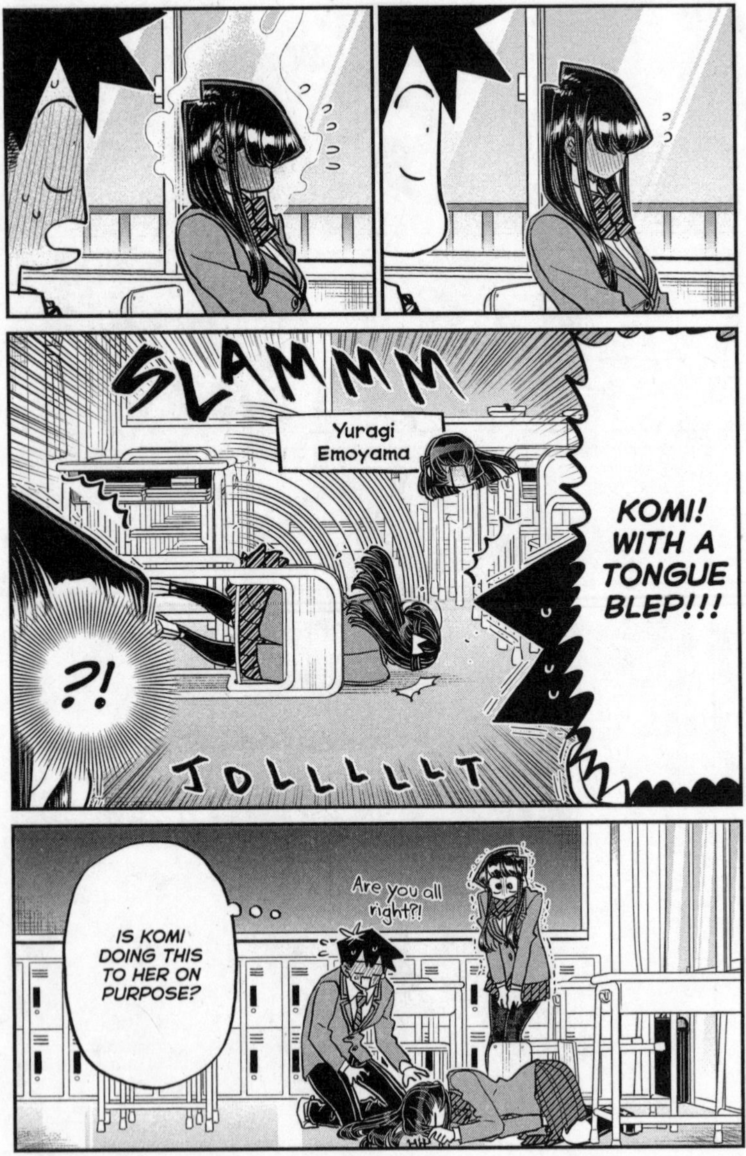
KOMI! WITH A TONGUE BLEP!!!
SLAMMM
Yuragi Emoyama
?!
JOLLLLLT
Are you all right?!
IS KOMI DOING THIS TO HER ON PURPOSE?

Communication 357 — The End

Communication 358: Selfie, Part 1

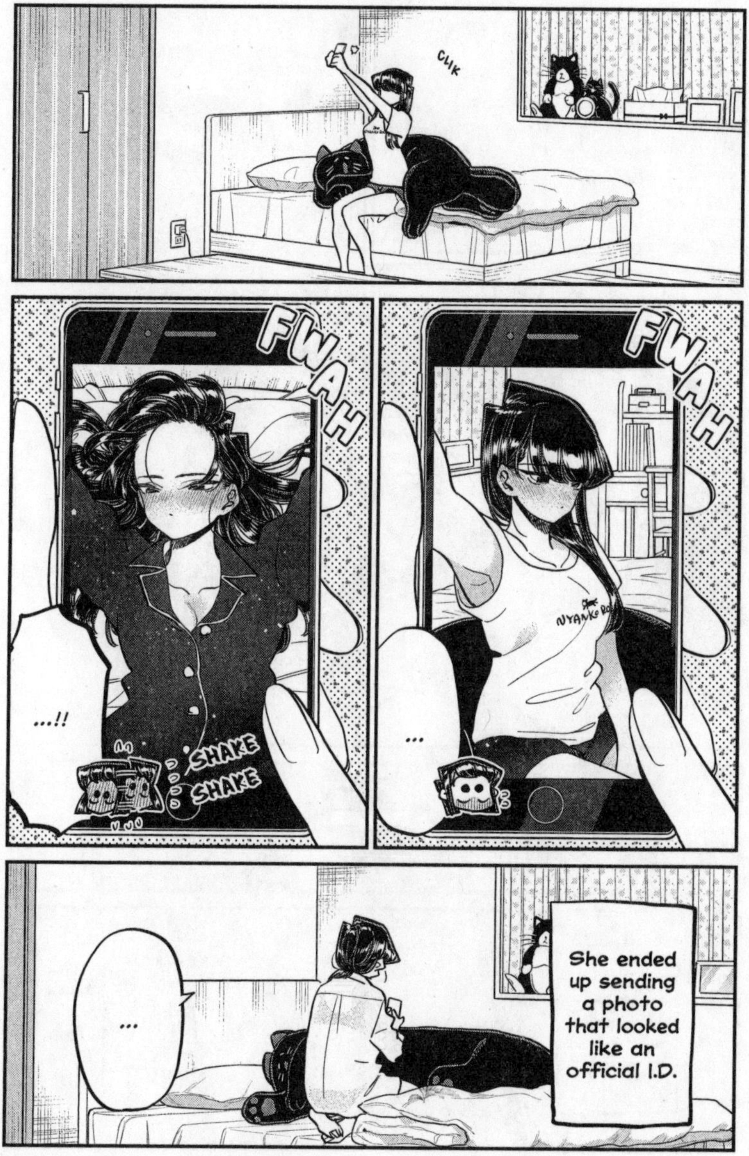
CLIK
FWAH
...
FWAH
...!!
SHAKE
SHAKE
She ended up sending a photo that looked like an official I.D.
...

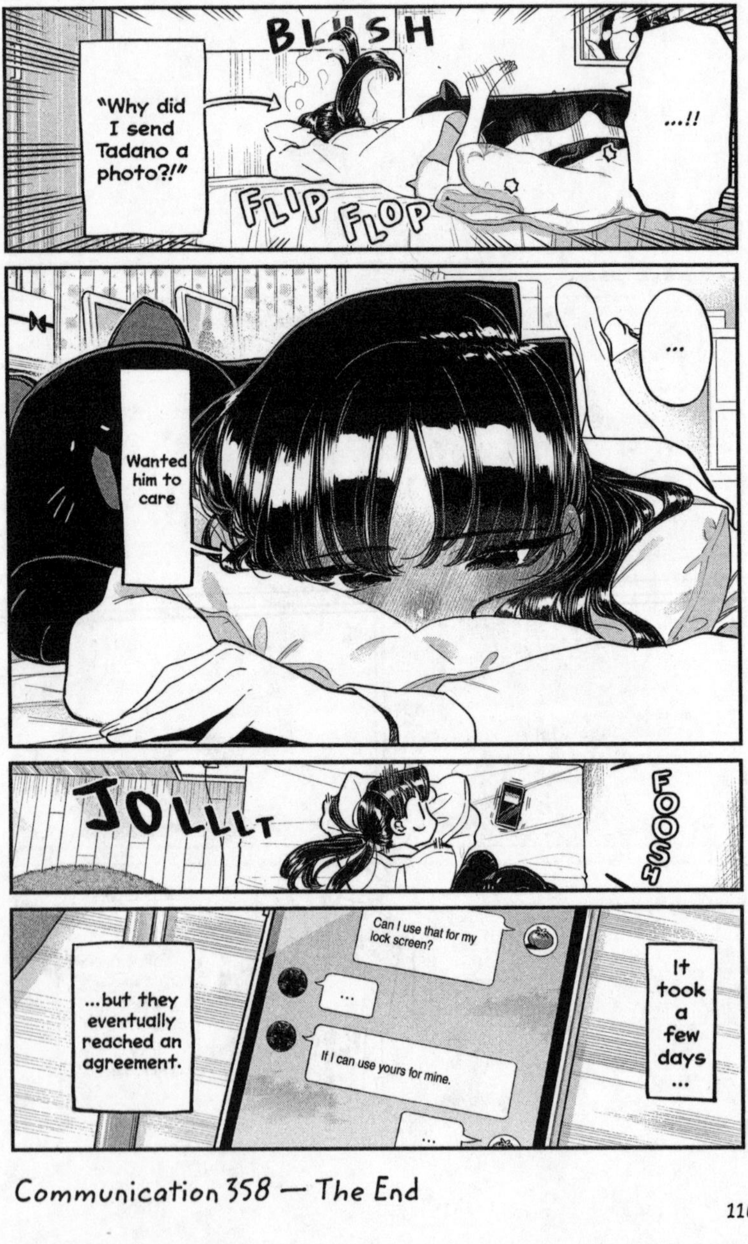
...!!
BLUSH
"Why did I send Tadano a photo?!"
FLIP FLOP
...
Wanted him to care
FOOSH
JOLLLT
It took a few days...
Can I use that for my lock screen?
...
If I can use yours for mine.
...
...but they eventually reached an agreement.

Communication 358 — The End

Hmmm???

They didn't want Najimi to see, so they changed their lock screens back to the default.

Komi Can't
Communicate

Komi Can't Communicate

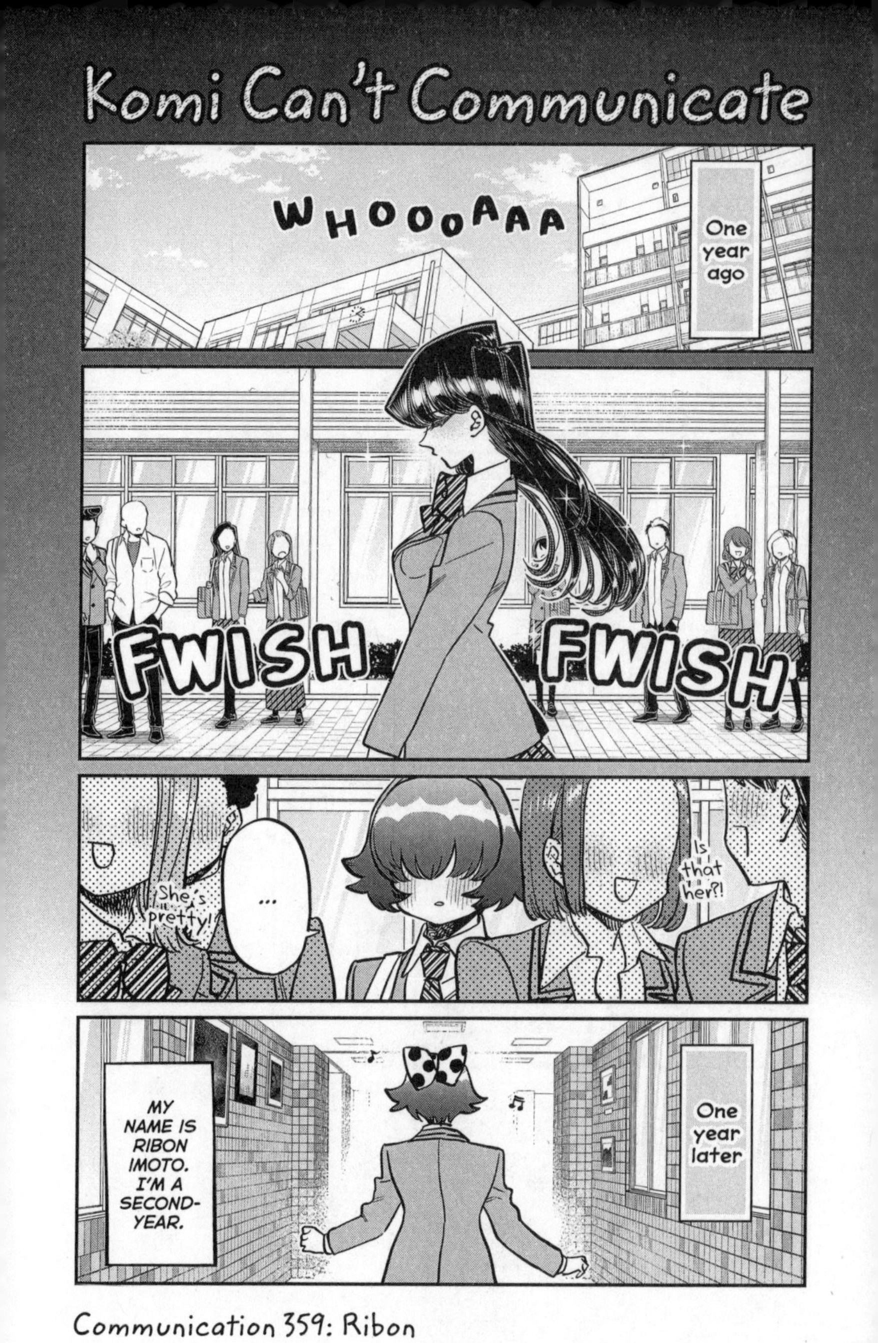
One year ago
WHOOOAAA
FWISH
FWISH
Is that her?!
...
She's pretty!
One year later
MY NAME IS RIBON IMOTO. I'M A SECOND-YEAR.

Communication 359: Ribon

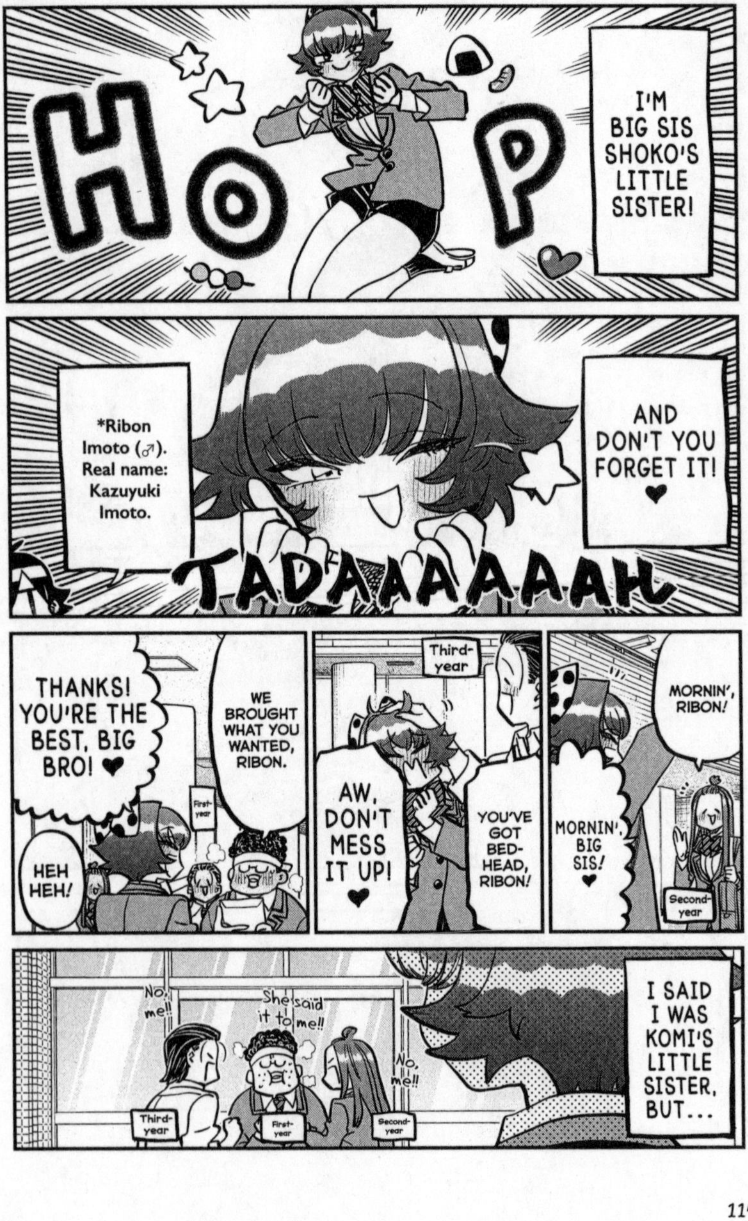
I'M BIG SIS SHOKO'S LITTLE SISTER!
HOP
AND DON'T YOU FORGET IT! ♥
*Ribon Imoto (♂). Real name: Kazuyuki Imoto.
TADAAAAAAH
MORNIN', RIBON!
MORNIN', BIG SIS! ♥
Second-year
Third-year
YOU'VE GOT BED-HEAD, RIBON!
AW, DON'T MESS IT UP! ♥
WE BROUGHT WHAT YOU WANTED, RIBON.
THANKS! YOU'RE THE BEST, BIG BRO! ♥
First-year
HEH HEH!
I SAID I WAS KOMI'S LITTLE SISTER, BUT...
No, me!!
She said it to me!!
No, me!!
Third-year
First-year
Second-year

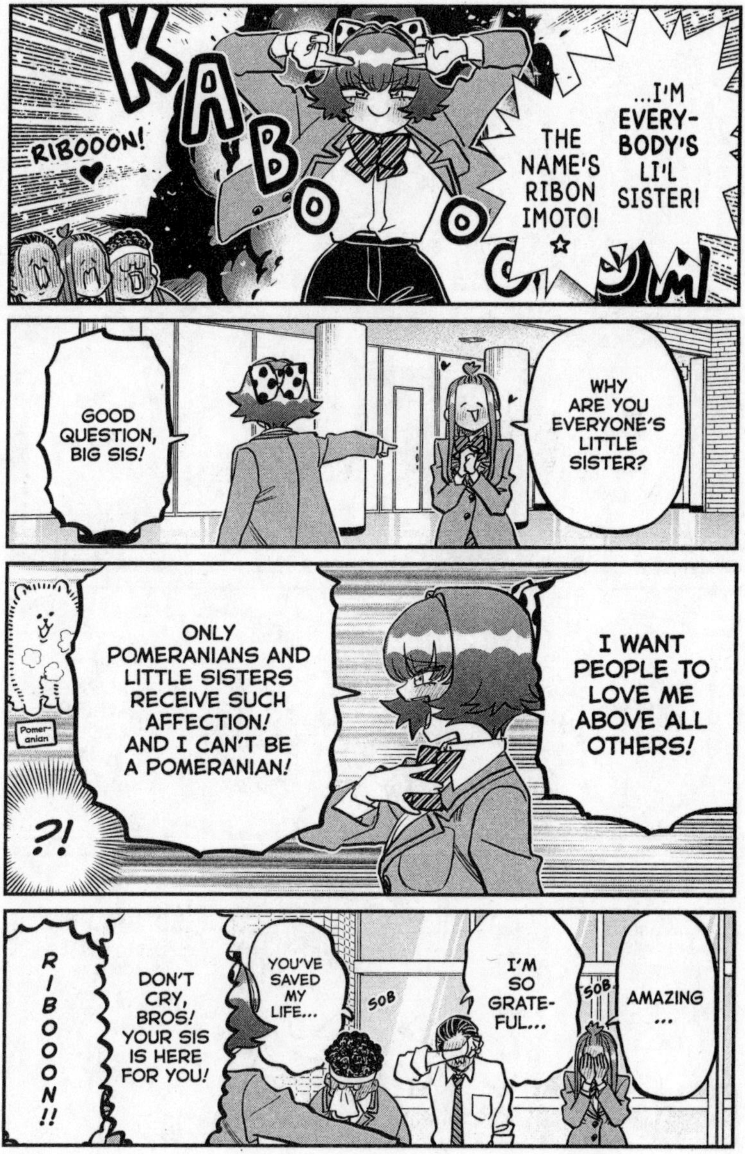
...I'M EVERY-BODY'S LI'L SISTER!
THE NAME'S RIBON IMOTO! ☆
KABOOOOM
RIBOOON! ♥
WHY ARE YOU EVERYONE'S LITTLE SISTER?
GOOD QUESTION, BIG SIS!
I WANT PEOPLE TO LOVE ME ABOVE ALL OTHERS!
ONLY POMERANIANS AND LITTLE SISTERS RECEIVE SUCH AFFECTION! AND I CAN'T BE A POMERANIAN!
Pomer-anian
?!
AMAZING...
SOB
I'M SO GRATE-FUL...
SOB
YOU'VE SAVED MY LIFE...
DON'T CRY, BROS! YOUR SIS IS HERE FOR YOU!
RIBOOOON!!

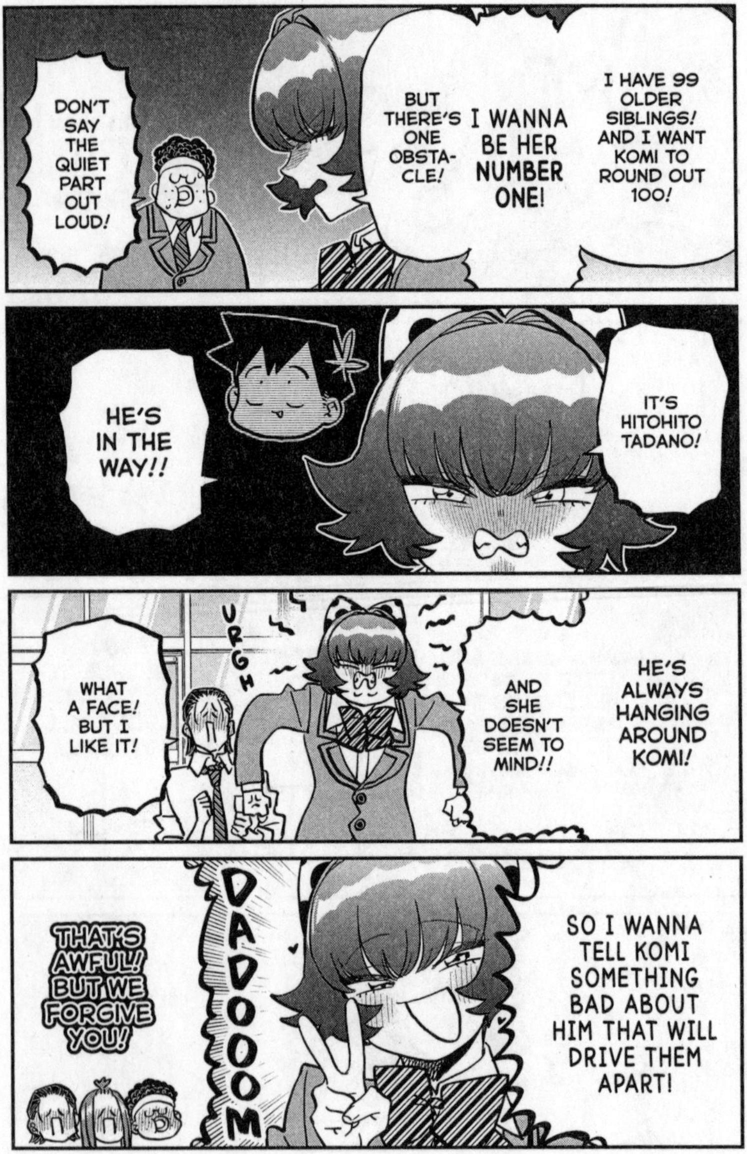
I HAVE 99 OLDER SIBLINGS! AND I WANT KOMI TO ROUND OUT 100!
I WANNA BE HER NUMBER ONE!
BUT THERE'S ONE OBSTA-CLE!
DON'T SAY THE QUIET PART OUT LOUD!
IT'S HITOHITO TADANO!
HE'S IN THE WAY!!
HE'S ALWAYS HANGING AROUND KOMI!
AND SHE DOESN'T SEEM TO MIND!!
URGH
WHAT A FACE! BUT I LIKE IT!
SO I WANNA TELL KOMI SOMETHING BAD ABOUT HIM THAT WILL DRIVE THEM APART!
DADOOOM
THAT'S AWFUL! BUT WE FORGIVE YOU!

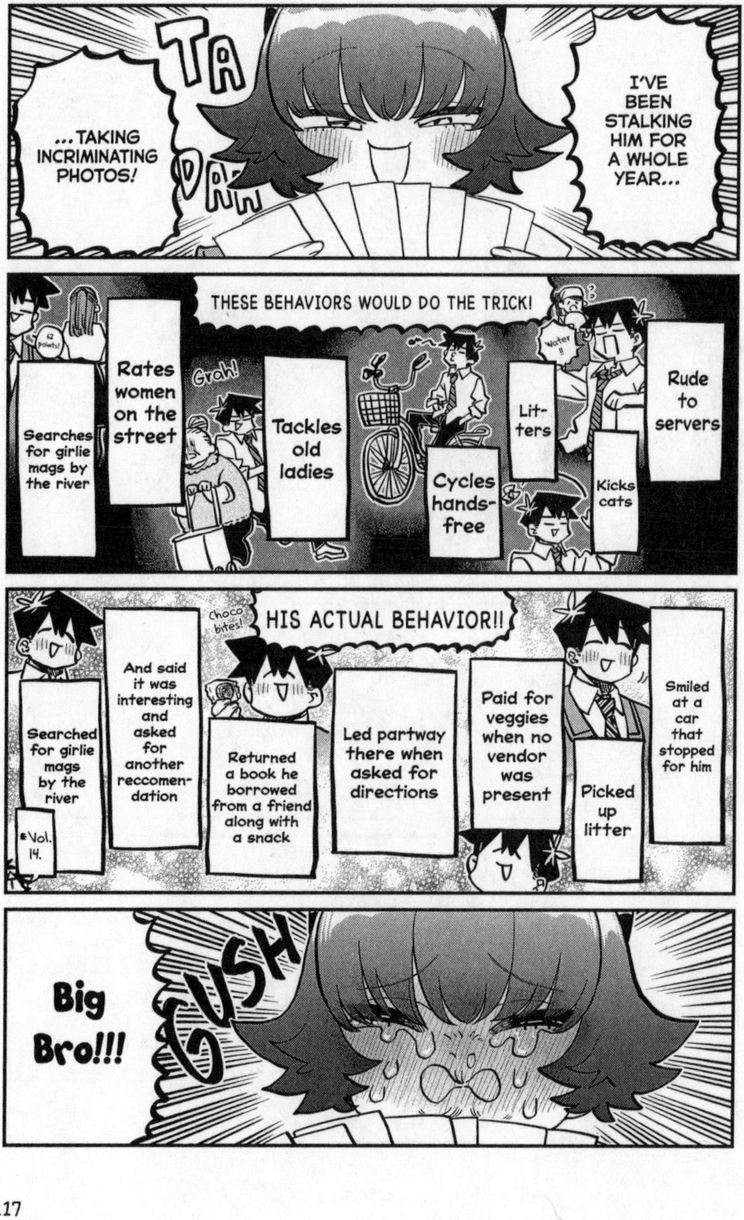
I'VE BEEN STALKING HIM FOR A WHOLE YEAR...
TA DAH
...TAKING INCRIMINATING PHOTOS!
THESE BEHAVIORS WOULD DO THE TRICK!
Rude to servers
Water!!
Kicks cats
Lit-ters
Cycles hands-free
Tackles old ladies
Grah!
Rates women on the street
62 points!
Searches for girlie mags by the river
HIS ACTUAL BEHAVIOR!!
Smiled at a car that stopped for him
Picked up litter
Paid for veggies when no vendor was present
Led partway there when asked for directions
Choco bites!
Returned a book he borrowed from a friend along with a snack
And said it was interesting and asked for another reccomen-dation
Searched for girlie mags by the river
*Vol. 14.
GUSH
Big Bro!!!

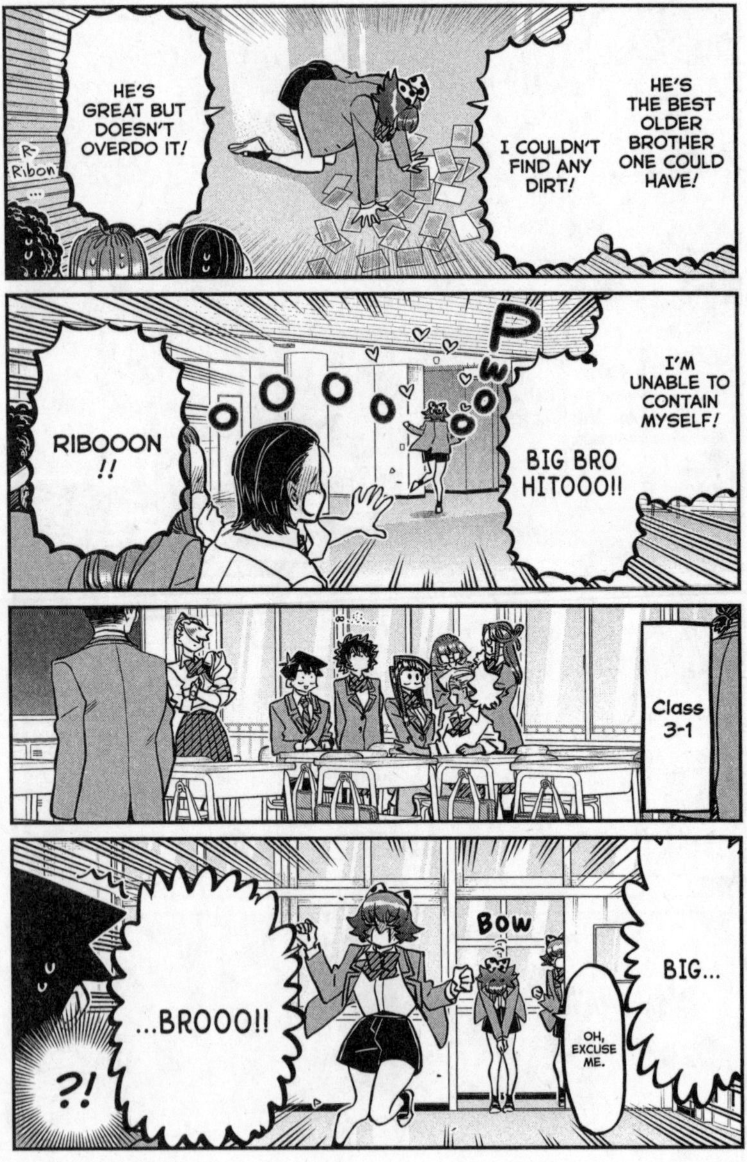
HE'S THE BEST OLDER BROTHER ONE COULD HAVE!
I COULDN'T FIND ANY DIRT!
HE'S GREAT BUT DOESN'T OVERDO IT!
R-Ribon...
I'M UNABLE TO CONTAIN MYSELF!
PWOOOOOO
BIG BRO HITOOO!!
RIBOOON!!
Class 3-1
BIG...
OH, EXCUSE ME.
BOW
...BROOO!!
?!

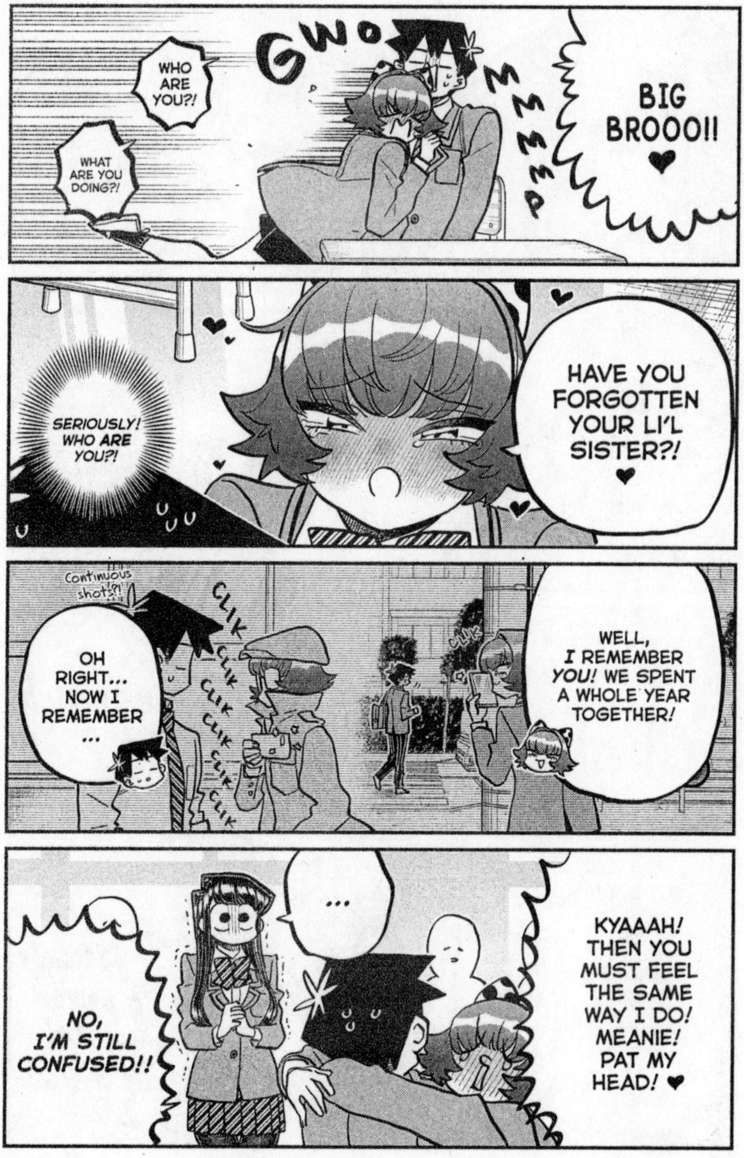
BIG BROOO!! ♥
GWOMMMMMP
WHO ARE YOU?!
WHAT ARE YOU DOING?!
HAVE YOU FORGOTTEN YOUR LI'L SISTER?! ♥
SERIOUSLY! WHO ARE YOU?!
WELL, I REMEMBER YOU! WE SPENT A WHOLE YEAR TOGETHER!
CLIK
CLIK CLIK CLIK CLIK CLIK CLIK CLIK CLIK
Continuous shots?!
OH RIGHT... NOW I REMEMBER ...
KYAAAH! THEN YOU MUST FEEL THE SAME WAY I DO! MEANIE! PAT MY HEAD! ♥
...
NO, I'M STILL CONFUSED!!

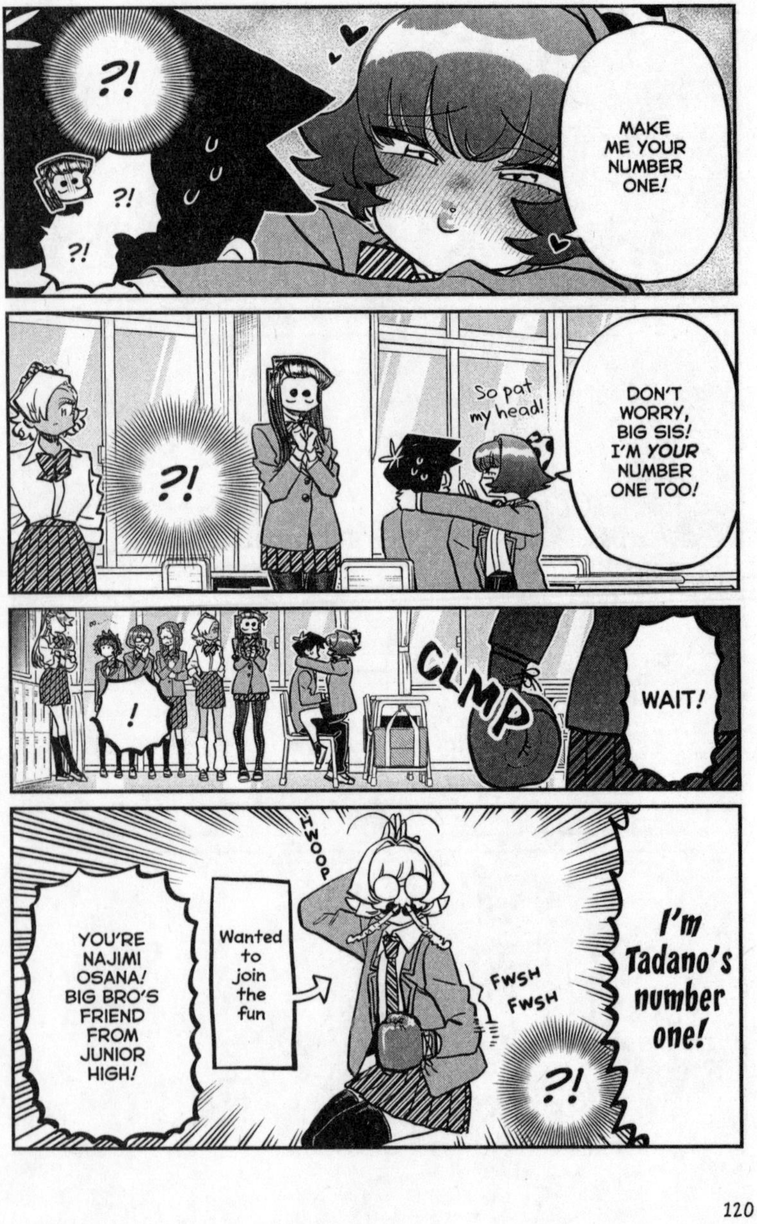
MAKE ME YOUR NUMBER ONE!
?!
?!
?!
DON'T WORRY, BIG SIS! I'M YOUR NUMBER ONE TOO!
So pat my head!
?!
WAIT!
CLMP
!
I'm Tadano's number one!
?!
FWSH FWSH
HWOOP
Wanted to join the fun
YOU'RE NAJIMI OSANA! BIG BRO'S FRIEND FROM JUNIOR HIGH!

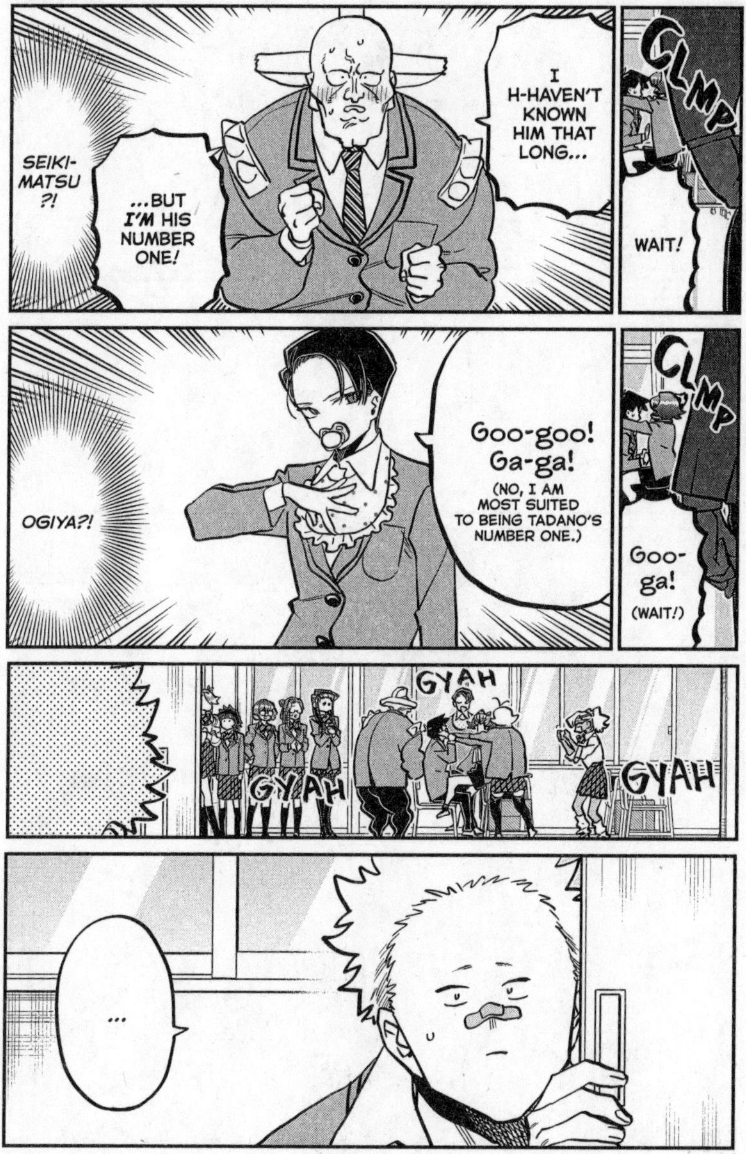
CLMP
WAIT!
I H-HAVEN'T KNOWN HIM THAT LONG...
...BUT *I'M* HIS NUMBER ONE!
SEIKI-MATSU?!
CLMP
Goo-ga! (WAIT!)
Goo-goo! Ga-ga! (NO, I AM MOST SUITED TO BEING TADANO'S NUMBER ONE.)
OGIYA?!
GYAH
GYAH
GYAH
...

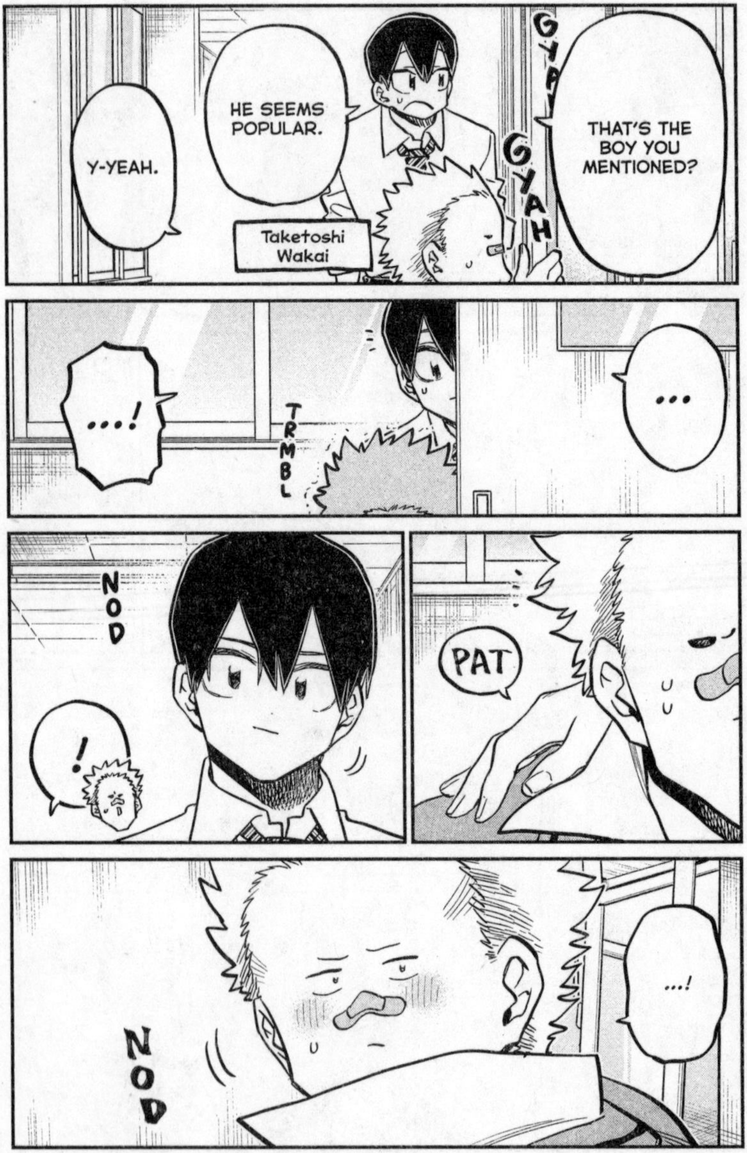
THAT'S THE BOY YOU MENTIONED?
GYA
GYAH
Taketoshi Wakai
HE SEEMS POPULAR.
Y-YEAH.
...
TRMBL
...!
PAT
NOD
!
...!
NOD

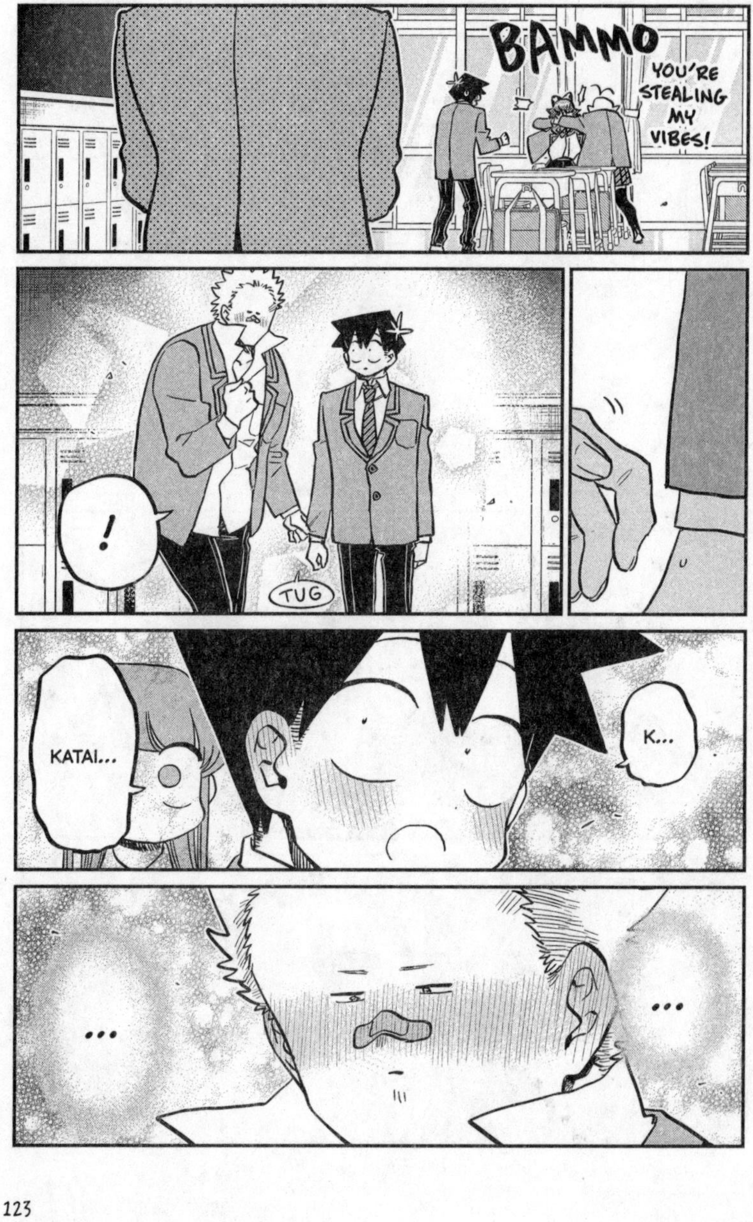

BAMMO
YOU'RE STEALING MY VIBES!
!
TUG
K...
KATAI...
...
...

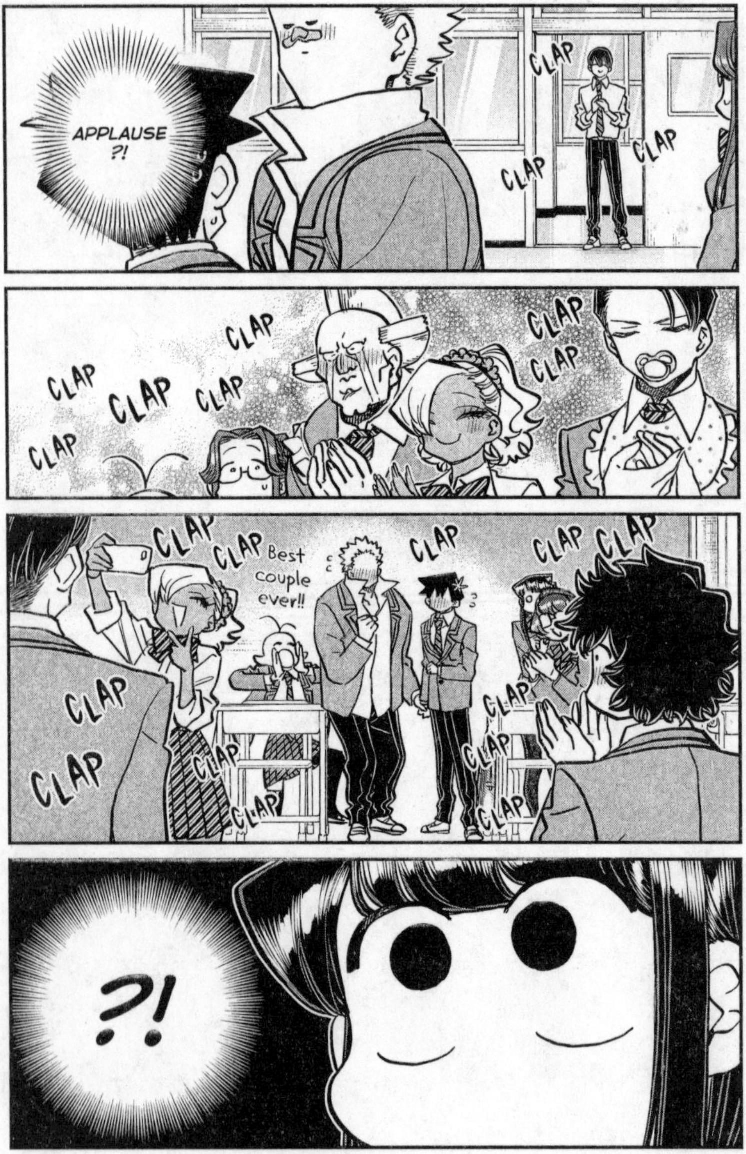
CLAP
CLAP
CLAP
APPLAUSE ?!
CLAP
CLAP
CLAP
CLAP
CLAP
CLAP
CLAP
CLAP
CLAP
CLAP
CLAP
CLAP
CLAP
CLAP
Best couple ever!!
CLAP
CLAP
CLAP
CLAP
CLAP
CLAP
?!

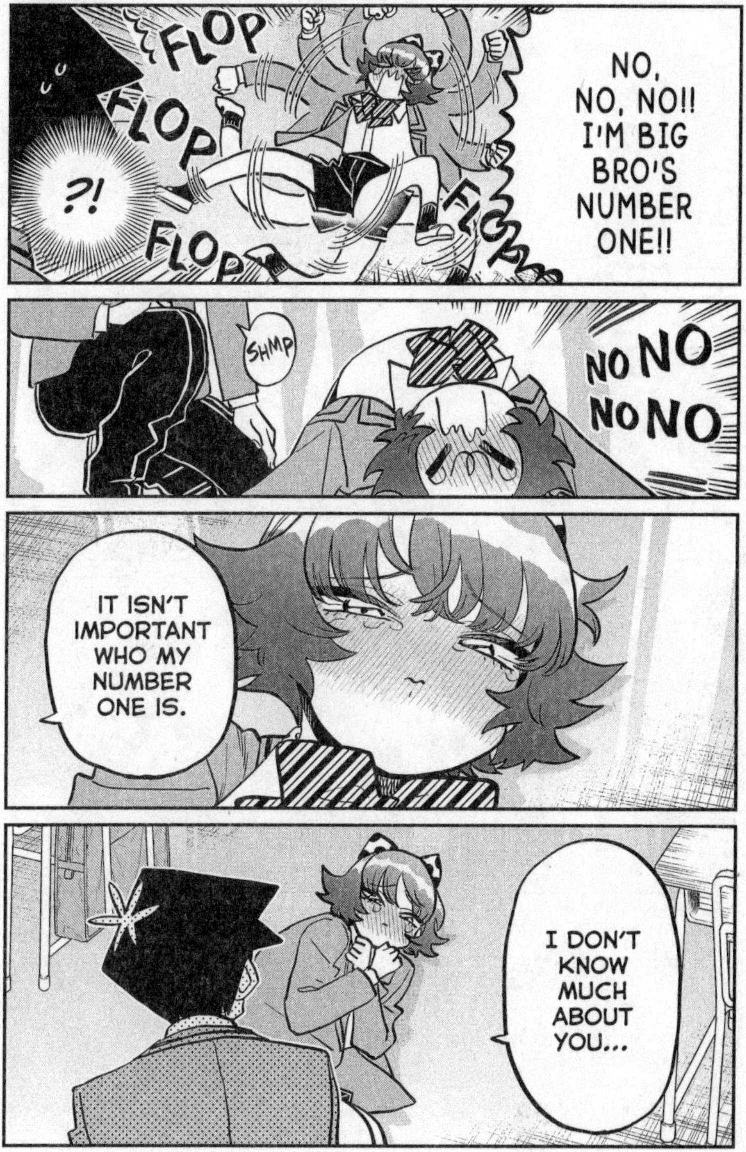
NO, NO, NO!! I'M BIG BRO'S NUMBER ONE!!
FLOP
FLOP
FLOP
FLOP
?!
NO NO NO NO
SHMP
IT ISN'T IMPORTANT WHO MY NUMBER ONE IS.
I DON'T KNOW MUCH ABOUT YOU...

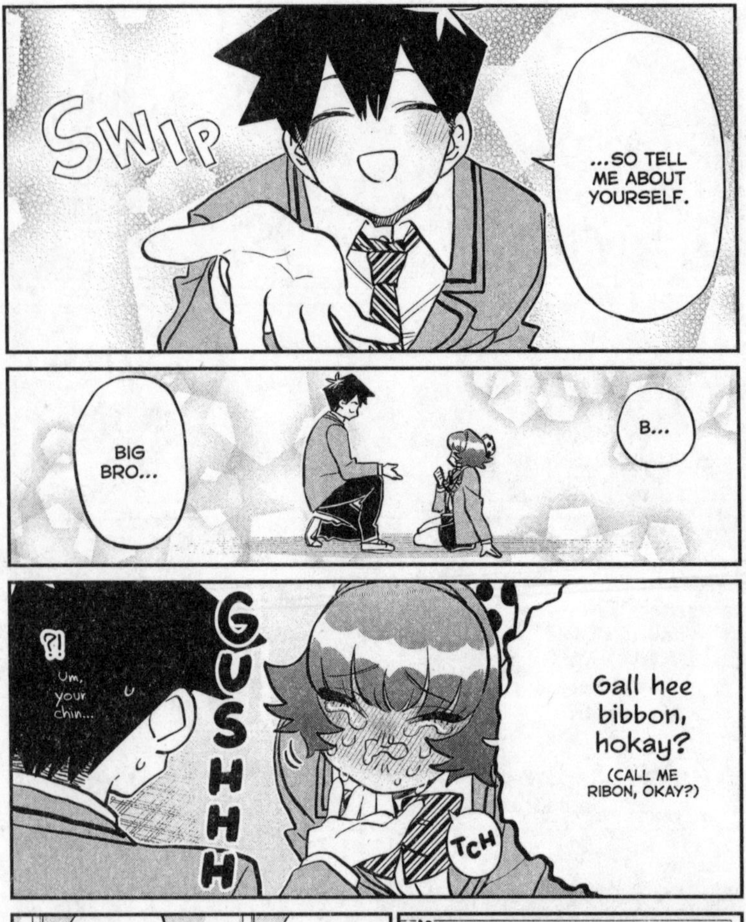
...SO TELL ME ABOUT YOURSELF.
SWIP
B...
BIG BRO...
Gall hee bibbon, hokay?
(CALL ME RIBON, OKAY?)
TCH
GUSHHH
?!
Um, your chin...
CLAP CLAP CLAP CLAP CLAP CLAP
?!
CLAP CLAP CLAP
WHEW! TADANO'S AMAZING!
HM? WHERE'S MAKOCCHI!?
GRUNT.

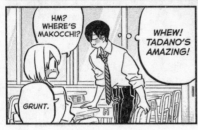

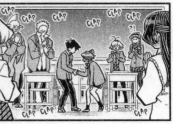

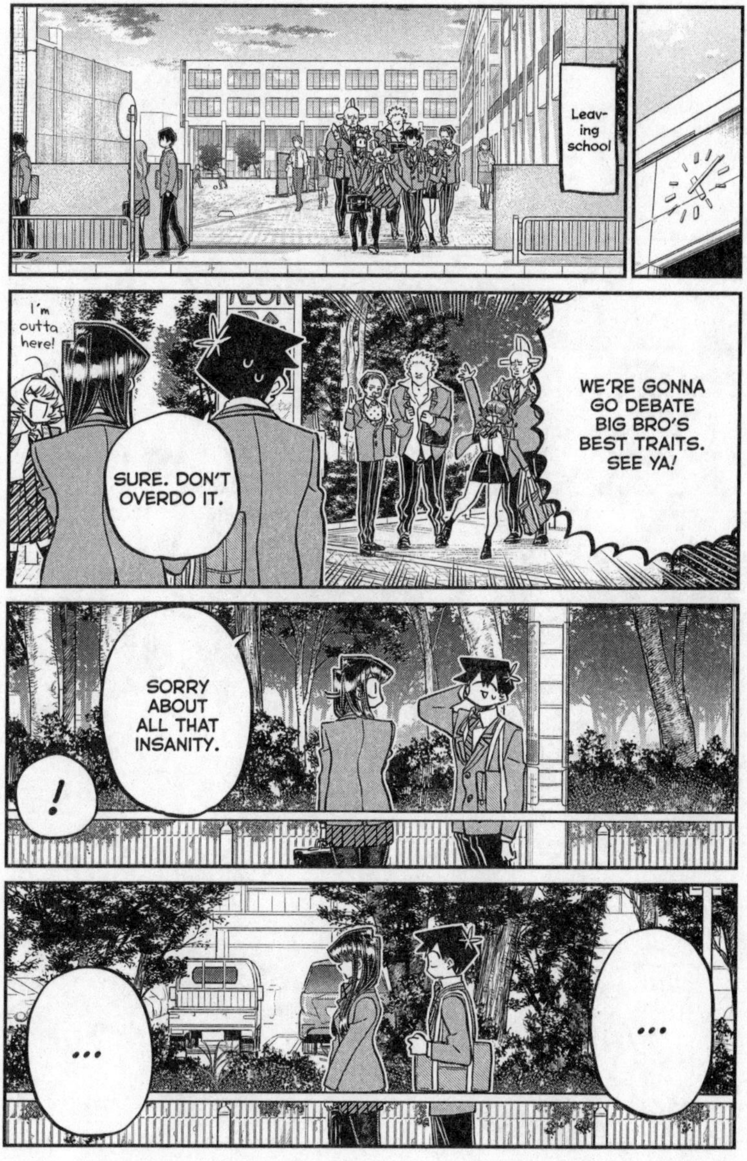
Leaving school
WE'RE GONNA GO DEBATE BIG BRO'S BEST TRAITS. SEE YA!
SURE. DON'T OVERDO IT.
I'm outta here!
SORRY ABOUT ALL THAT INSANITY.
!
...
...

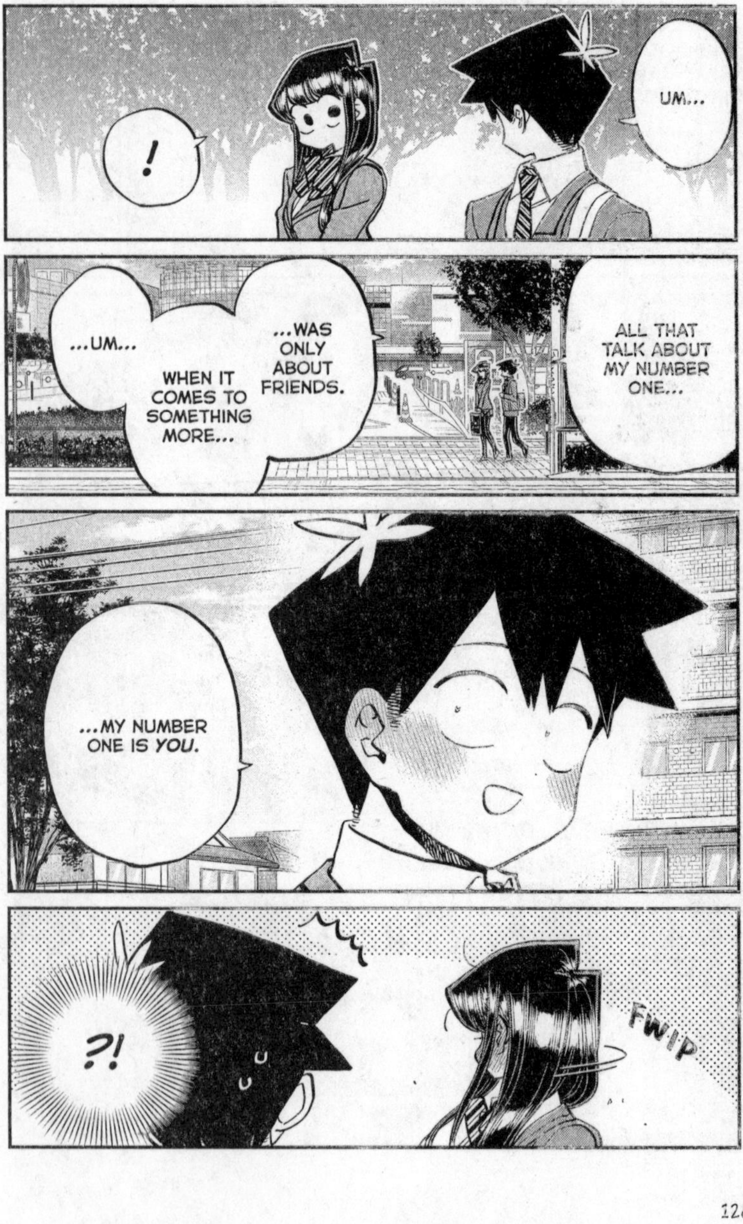
UM...
!
ALL THAT TALK ABOUT MY NUMBER ONE...
...WAS ONLY ABOUT FRIENDS.
...UM...
WHEN IT COMES TO SOMETHING MORE...
...MY NUMBER ONE IS *YOU*.
FWIP
?!

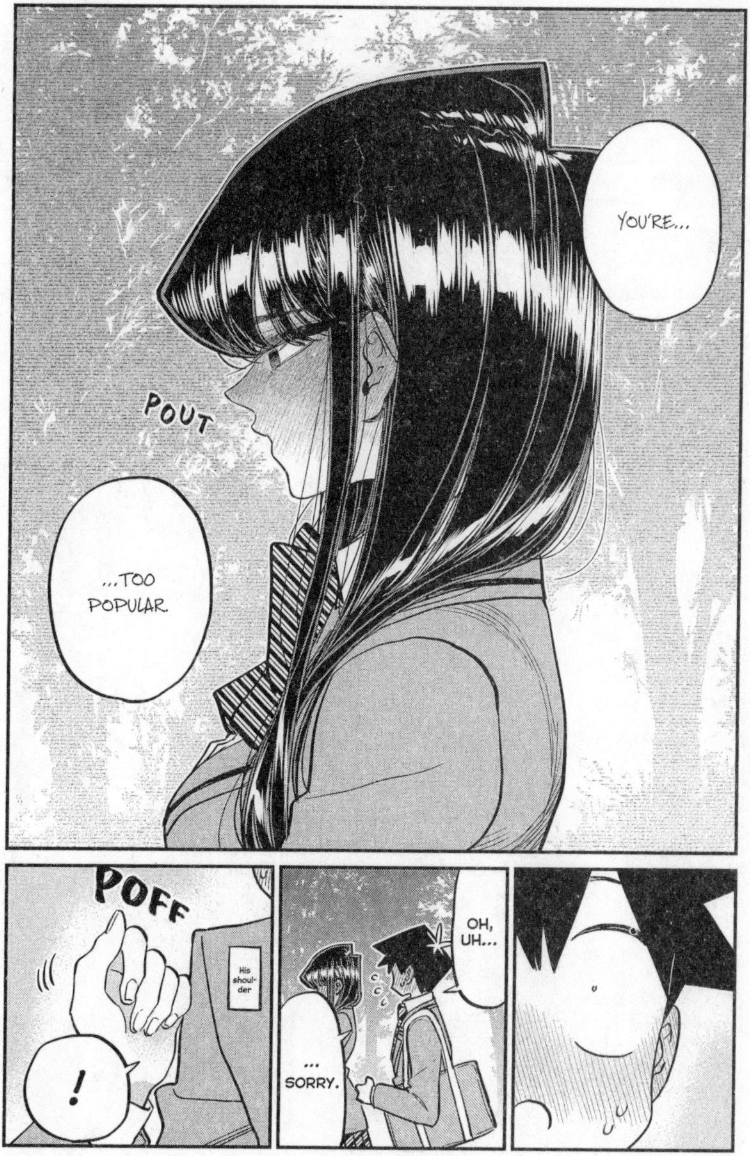
YOU'RE...
POUT
...TOO POPULAR.
OH, UH...
... SORRY.
POFF
His shoulder
!

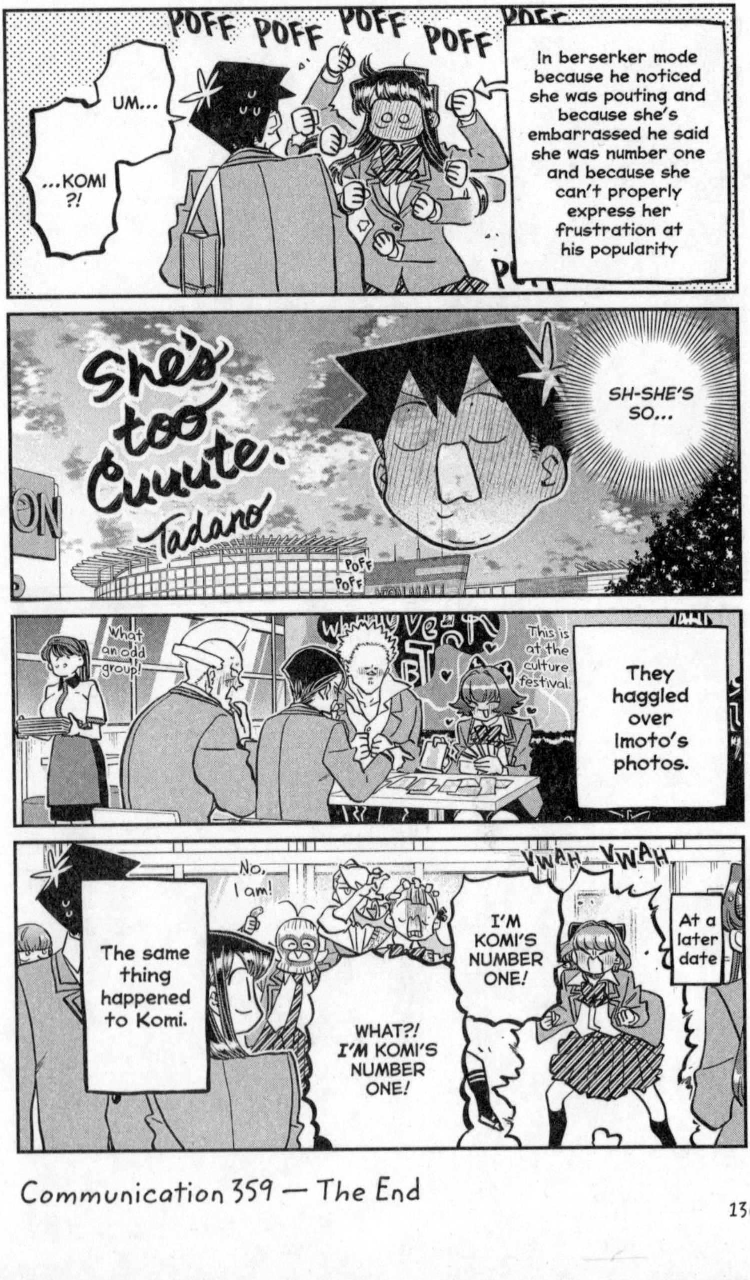
In berserker mode because he noticed she was pouting and because she's embarrassed he said she was number one and because she can't properly express her frustration at his popularity
POFF POFF POFF POFF
UM...
...KOMI ?!
SH-SHE'S SO...
She's too Cuuute.
Tadano
POFF POFF
They haggled over Imoto's photos.
This is at the culture festival.
What an odd group!
At a later date
I'M KOMI'S NUMBER ONE!
VWAH VWAH
WHAT?! I'M KOMI'S NUMBER ONE!
No, I am!
The same thing happened to Komi.

Communication 359 — The End

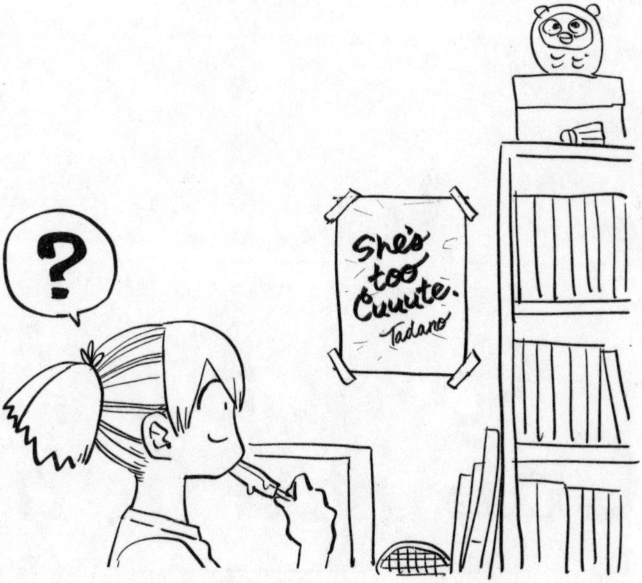
?
She's too Cuuute.
Tadano

Komi Can't
Communicate

Komi Can't Communicate

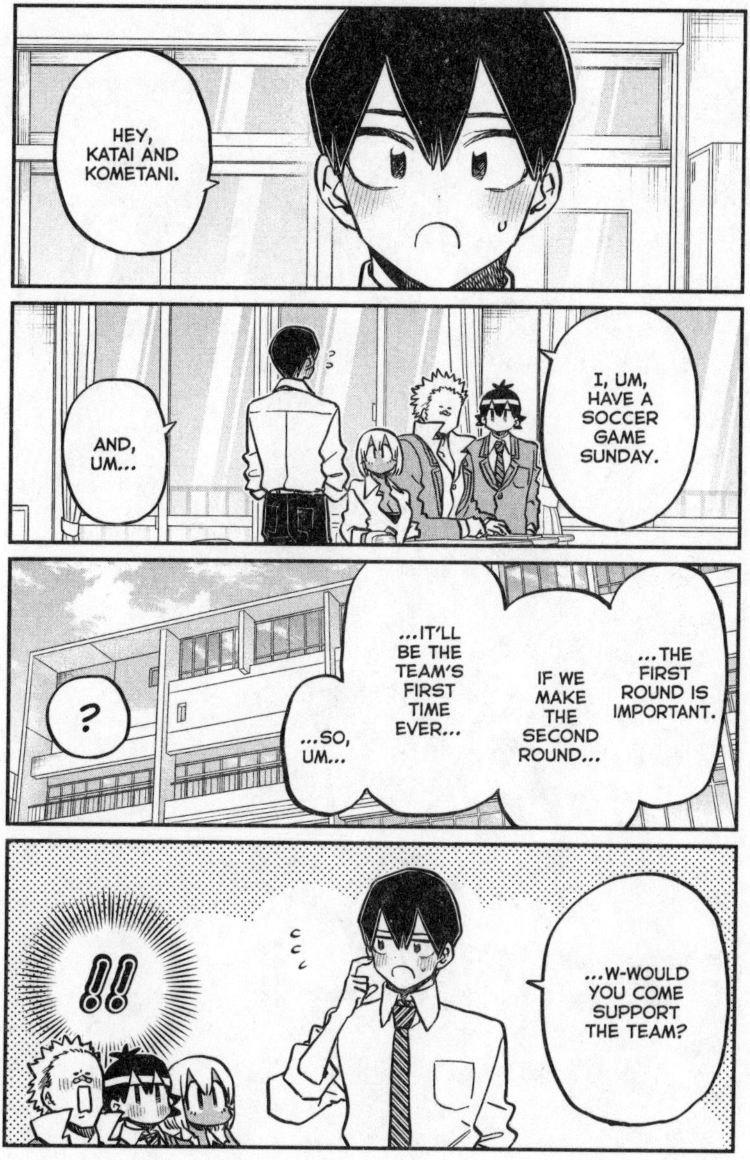
HEY, KATAI AND KOMETANI.
I, UM, HAVE A SOCCER GAME SUNDAY.
AND, UM...
...THE FIRST ROUND IS IMPORTANT.
IF WE MAKE THE SECOND ROUND...
...IT'LL BE THE TEAM'S FIRST TIME EVER...
...SO, UM...
?
...W-WOULD YOU COME SUPPORT THE TEAM?
!!

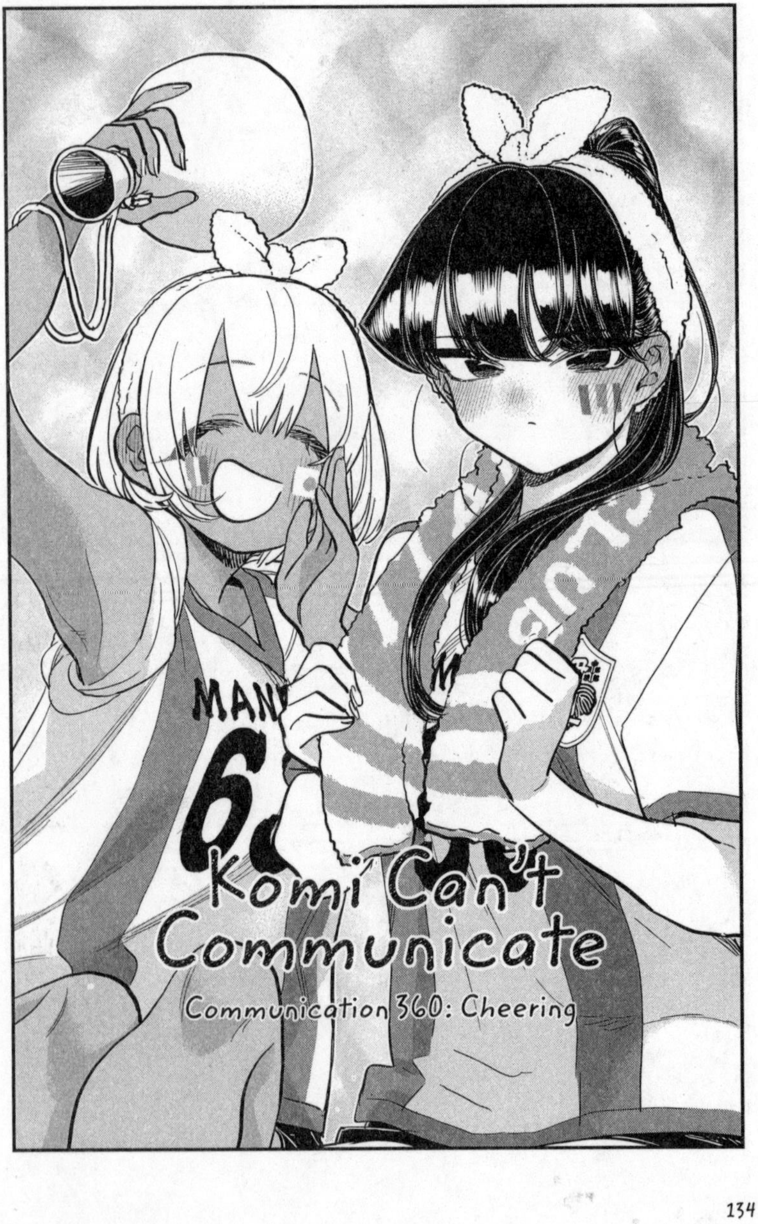
MAN
Komi Can't Communicate
Communication 360: Cheering

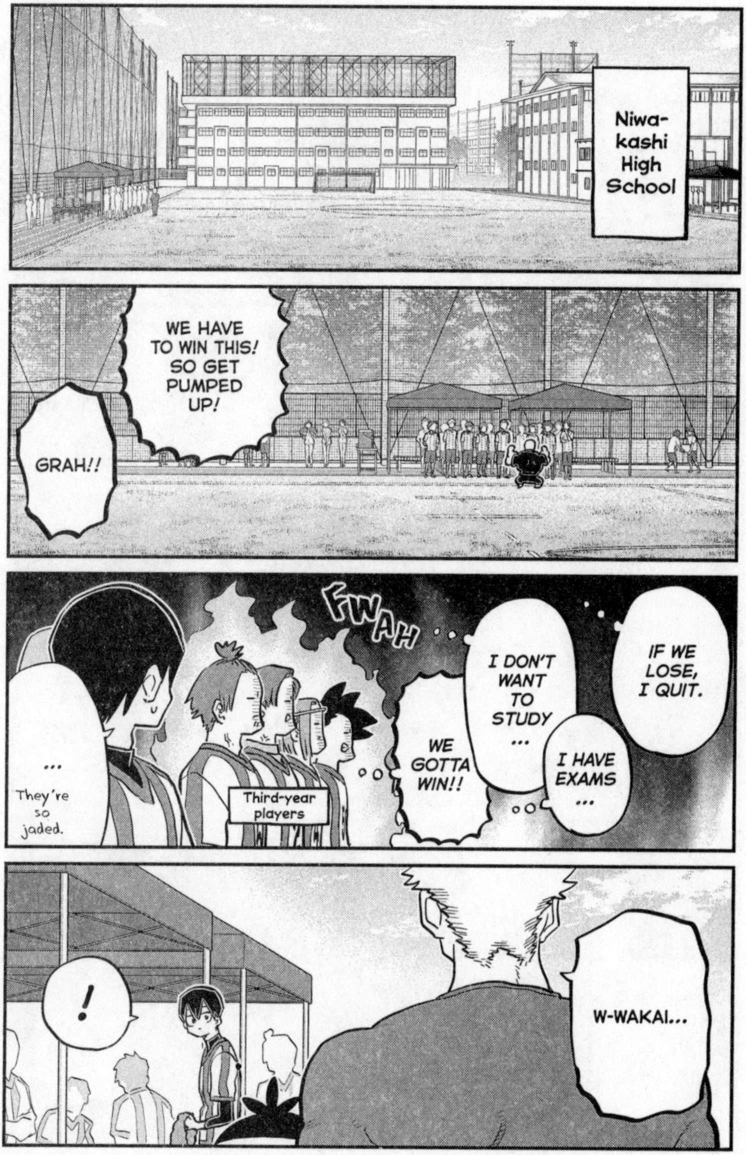
Niwa-kashi High School
WE HAVE TO WIN THIS! SO GET PUMPED UP!
GRAH!!
IF WE LOSE, I QUIT.
I DON'T WANT TO STUDY...
I HAVE EXAMS...
WE GOTTA WIN!!
FWAH
Third-year players
...
They're so jaded.
W-WAKAI...
!

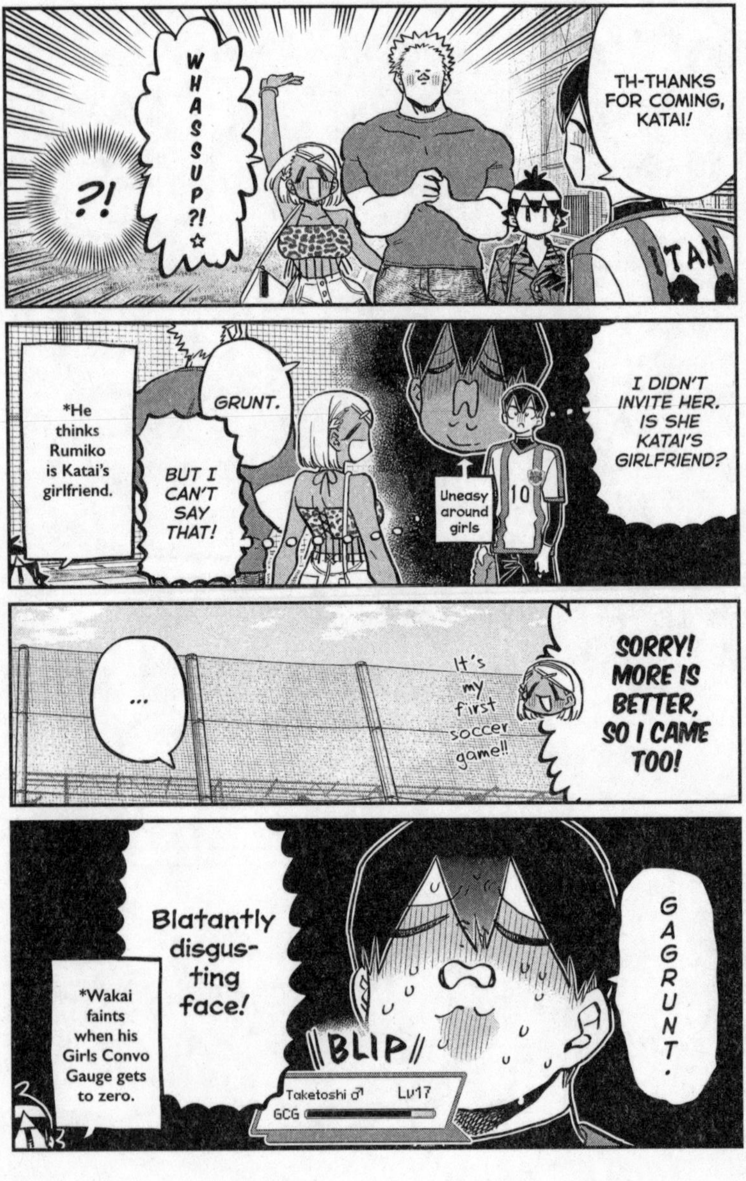
TH-THANKS FOR COMING, KATAI!
ITAN
WHASSUP?!☆
?!
I DIDN'T INVITE HER. IS SHE KATAI'S GIRLFRIEND?
Uneasy around girls
GRUNT.
BUT I CAN'T SAY THAT!
*He thinks Rumiko is Katai's girlfriend.
SORRY! MORE IS BETTER, SO I CAME TOO!
It's my first soccer game!!
...
GAGRUNT.
Blatantly disgus-ting face!
BLIP
Taketoshi ♂ Lv17
GCG
*Wakai faints when his Girls Convo Gauge gets to zero.

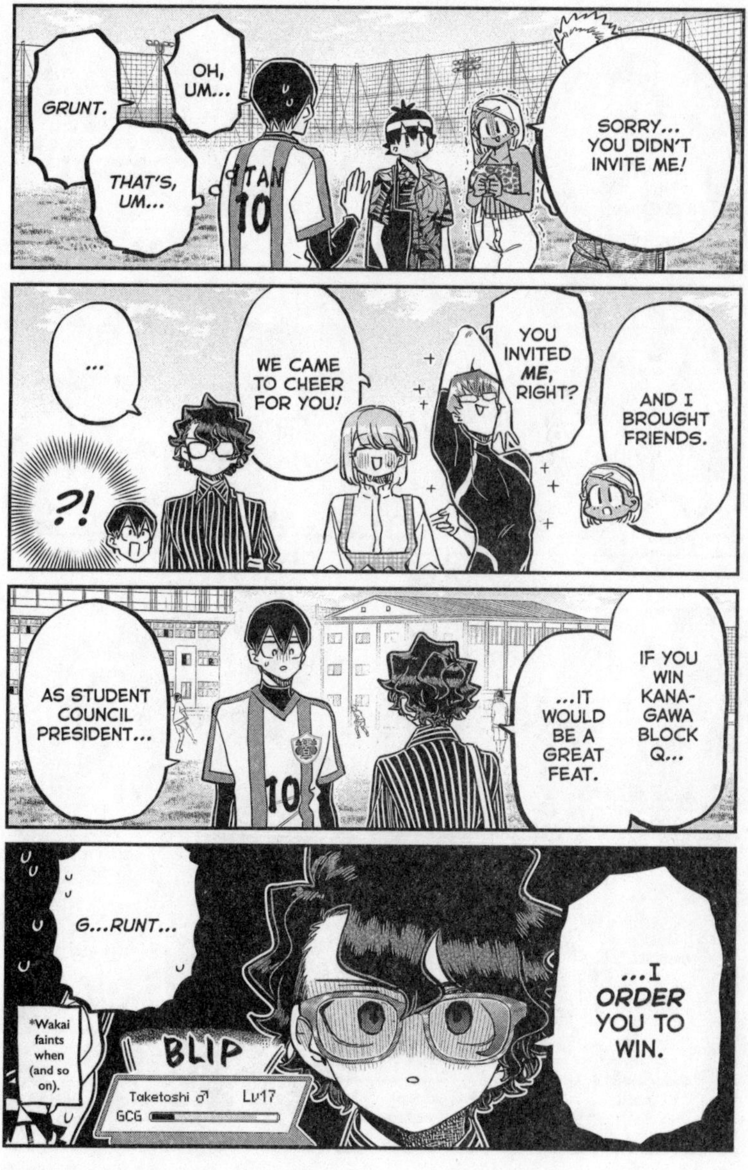
SORRY... YOU DIDN'T INVITE ME!
OH, UM...
GRUNT.
THAT'S, UM...
TAN 10
YOU INVITED ME, RIGHT?
AND I BROUGHT FRIENDS.
WE CAME TO CHEER FOR YOU!
...
?!
IF YOU WIN KANAGAWA BLOCK Q...
...IT WOULD BE A GREAT FEAT.
AS STUDENT COUNCIL PRESIDENT...
10
...I ORDER YOU TO WIN.
G...RUNT...
BLIP
*Wakai faints when (and so on).
Taketoshi ♂ Lv17
GCG

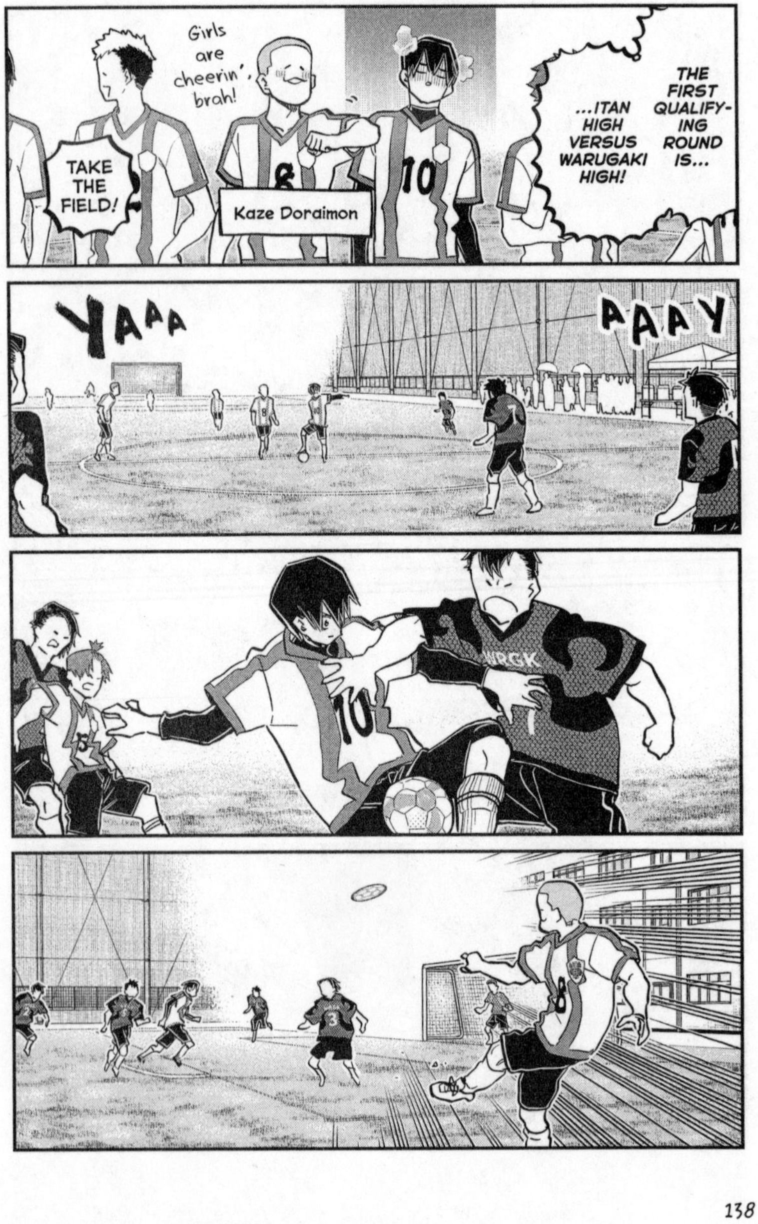
THE FIRST QUALIFYING ROUND IS...
...ITAN HIGH VERSUS WARUGAKI HIGH!
Girls are cheerin', brah!
Kaze Doraimon
TAKE THE FIELD!
YAAA
AAAY
WRGK

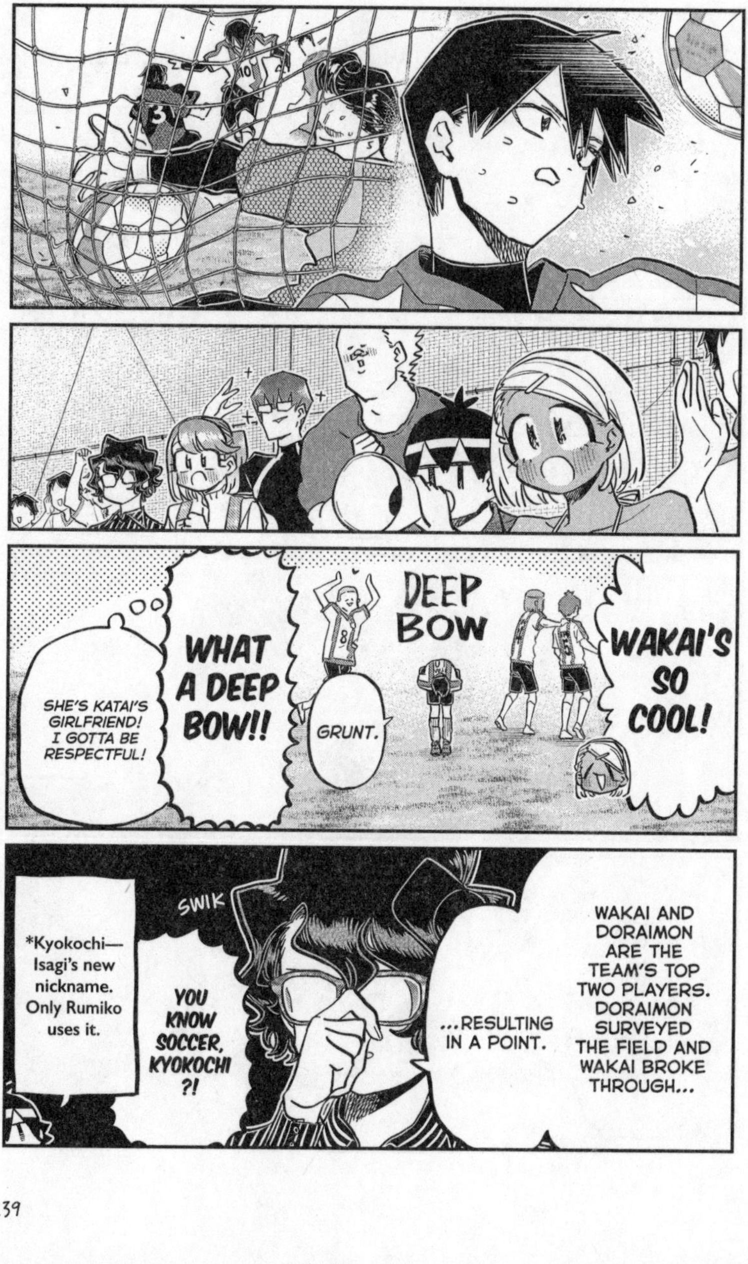
WAKAI'S SO COOL!
DEEP BOW
WHAT A DEEP BOW!!
GRUNT.
SHE'S KATAI'S GIRLFRIEND! I GOTTA BE RESPECTFUL!
WAKAI AND DORAIMON ARE THE TEAM'S TOP TWO PLAYERS. DORAIMON SURVEYED THE FIELD AND WAKAI BROKE THROUGH...
...RESULTING IN A POINT.
SWIK
YOU KNOW SOCCER, KYOKOCHI?!
*Kyokochi—Isagi's new nickname. Only Rumiko uses it.

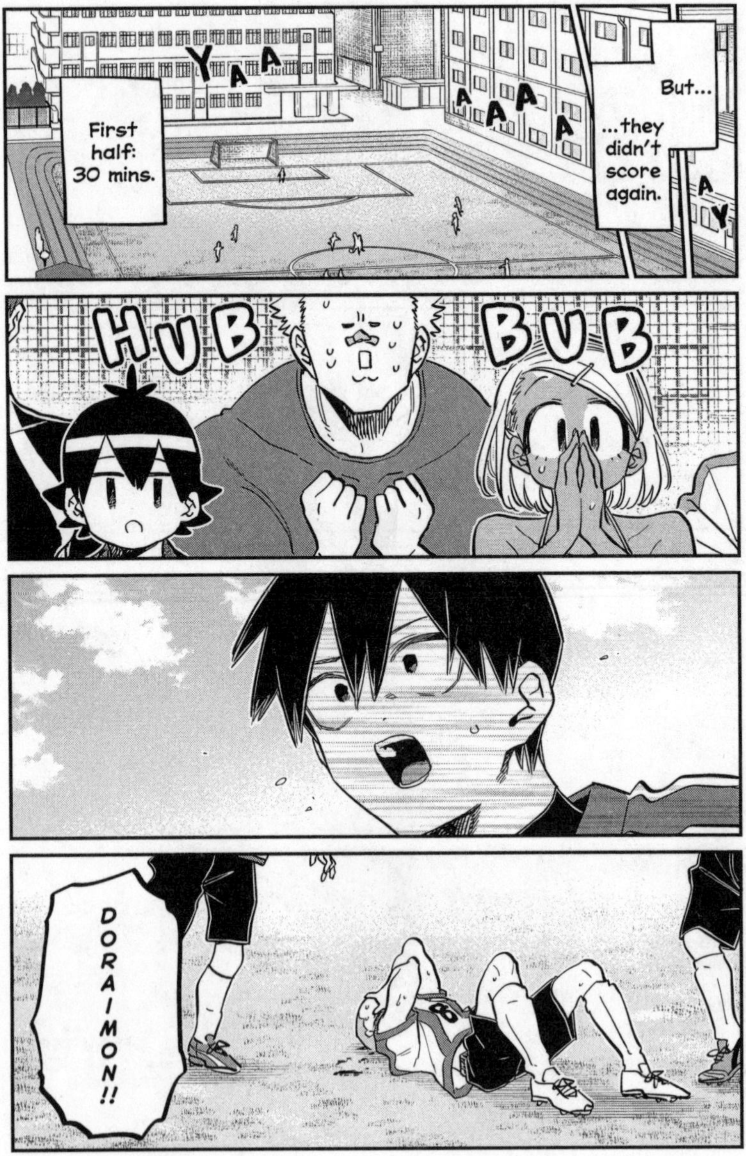
First half: 30 mins.
But...
...they didn't score again.
YAAAAAAA
AY
HUB BUB
DORAIMON!!

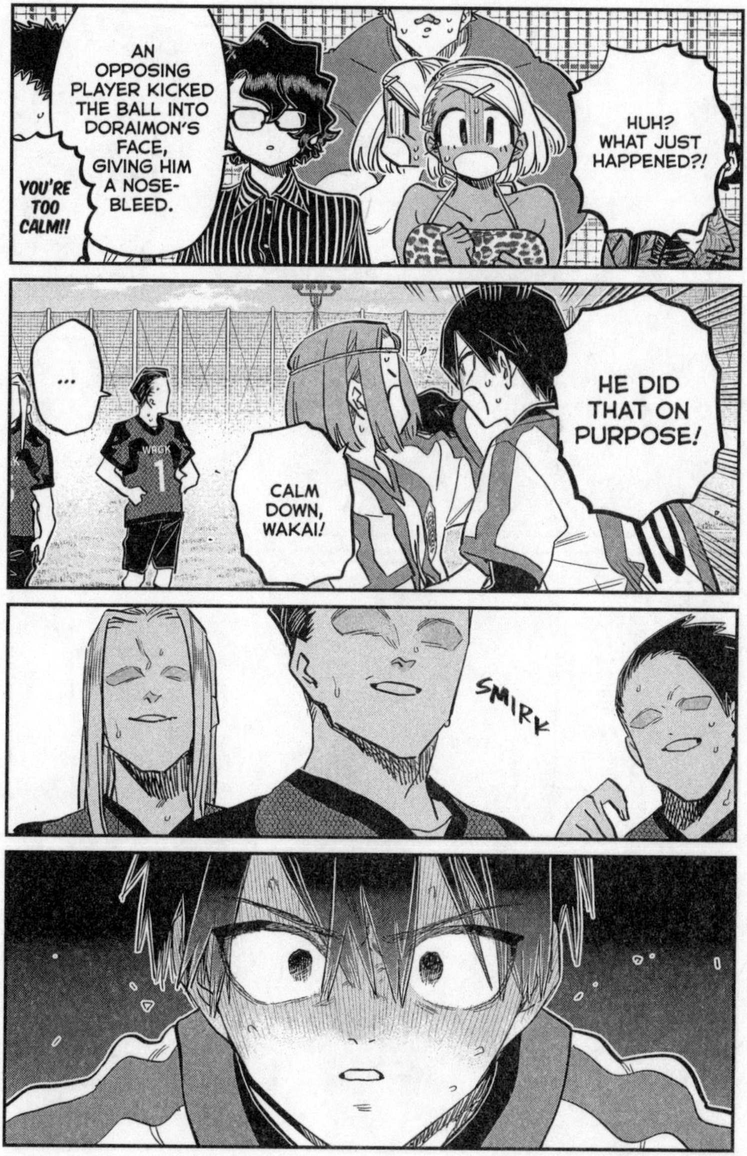
HUH? WHAT JUST HAPPENED?!
AN OPPOSING PLAYER KICKED THE BALL INTO DORAIMON'S FACE, GIVING HIM A NOSE-BLEED.
YOU'RE TOO CALM!!
HE DID THAT ON PURPOSE!
CALM DOWN, WAKAI!
...
SMIRK

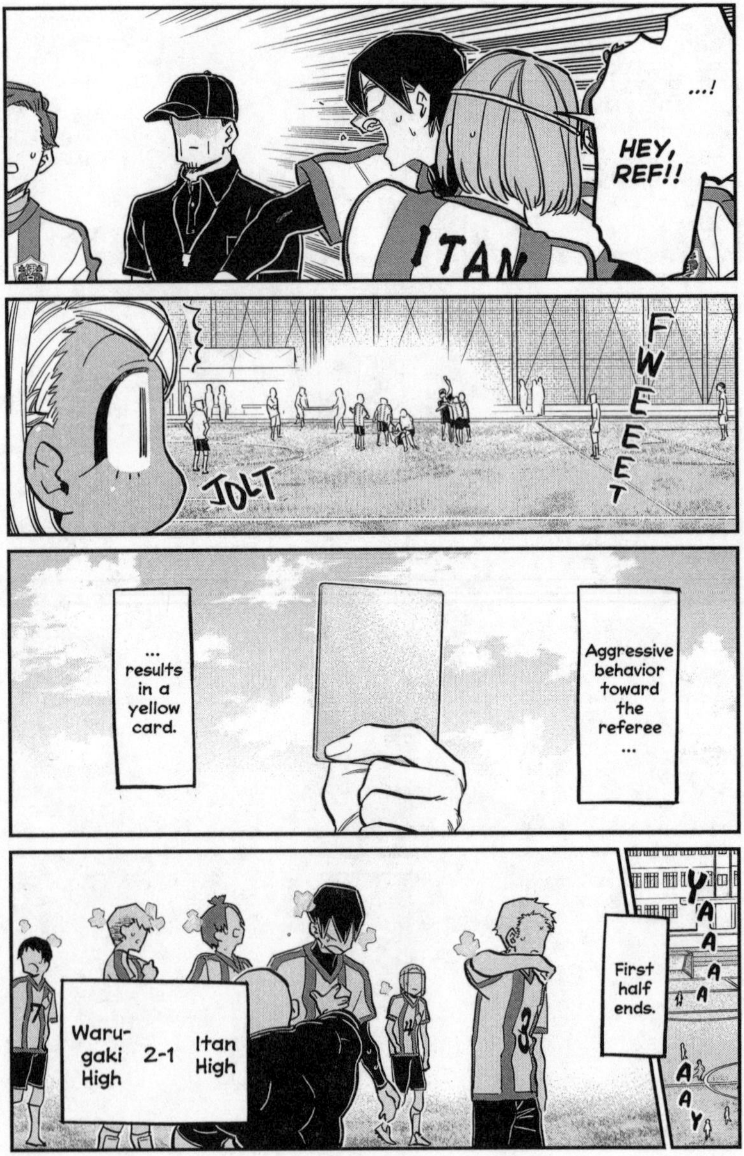
...!
HEY, REF!!
FWEEEET
JOLT
Aggressive behavior toward the referee ...
... results in a yellow card.
YAAAAA AAAY
First half ends.
Waru-gaki High 2-1 Itan High
ITAN

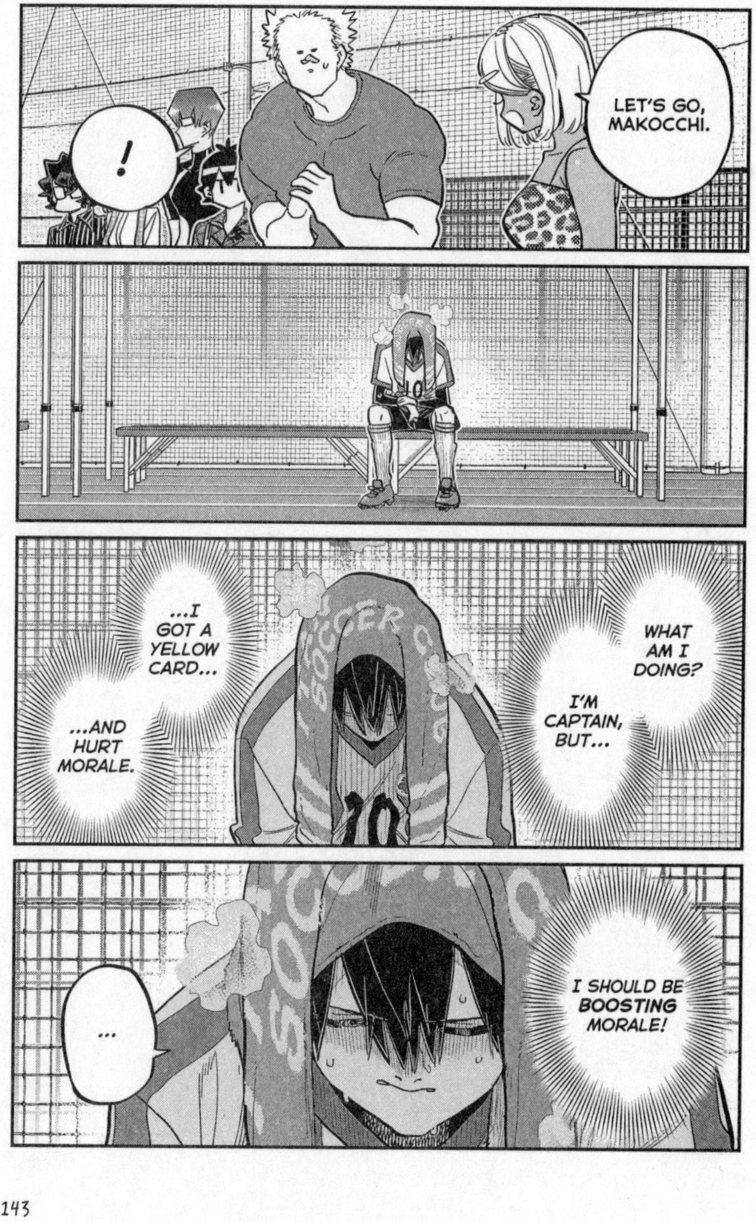
LET'S GO, MAKOCCHI.
!
WHAT AM I DOING?
I'M CAPTAIN, BUT...
...I GOT A YELLOW CARD...
...AND HURT MORALE.
I SHOULD BE BOOSTING MORALE!
...

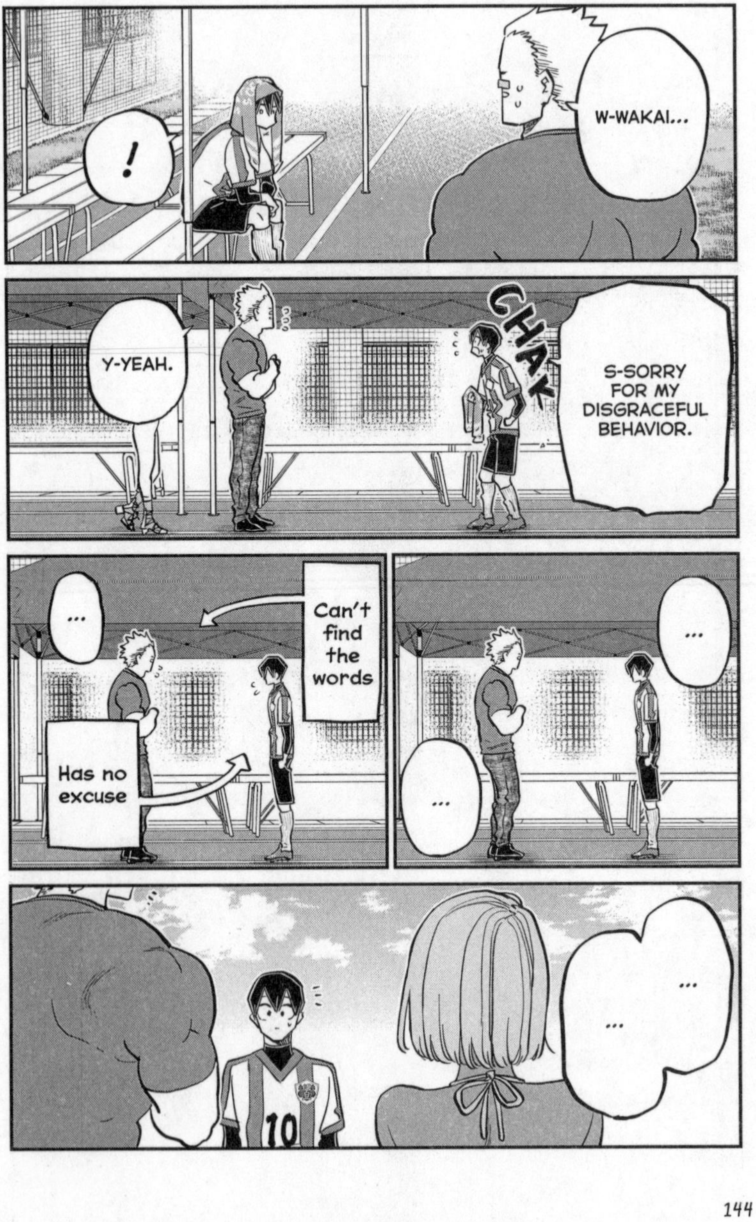
W-WAKAI...
!
S-SORRY FOR MY DISGRACEFUL BEHAVIOR.
CHAK
Y-YEAH.
...
...
Can't find the words
...
Has no excuse
...
...

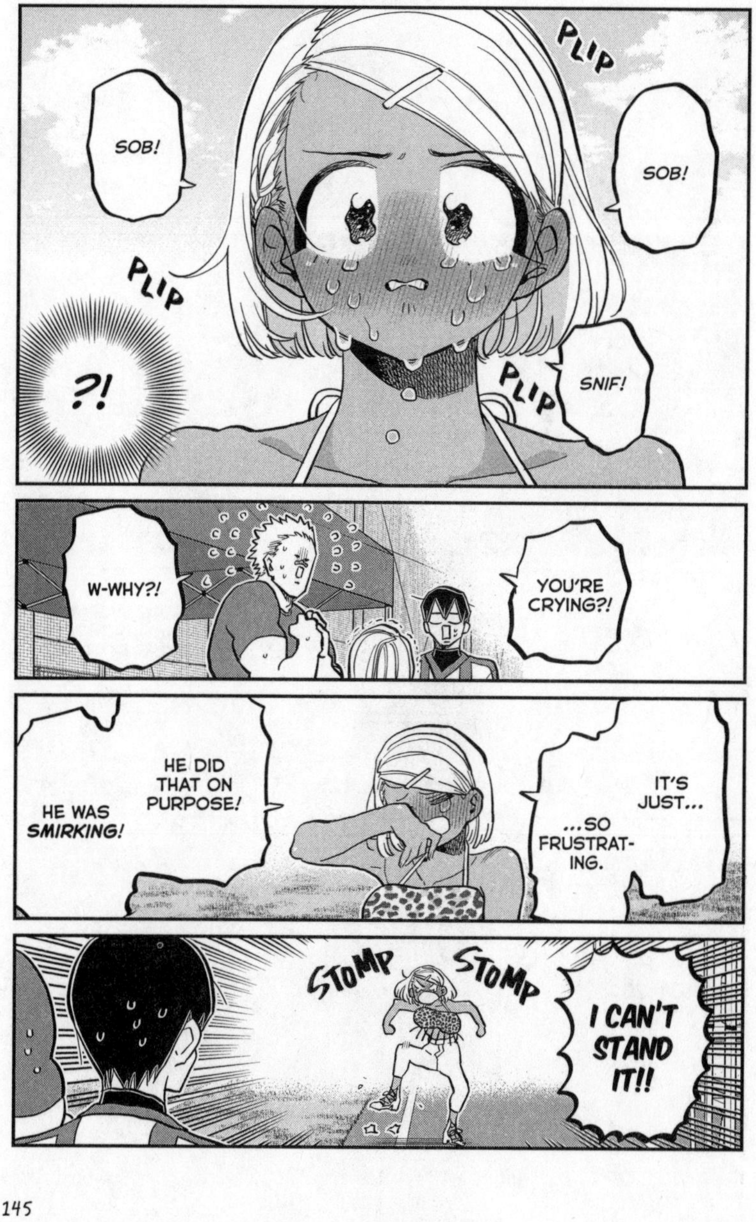
PLIP
SOB!
SNIF!
PLIP
SOB!
PLIP
?!
YOU'RE CRYING?!
W-WHY?!
IT'S JUST...
...SO FRUSTRAT-ING.
HE DID THAT ON PURPOSE!
HE WAS SMIRKING!
I CAN'T STAND IT!!
STOMP
STOMP

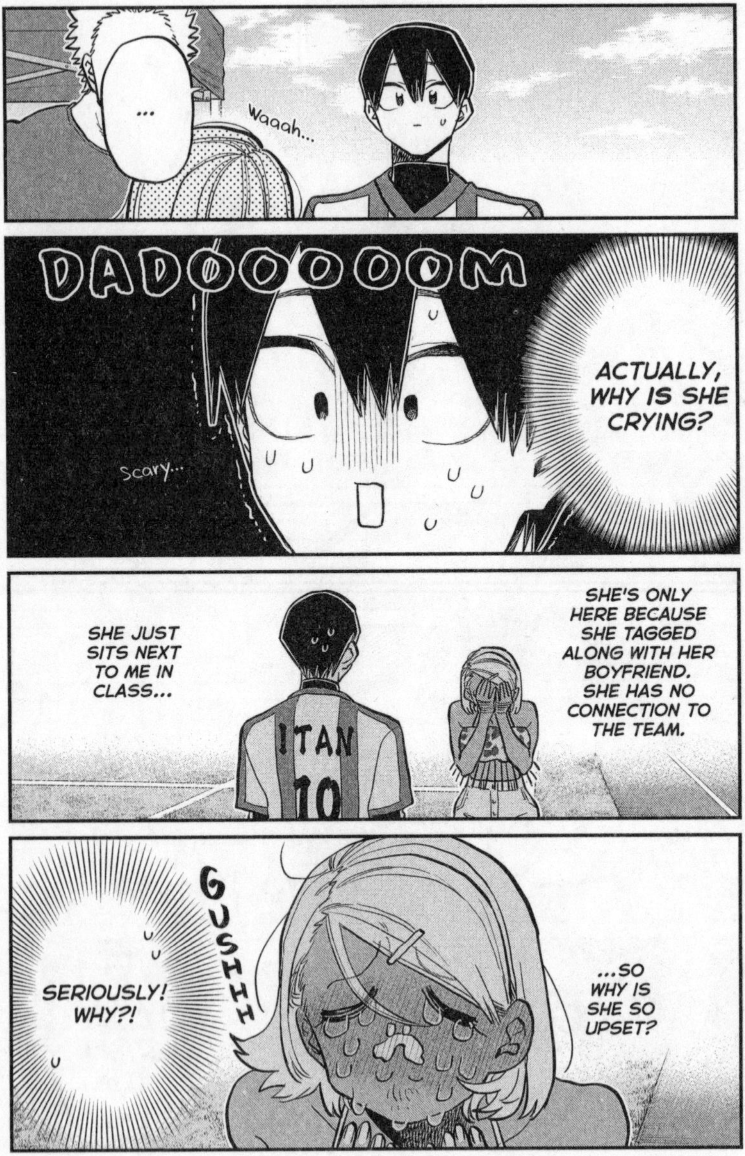
Waaah...
...
ACTUALLY, WHY IS SHE CRYING?
DADOOOOOM
Scary...
SHE'S ONLY HERE BECAUSE SHE TAGGED ALONG WITH HER BOYFRIEND. SHE HAS NO CONNECTION TO THE TEAM.
SHE JUST SITS NEXT TO ME IN CLASS...
ITAN
10
...SO WHY IS SHE SO UPSET?
GUSHHH
SERIOUSLY! WHY?!

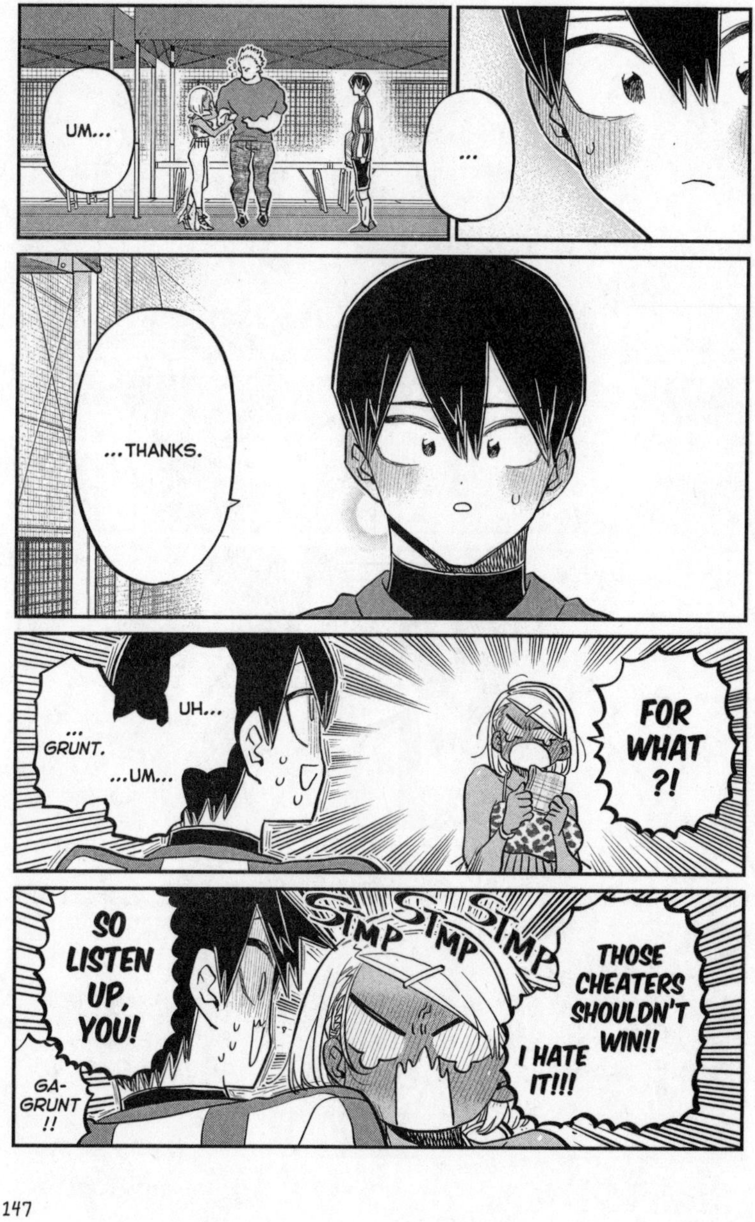
...
UM...
...THANKS.
FOR WHAT ?!
UH...
... GRUNT.
...UM...
STIMP STIMP STIMP
THOSE CHEATERS SHOULDN'T WIN!!
I HATE IT!!!
SO LISTEN UP, YOU!
GA-GRUNT !!

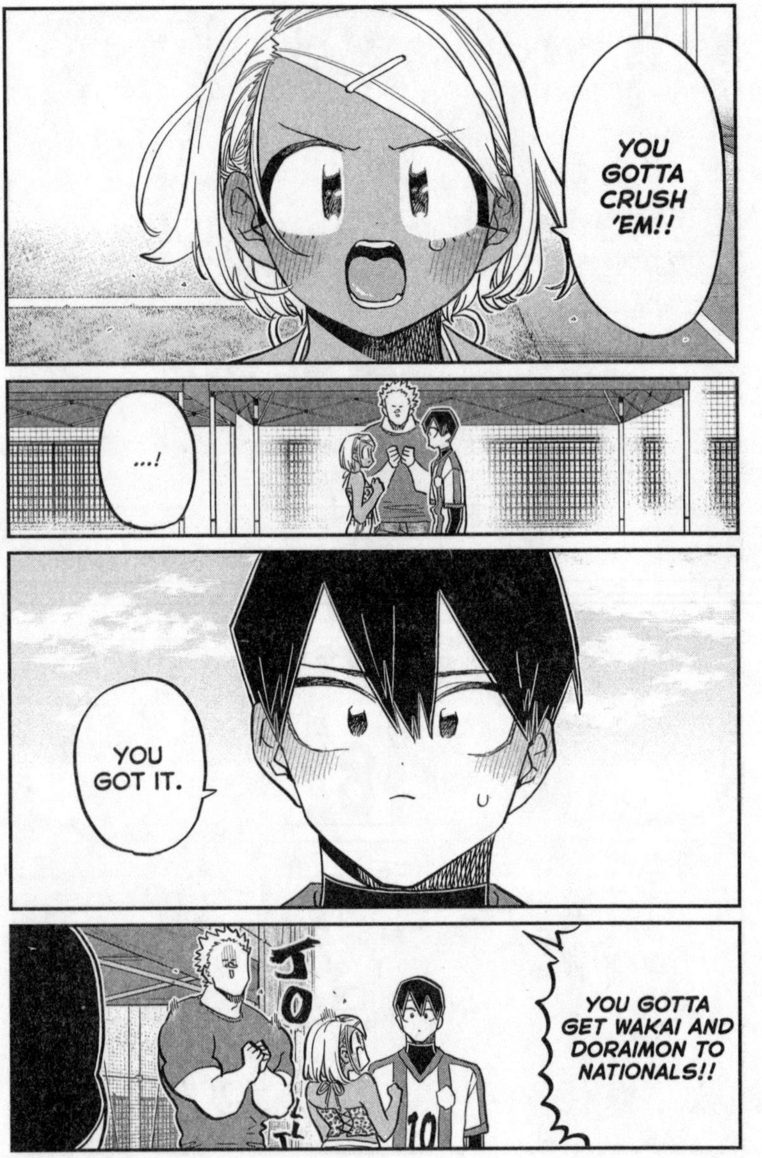
YOU GOTTA CRUSH 'EM!!
...!
YOU GOT IT.
YOU GOTTA GET WAKAI AND DORAIMON TO NATIONALS!!

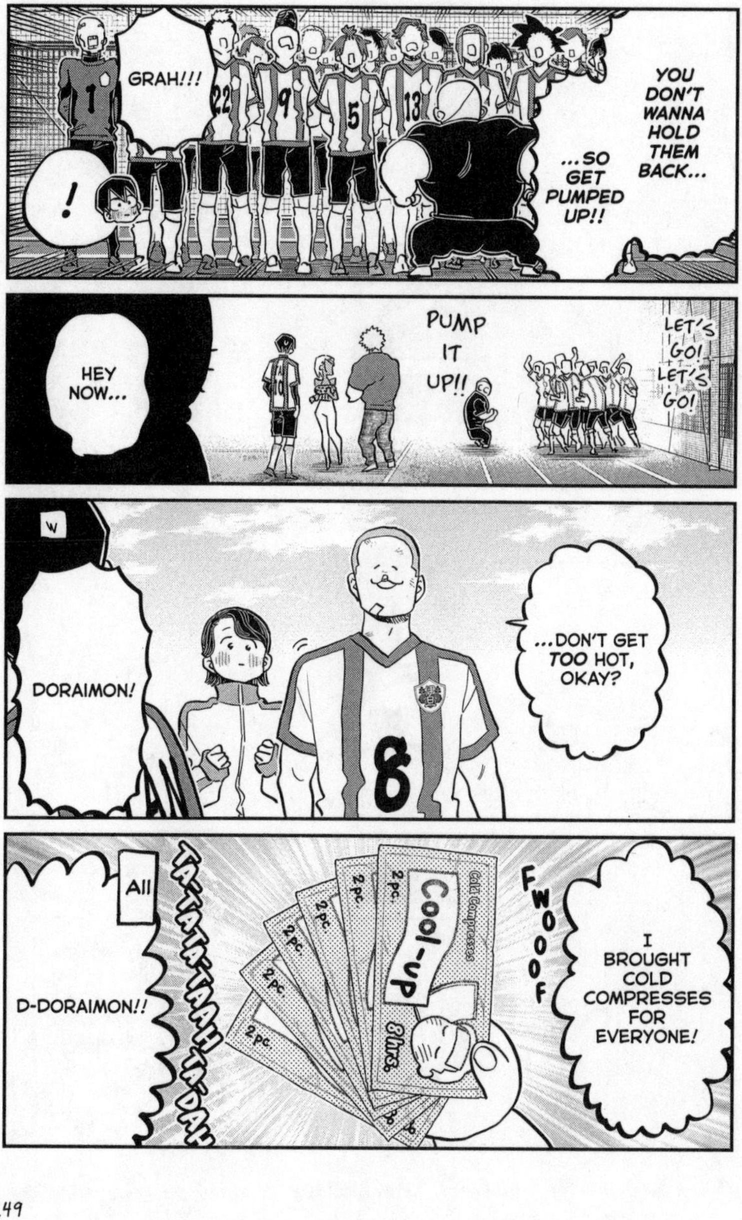
YOU DON'T WANNA HOLD THEM BACK...
...SO GET PUMPED UP!!
GRAH!!!
!
LET'S GO! LET'S GO!
PUMP IT UP!!
HEY NOW...
...DON'T GET TOO HOT, OKAY?
DORAIMON!
W
I BROUGHT COLD COMPRESSES FOR EVERYONE!
FWOOOF
Cold Compresses
COOL-UP
2pc.
8hrs.
TA-TA-TA-TAAAH TA-DAH
D-DORAIMON!!
All

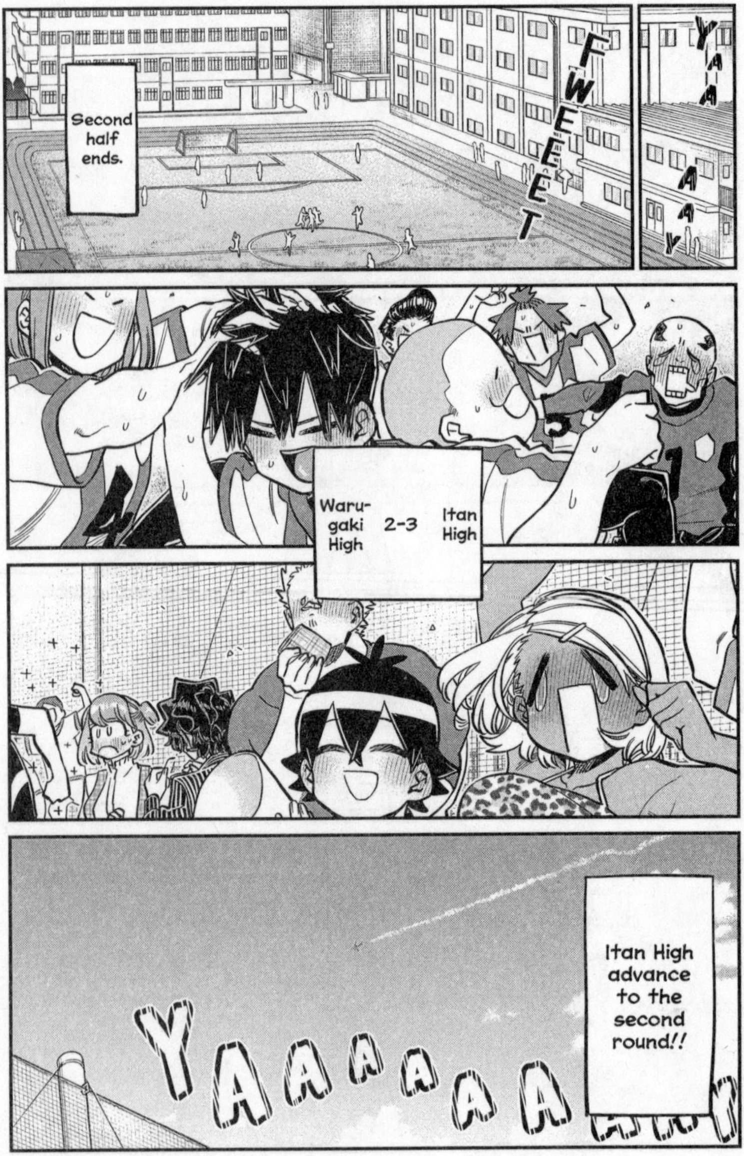
YAAAAY
FWEEET
Second half ends.
Waru-gaki High 2-3 Itan High
Itan High advance to the second round!!
YAAAAAAAAY

Communication 360 — The End

Komi Can't Communicate

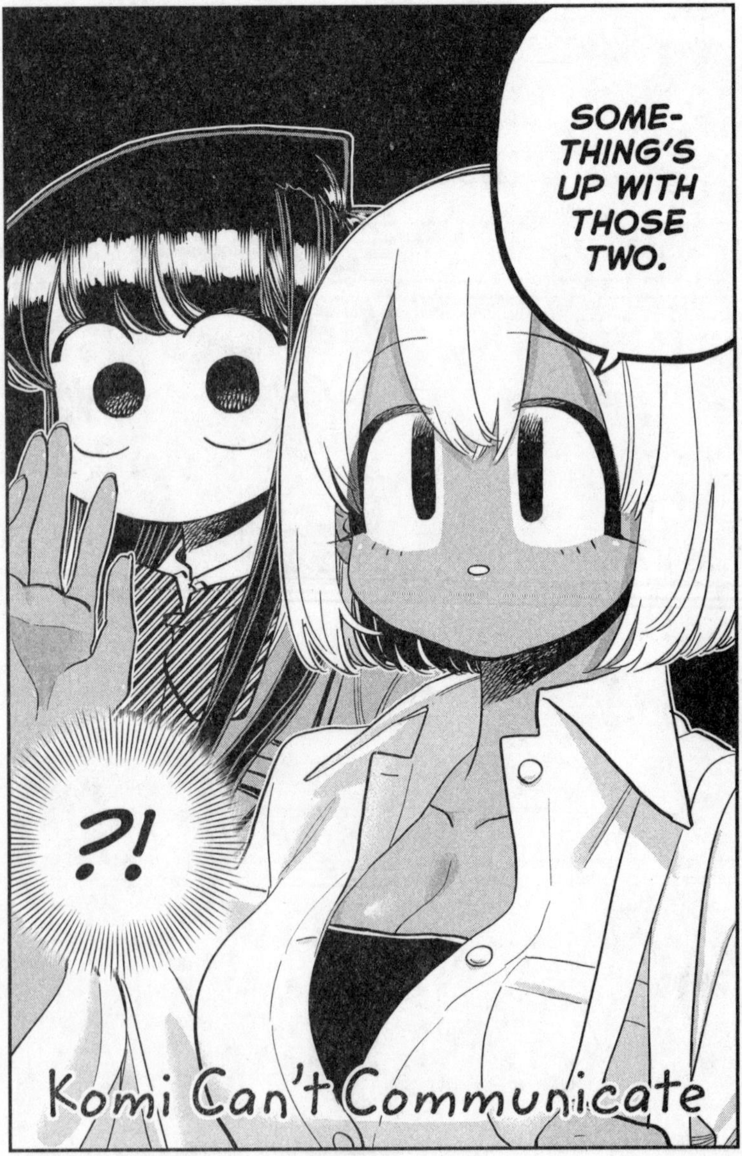
SOME-THING'S UP WITH THOSE TWO.
?!
Komi Can't Communicate

Communication 363: Ase Girls' Convo

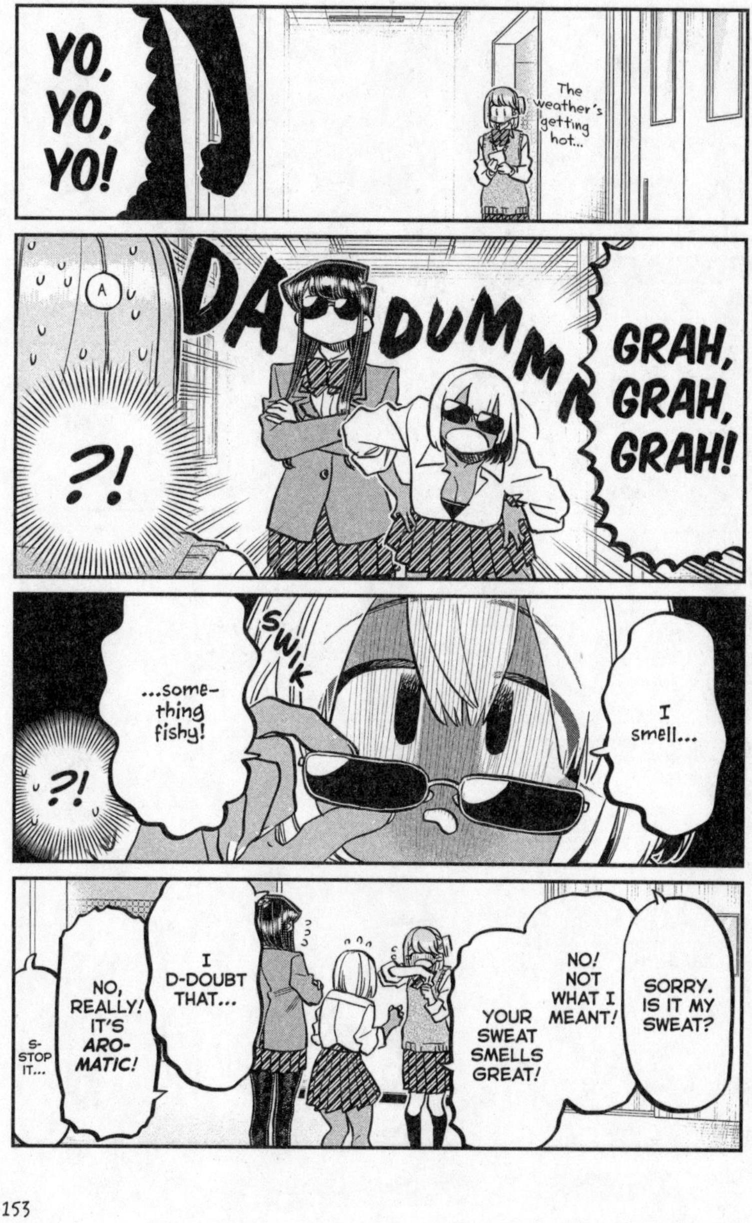
The weather's getting hot...
YO, YO, YO!
GRAH, GRAH, GRAH!
DA DUMM
A
?!
I smell...
SWIK
...some-thing fishy!
?!
SORRY. IS IT MY SWEAT?
NO! NOT WHAT I MEANT!
YOUR SWEAT SMELLS GREAT!
I D-DOUBT THAT...
NO, REALLY! IT'S ARO-MATIC!
S-STOP IT...

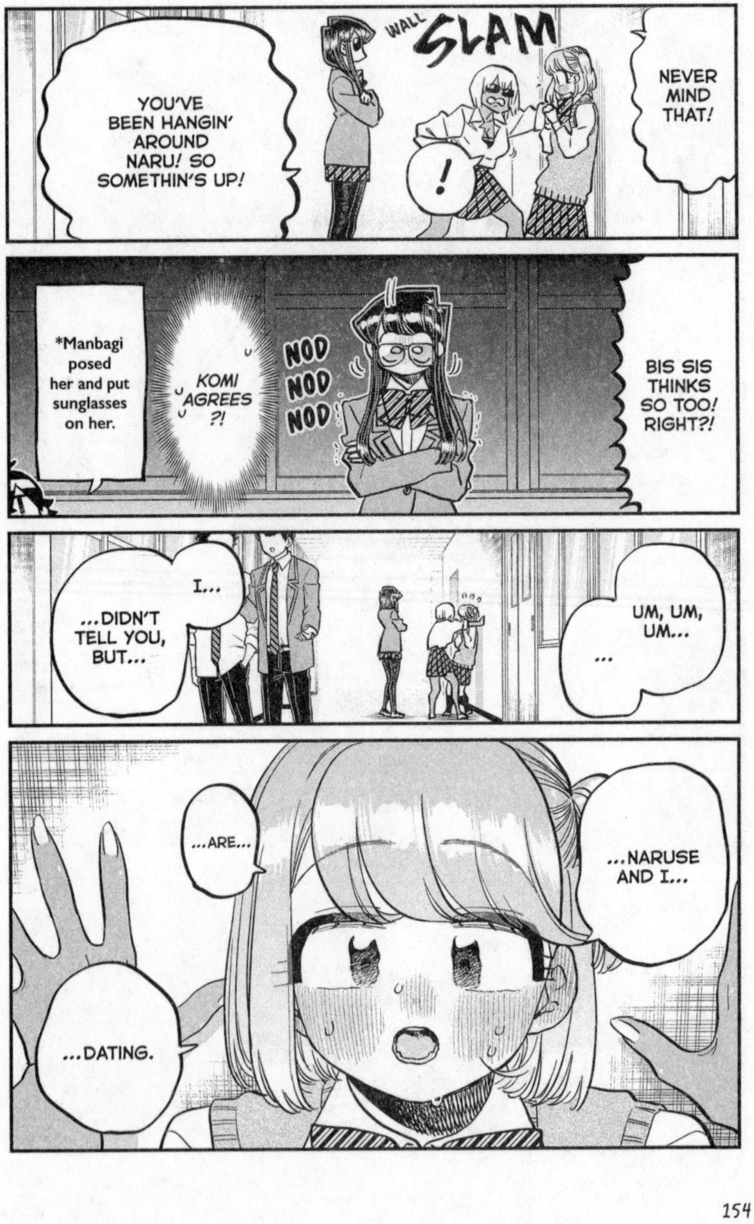
NEVER MIND THAT!
WALL
SLAM
!
YOU'VE BEEN HANGIN' AROUND NARU! SO SOMETHIN'S UP!
BIS SIS THINKS SO TOO! RIGHT?!
NOD NOD NOD
KOMI AGREES?!
*Manbagi posed her and put sunglasses on her.
UM, UM, UM...
...
I...
...DIDN'T TELL YOU, BUT...
...NARUSE AND I...
...ARE...
...DATING.

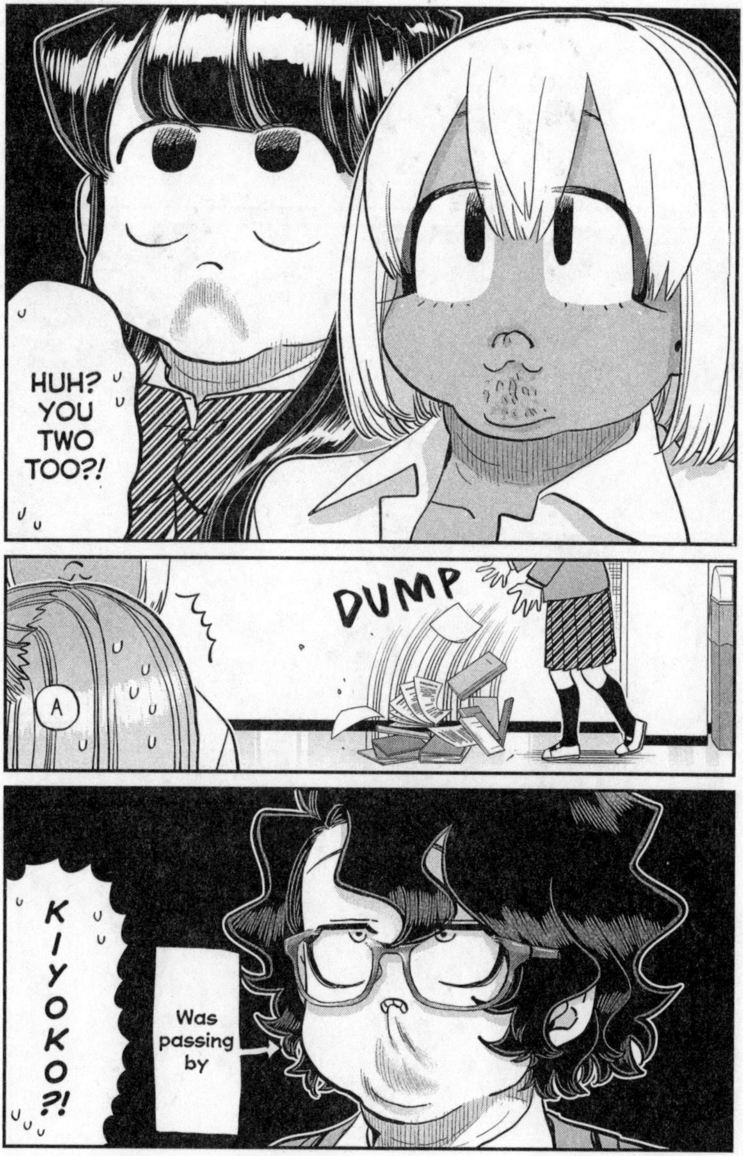
HUH? YOU TWO TOO?!
A
DUMP
KIYOKO?!
Was passing by

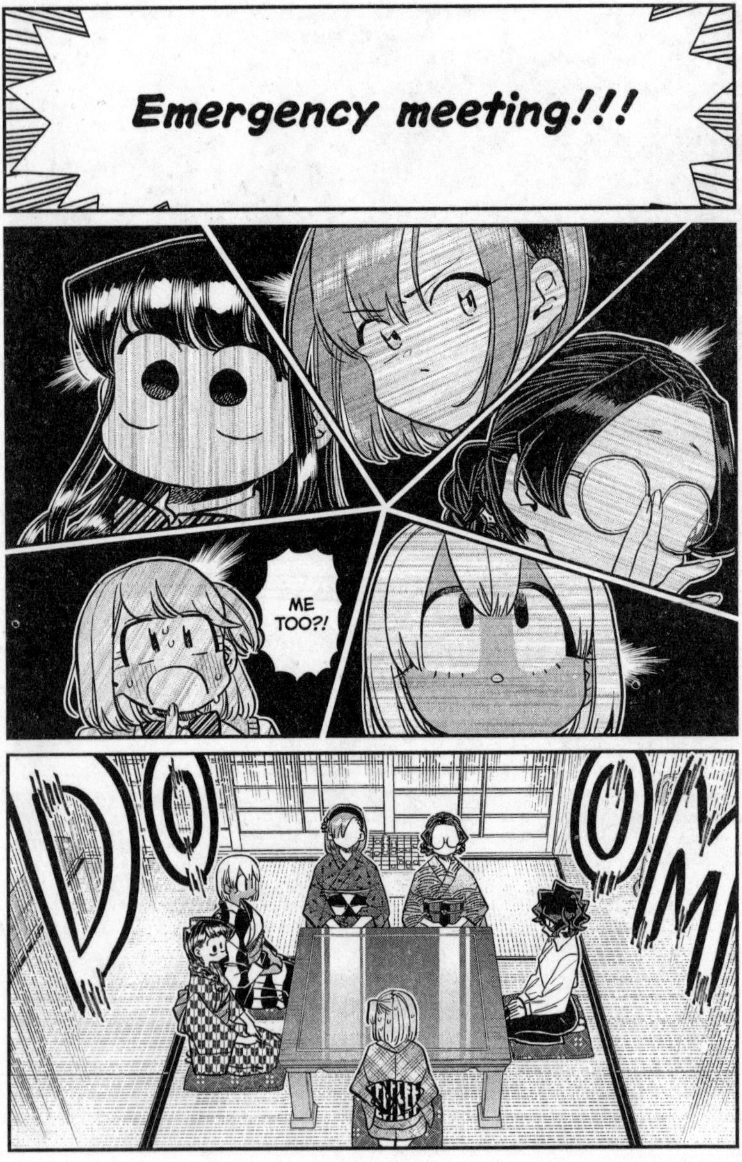
Emergency meeting!!!
ME TOO?!
DOOM

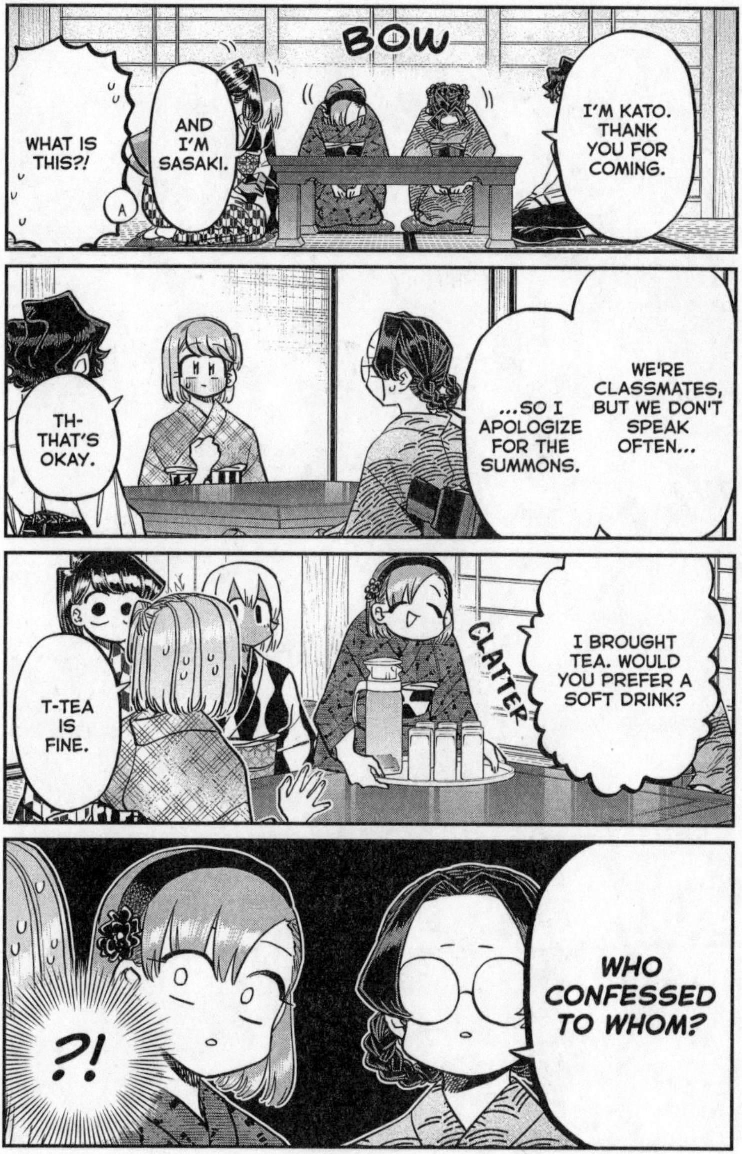
BOW
I'M KATO. THANK YOU FOR COMING.
AND I'M SASAKI.
WHAT IS THIS?!
A
WE'RE CLASSMATES, BUT WE DON'T SPEAK OFTEN...
...SO I APOLOGIZE FOR THE SUMMONS.
TH- THAT'S OKAY.
I BROUGHT TEA. WOULD YOU PREFER A SOFT DRINK?
CLATTER
T-TEA IS FINE.
WHO CONFESSED TO WHOM?
?!

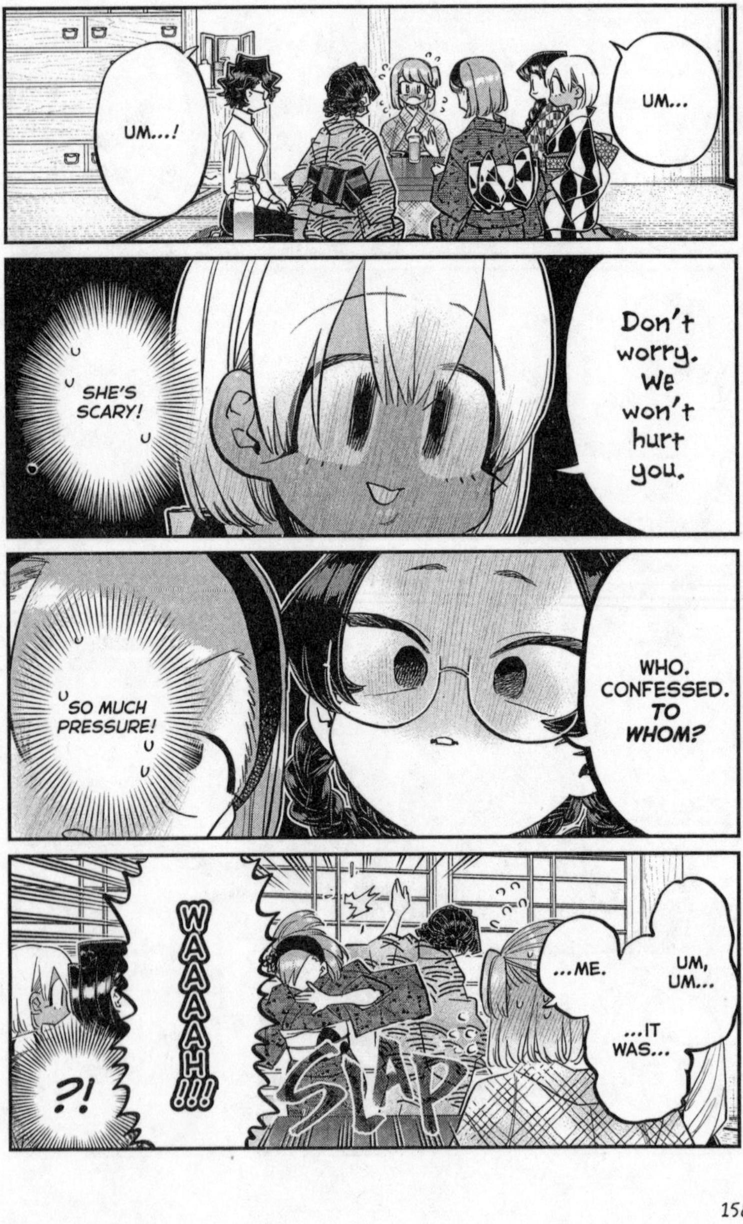
UM...
UM...!
Don't worry. We won't hurt you.
SHE'S SCARY!
WHO. CONFESSED. TO WHOM?
SO MUCH PRESSURE!
UM, UM...
...IT WAS...
...ME.
SLAP
WAAAAAH!!!
?!

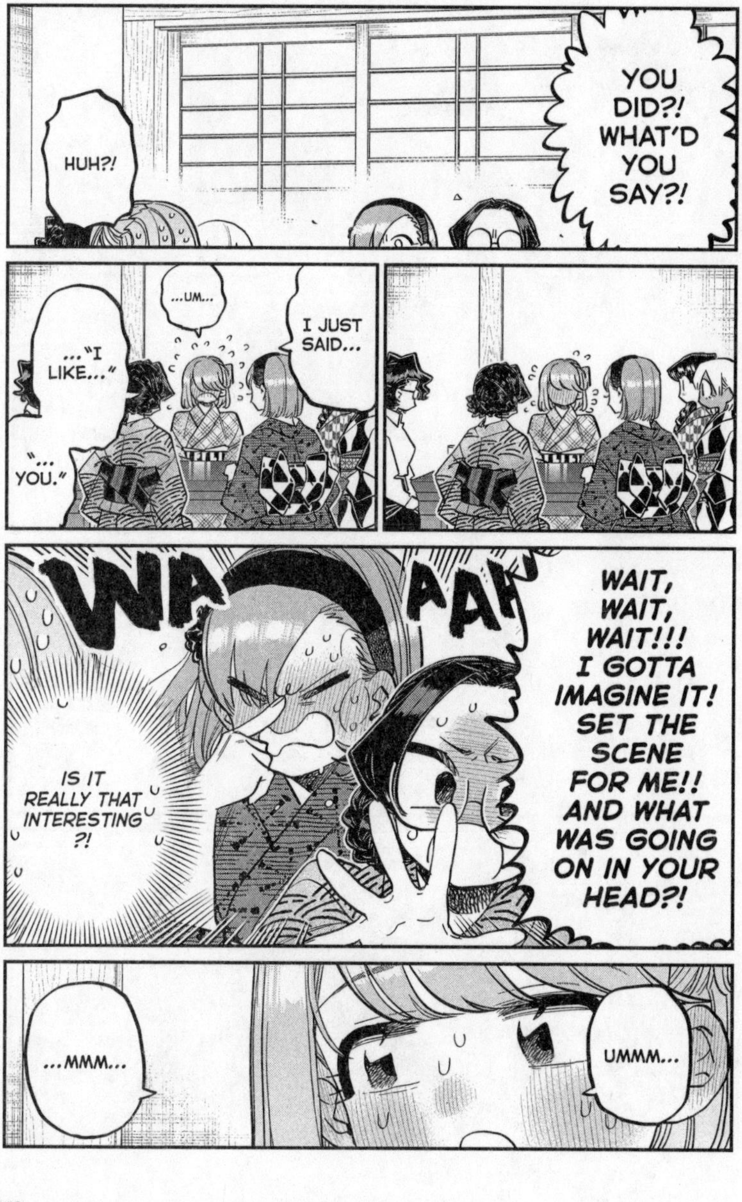
YOU DID?! WHAT'D YOU SAY?!
HUH?!
I JUST SAID...
...UM...
..."I LIKE..."
"...YOU."
WAIT, WAIT, WAIT!!! I GOTTA IMAGINE IT! SET THE SCENE FOR ME!! AND WHAT WAS GOING ON IN YOUR HEAD?!
IS IT REALLY THAT INTERESTING?!
UMMM...
...MMM...

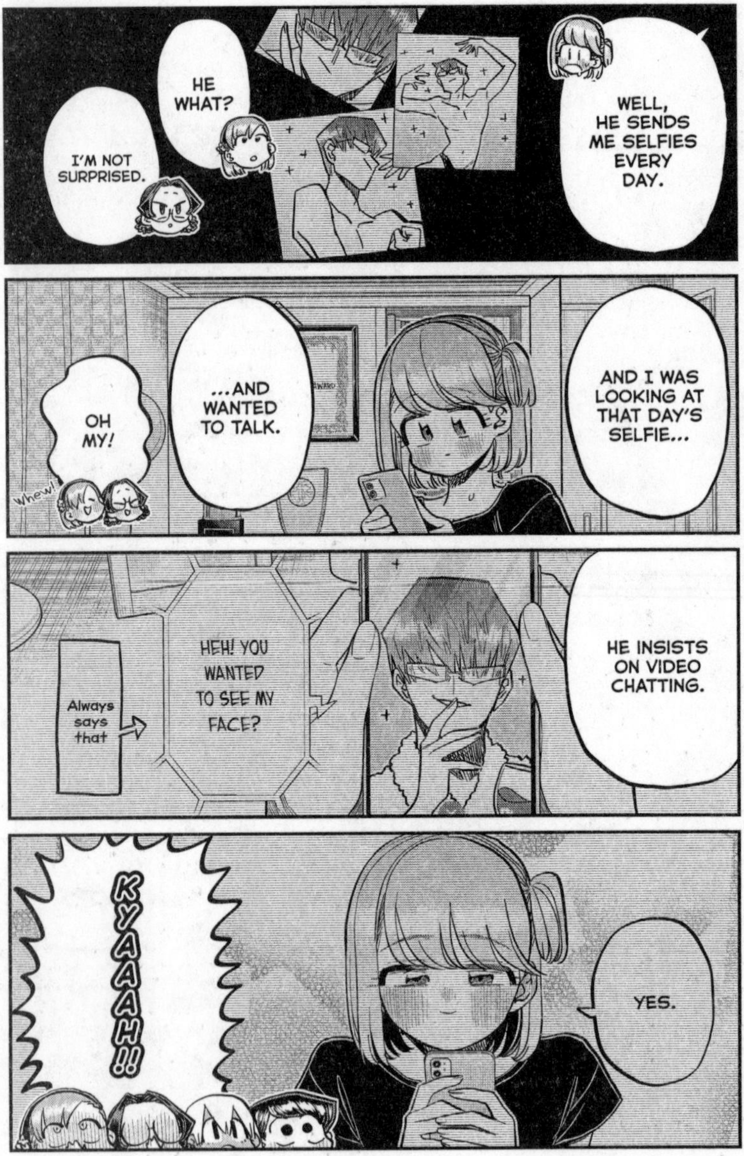
WELL, HE SENDS ME SELFIES EVERY DAY.
HE WHAT?
I'M NOT SURPRISED.
AND I WAS LOOKING AT THAT DAY'S SELFIE...
...AND WANTED TO TALK.
OH MY!
Whew!
HE INSISTS ON VIDEO CHATTING.
HEH! YOU WANTED TO SEE MY FACE?
Always says that
YES.
KYAAAAH!!

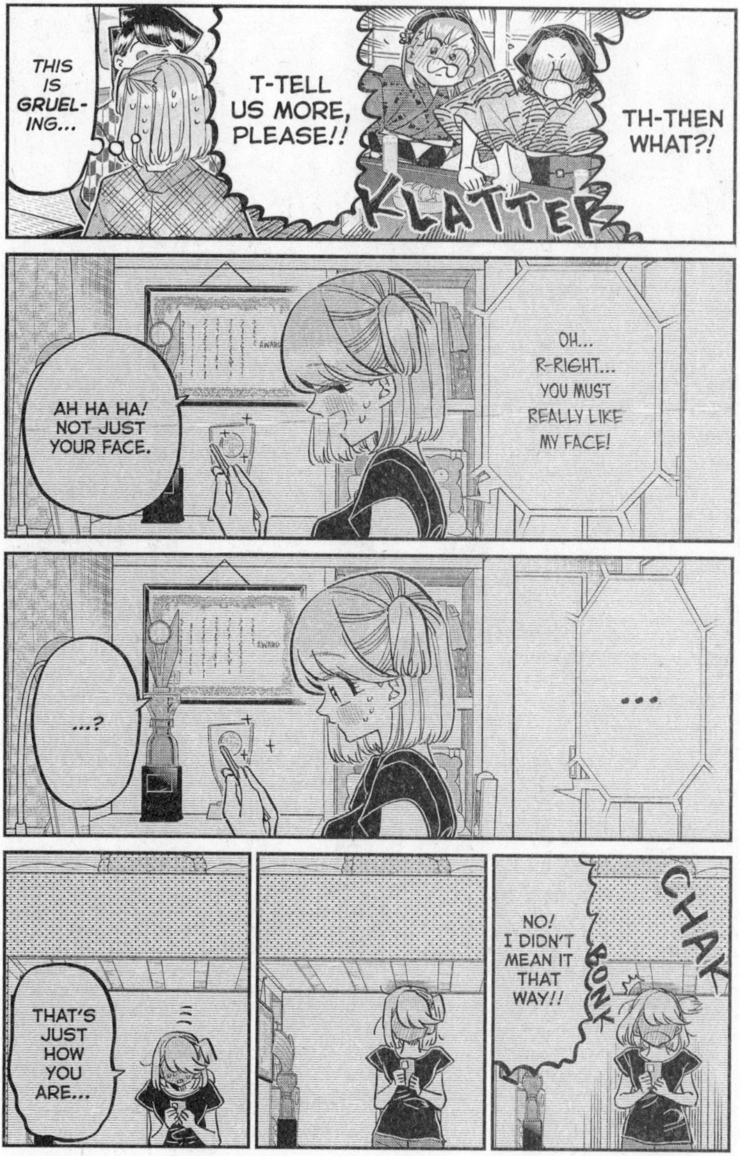
TH-THEN WHAT?!
T-TELL US MORE, PLEASE!!
KLATTER
THIS IS GRUEL-ING...
OH... R-RIGHT... YOU MUST REALLY LIKE MY FACE!
AH HA HA! NOT JUST YOUR FACE.
...
...?
CHAK
BONK
NO! I DIDN'T MEAN IT THAT WAY!!
THAT'S JUST HOW YOU ARE...

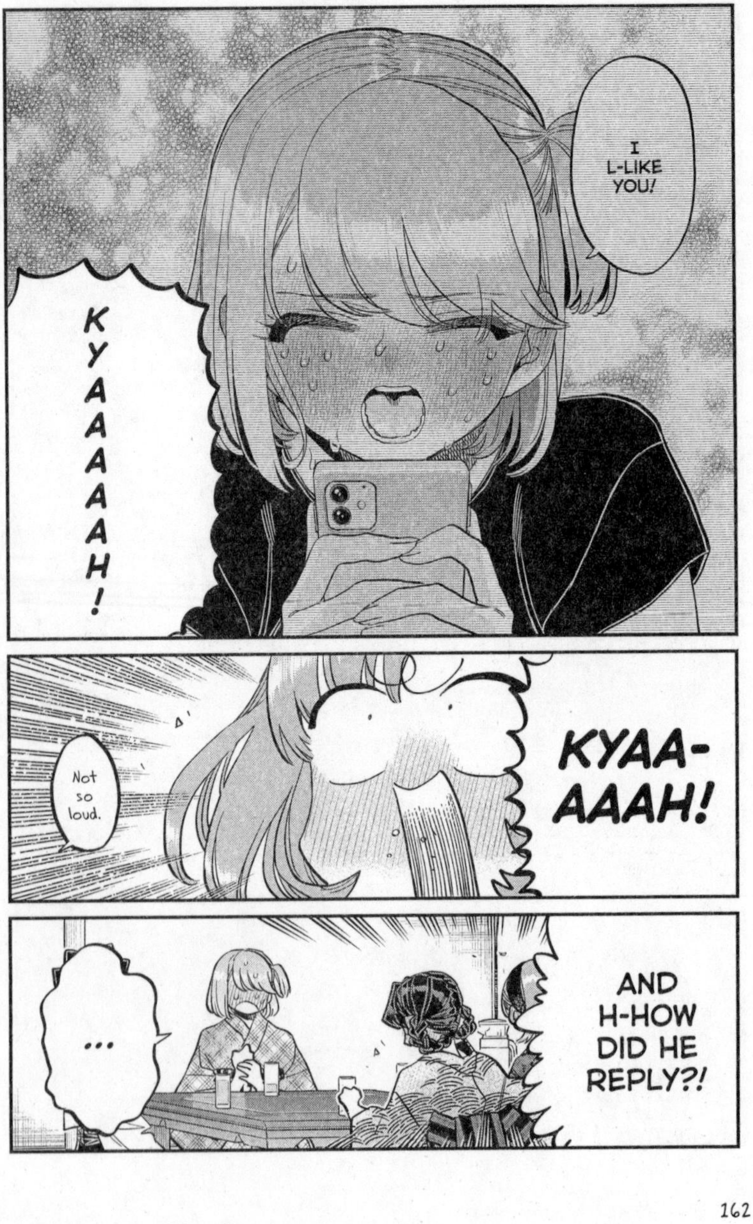
I L-LIKE YOU!
KYAAAAAAAH!
KYAA-AAAH!
Not so loud.
AND H-HOW DID HE REPLY?!
...

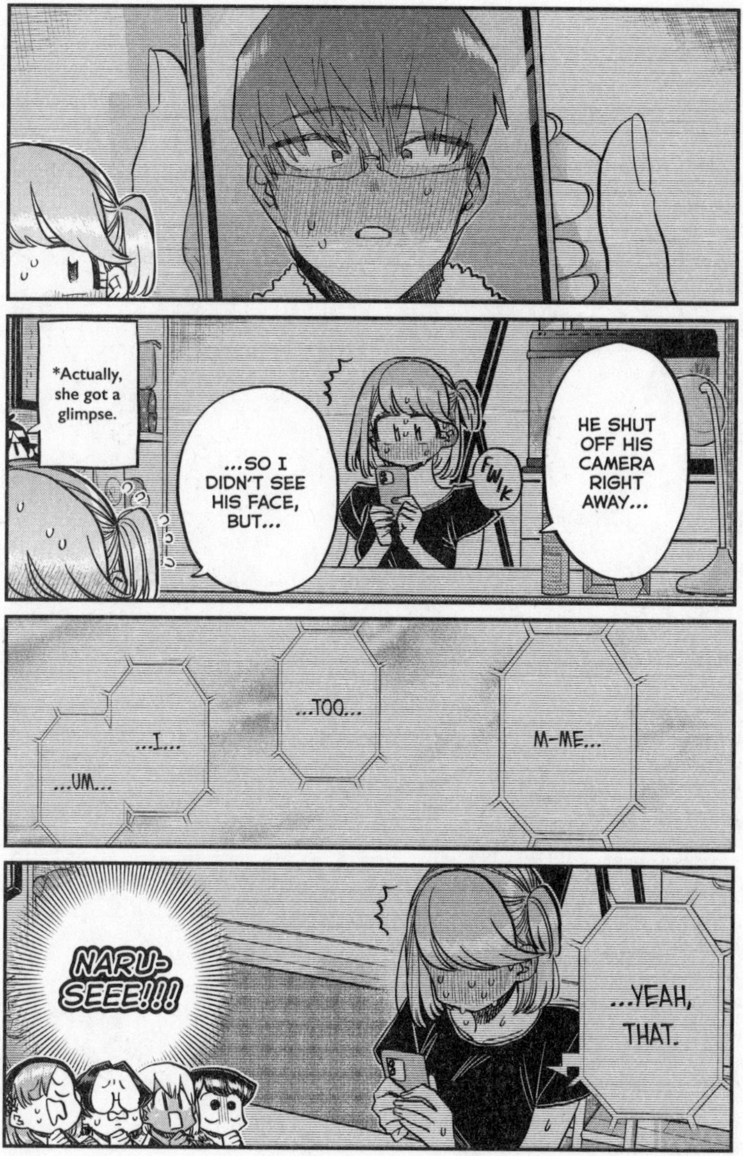
HE SHUT OFF HIS CAMERA RIGHT AWAY...
FWIK
...SO I DIDN'T SEE HIS FACE, BUT...
*Actually, she got a glimpse.
M-ME...
...TOO...
...I...
...UM...
...YEAH, THAT.
NARU-SEEE!!!

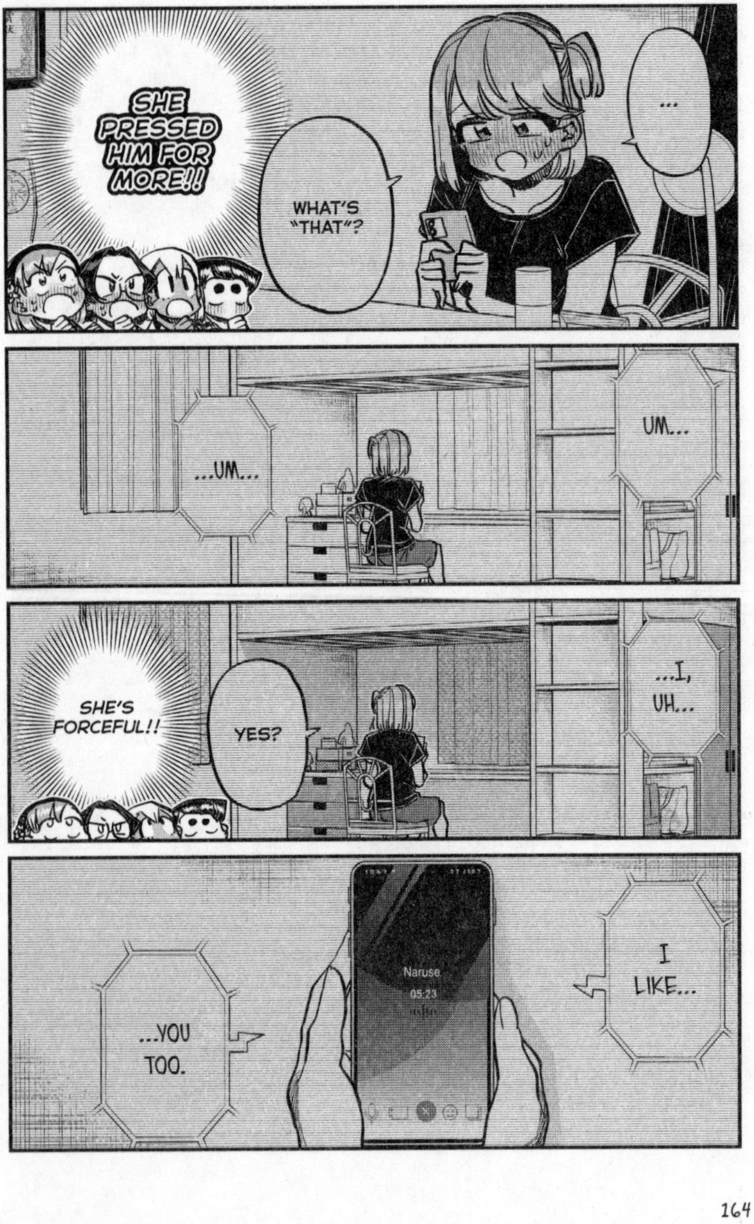
...
WHAT'S "THAT"?
SHE PRESSED HIM FOR MORE!!
UM...
...UM...
...I, UH...
YES?
SHE'S FORCEFUL!!
I LIKE...
Naruse
05:23
...YOU TOO.

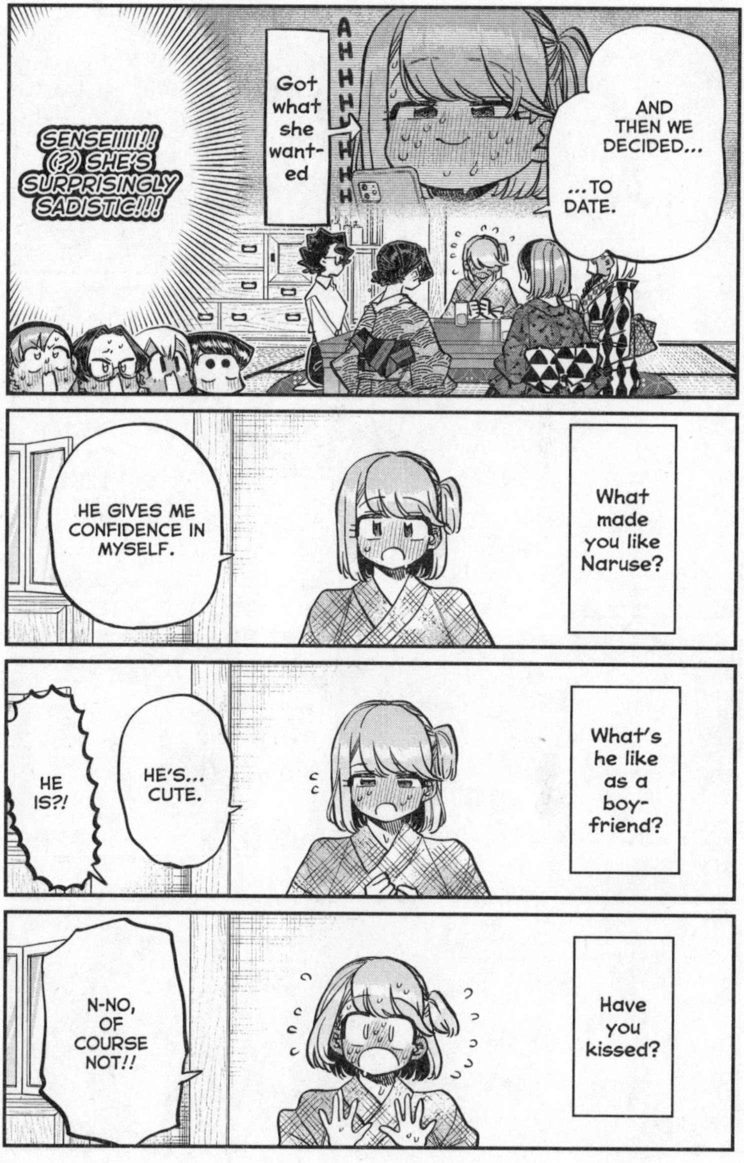
AND THEN WE DECIDED...
...TO DATE.
AHHHHHHH
Got what she want-ed
SENSEI!!!!!! (?) SHE'S SURPRISINGLY SADISTIC!!!
What made you like Naruse?
HE GIVES ME CONFIDENCE IN MYSELF.
What's he like as a boy-friend?
HE'S... CUTE.
HE IS?!
Have you kissed?
N-NO, OF COURSE NOT!!

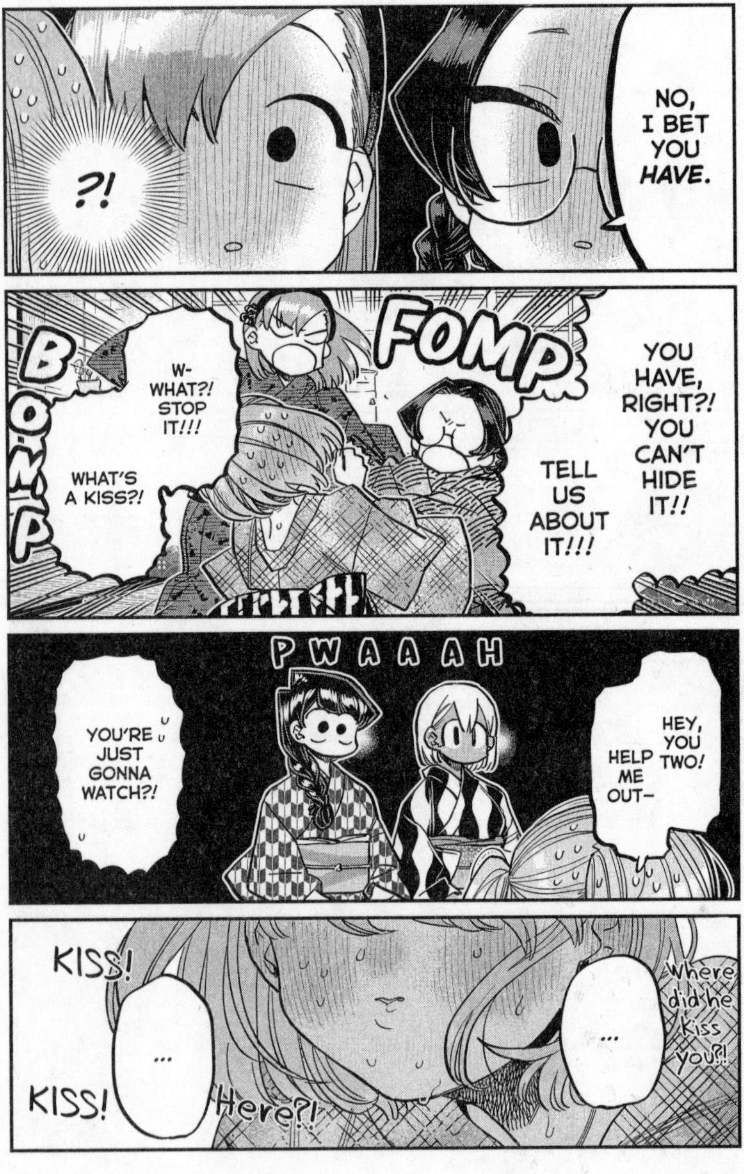
NO, I BET YOU HAVE.
?!
YOU HAVE, RIGHT?! YOU CAN'T HIDE IT!!
TELL US ABOUT IT!!!
FOMP
W-WHAT?! STOP IT!!!
WHAT'S A KISS?!
BOMP
PWAAAAH
HEY, YOU TWO! HELP ME OUT–
YOU'RE JUST GONNA WATCH?!
Where did he kiss you?!
...
Here?!
KISS!
...
KISS!

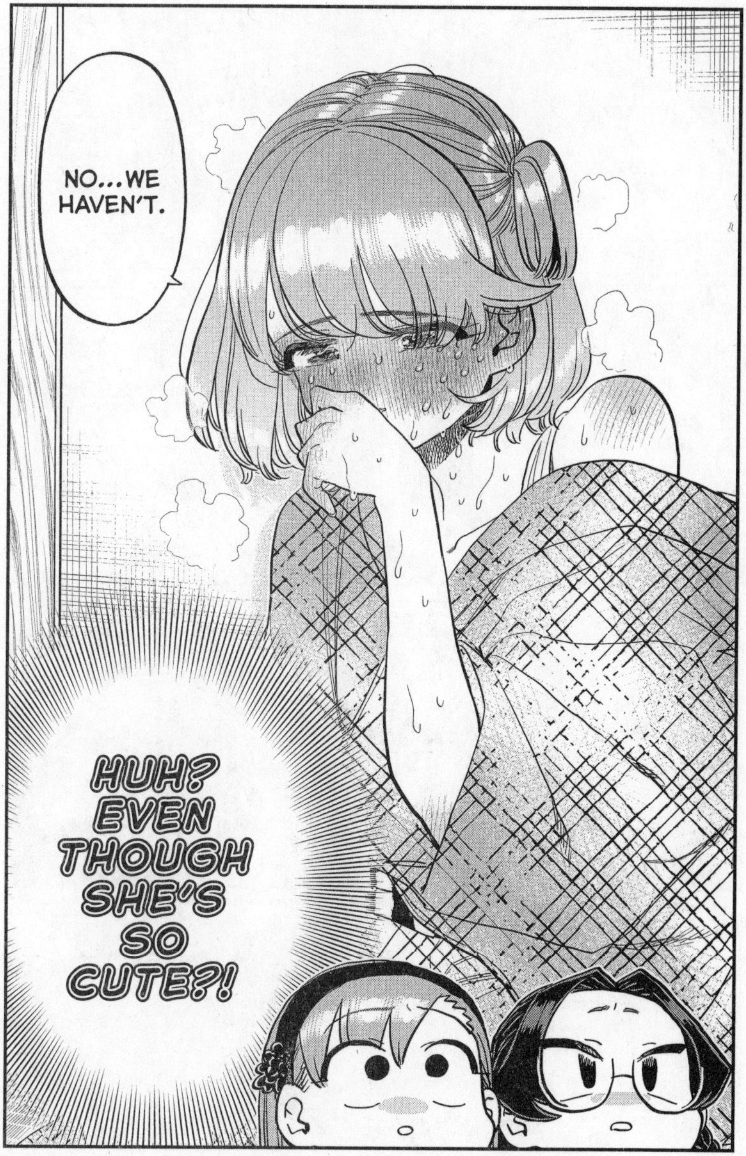
NO...WE HAVEN'T.
HUH? EVEN THOUGH SHE'S SO CUTE?!

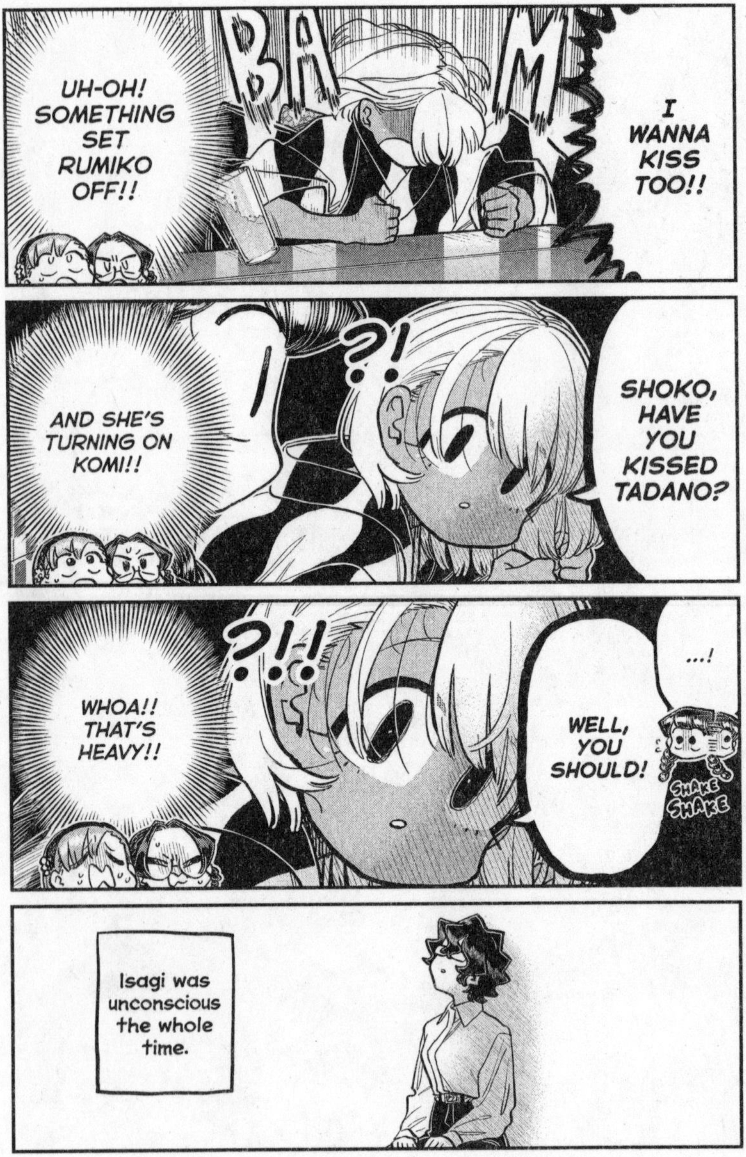
I WANNA KISS TOO!!
BAM
UH-OH! SOMETHING SET RUMIKO OFF!!
SHOKO, HAVE YOU KISSED TADANO?
?!
AND SHE'S TURNING ON KOMI!!
...!
SHAKE SHAKE
WELL, YOU SHOULD!
?!!
WHOA!! THAT'S HEAVY!!
Isagi was unconscious the whole time.

Communication 361 — The End

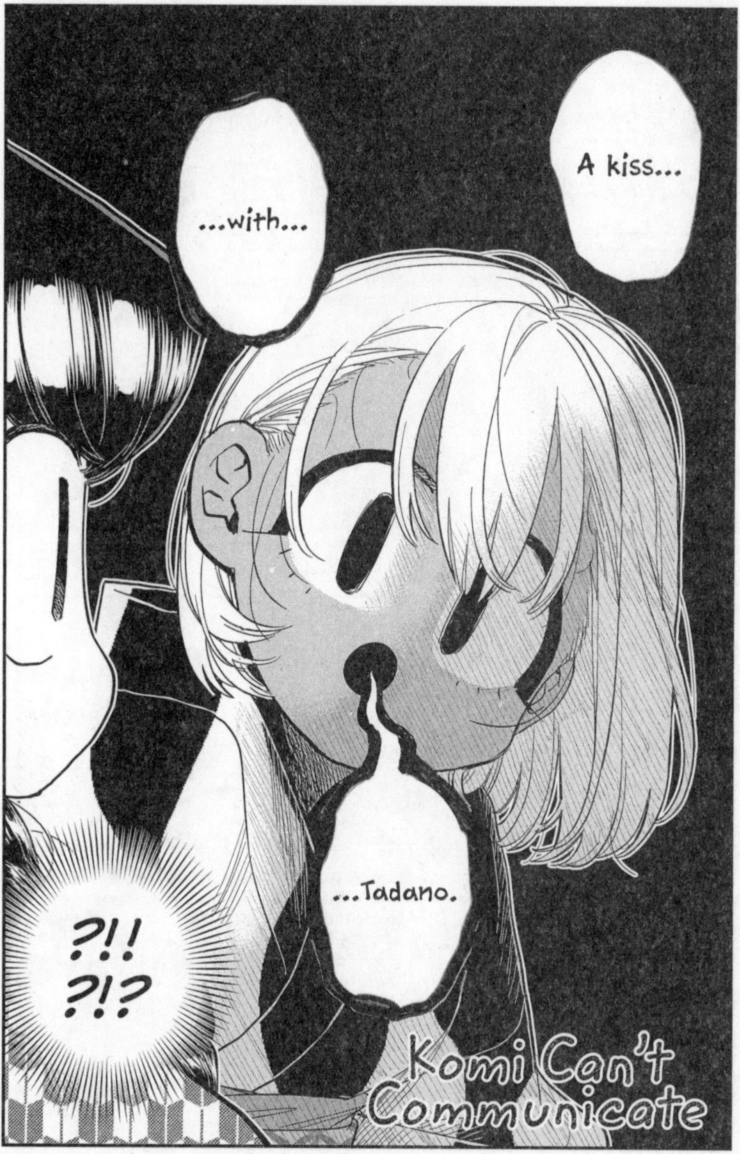
A kiss...
...with...
...Tadano.
?!! ?!?
Komi Can't Communicate

Communication 362: Kiss

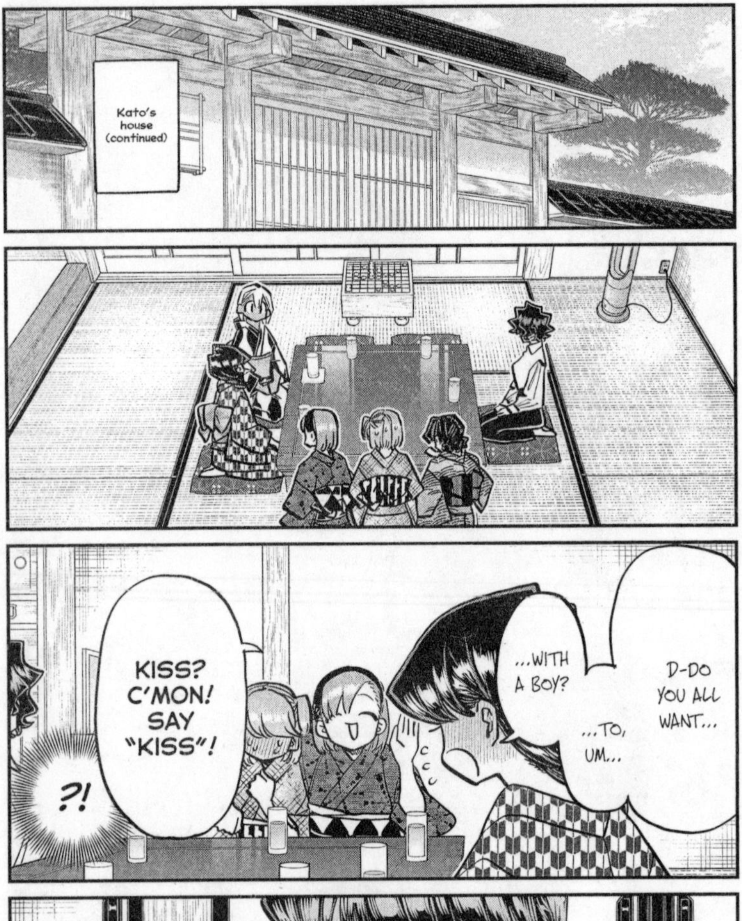
Kato's house (continued)
D-DO YOU ALL WANT...
...TO, UM...
...WITH A BOY?
KISS? C'MON! SAY "KISS"!
?!
K...

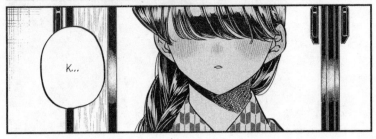

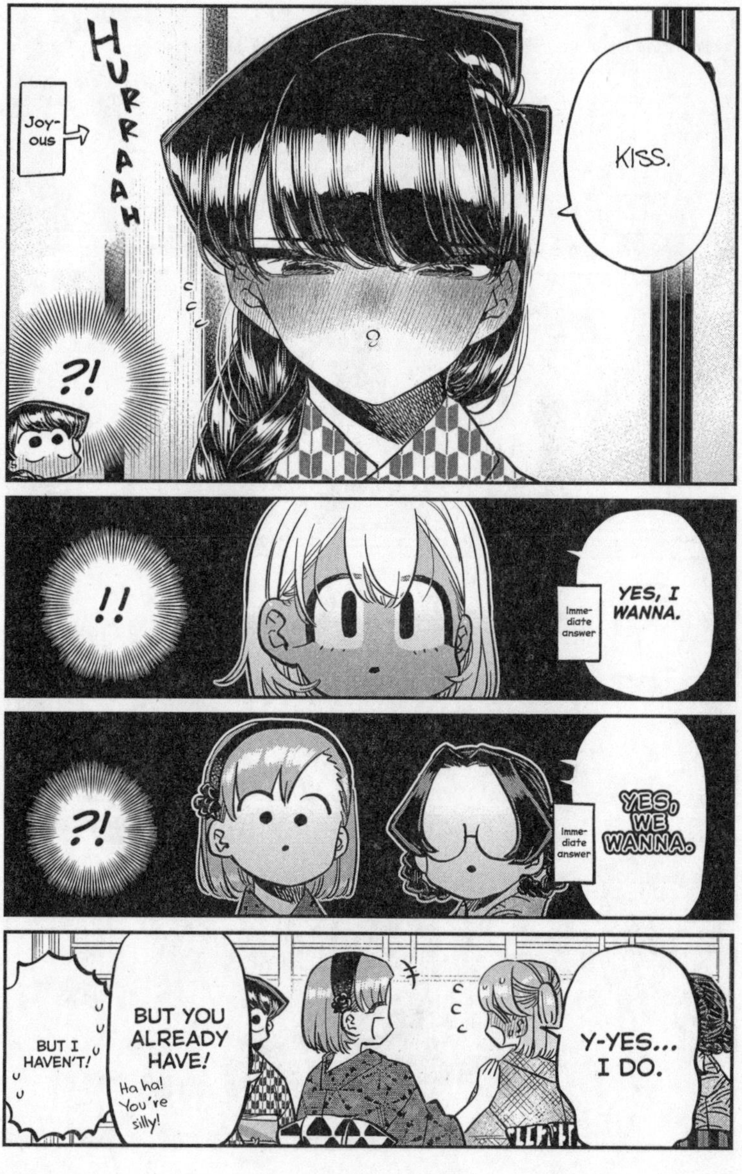
KISS.
HURRAAH
Joy-ous
?!
YES, I WANNA.
Imme-diate answer
!!
YES, WE WANNA.
Imme-diate answer
?!
Y-YES... I DO.
BUT YOU ALREADY HAVE!
Ha ha! You're silly!
BUT I HAVEN'T!

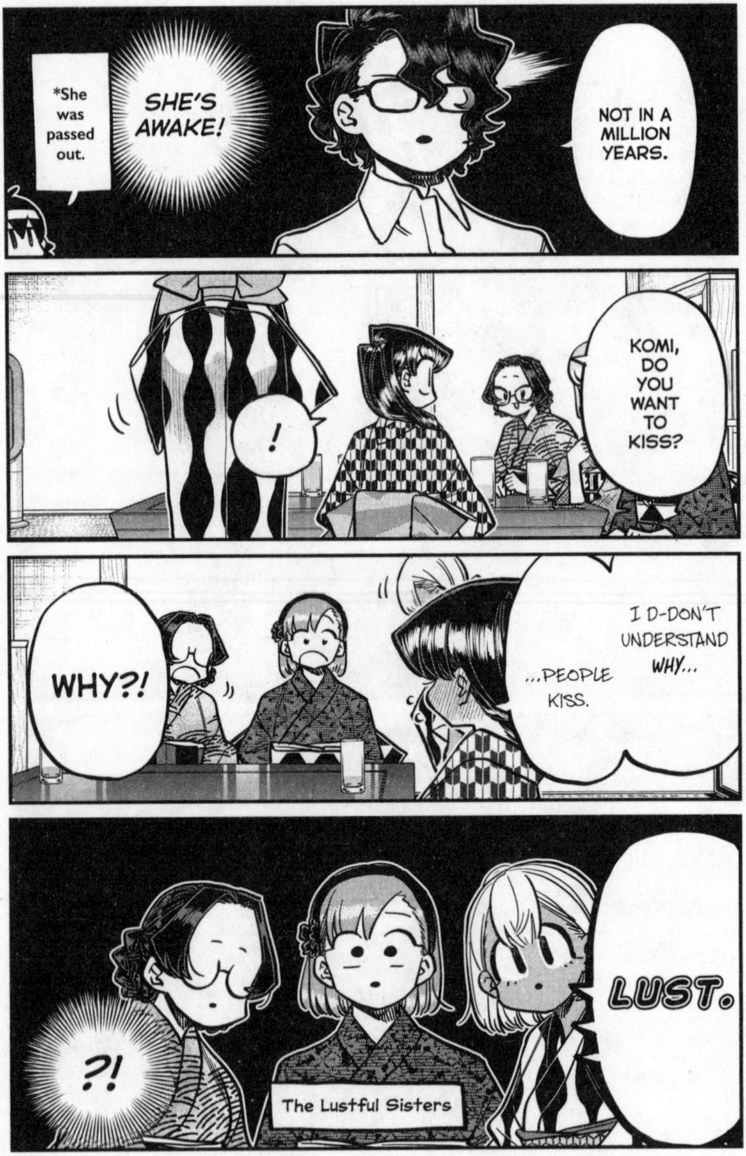
NOT IN A MILLION YEARS.
SHE'S AWAKE!
*She was passed out.
KOMI, DO YOU WANT TO KISS?
!
I D-DON'T UNDERSTAND WHY...
...PEOPLE KISS.
WHY?!
LUST.
?!
The Lustful Sisters

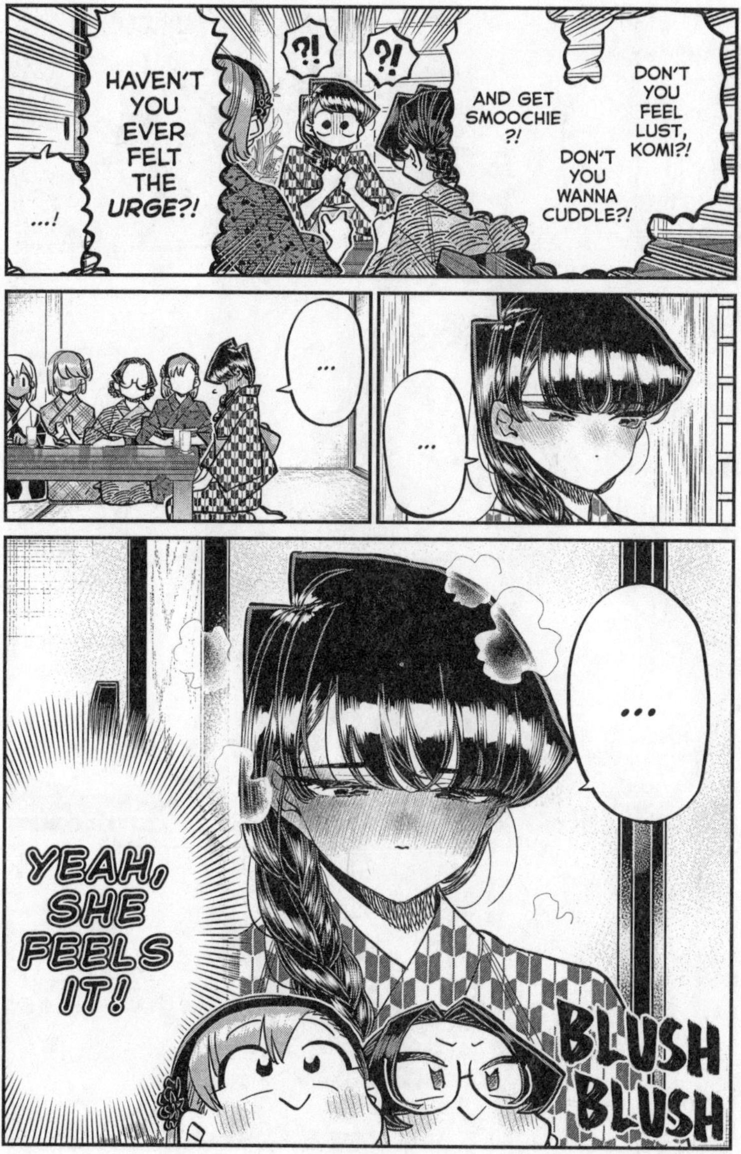
DON'T YOU FEEL LUST, KOMI?!
DON'T YOU WANNA CUDDLE?!
AND GET SMOOCHIE ?!
?!
?!
HAVEN'T YOU EVER FELT THE URGE?!
...!
...
...
...
BLUSH BLUSH
YEAH, SHE FEELS IT!

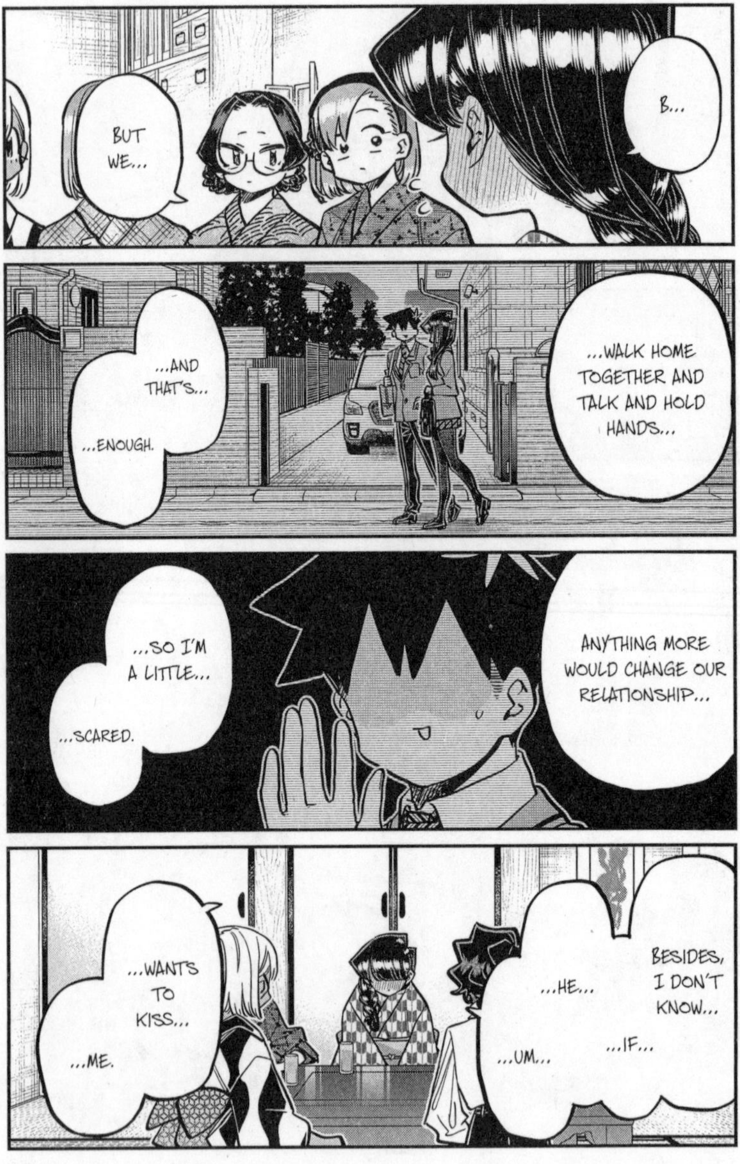
B...
BUT WE...
...WALK HOME TOGETHER AND TALK AND HOLD HANDS...
...AND THAT'S... ...ENOUGH.
ANYTHING MORE WOULD CHANGE OUR RELATIONSHIP...
...SO I'M A LITTLE... ...SCARED.
BESIDES, I DON'T KNOW... ...IF... ...HE... ...UM...
...WANTS TO KISS... ...ME.

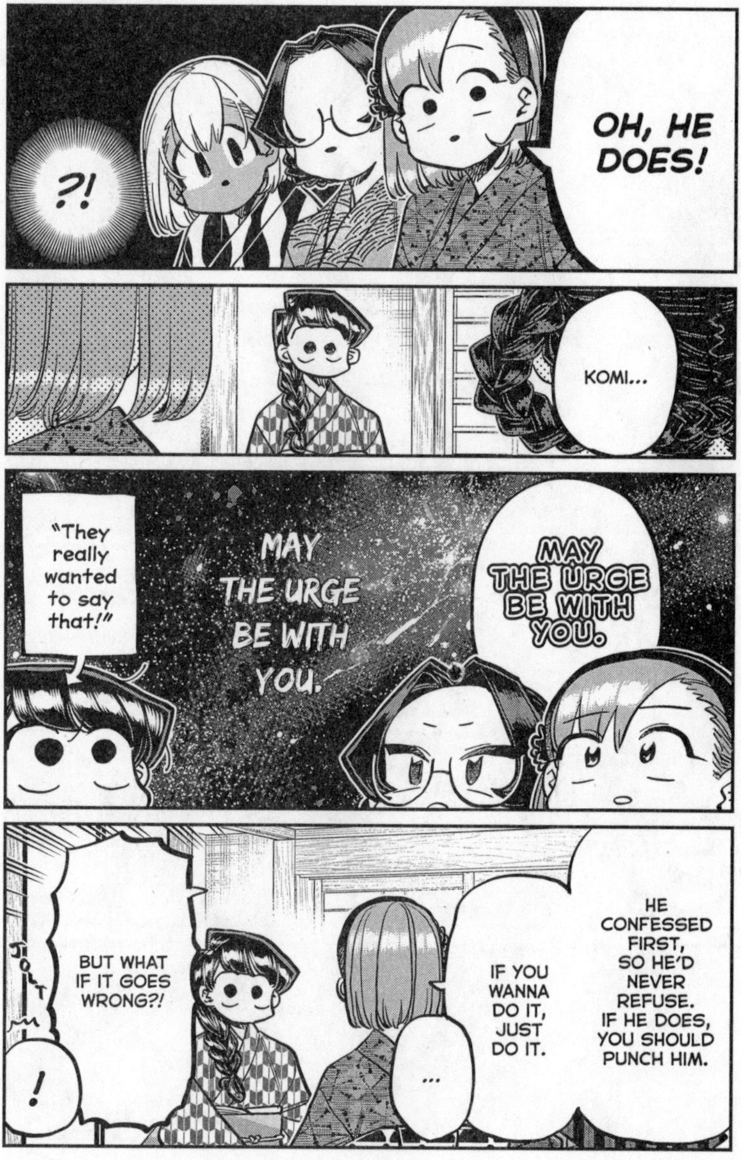
OH, HE DOES!
?!
KOMI...
MAY THE URGE BE WITH YOU.
MAY THE URGE BE WITH YOU.
"They really wanted to say that!"
HE CONFESSED FIRST, SO HE'D NEVER REFUSE. IF HE DOES, YOU SHOULD PUNCH HIM.
IF YOU WANNA DO IT, JUST DO IT.
...
BUT WHAT IF IT GOES WRONG?!
JOLT
!

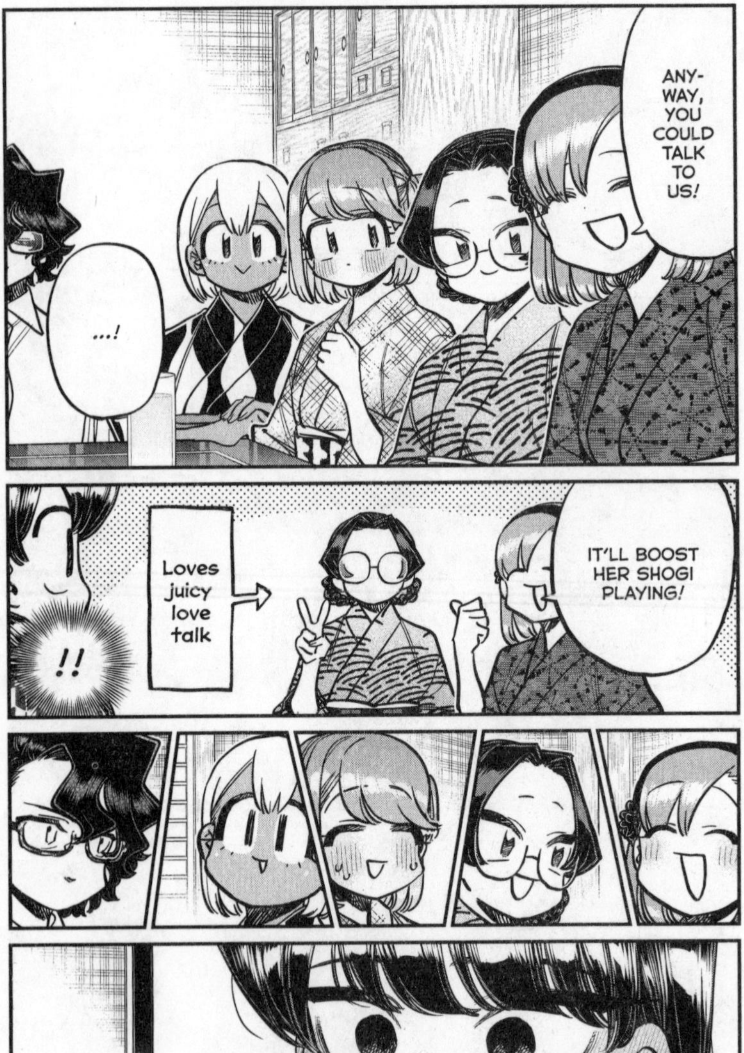
ANY-WAY, YOU COULD TALK TO US!
...!
IT'LL BOOST HER SHOGI PLAYING!
Loves juicy love talk
!!

YES.

WHAT'S A FIRST KISS TASTE LIKE?! LET'S GUESS!!!

?!

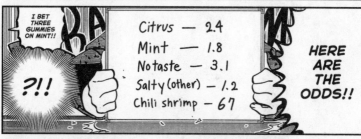

I BET THREE GUMMIES ON MINT!!

?!!

Citrus	—	2.4
Mint	—	1.8
Notaste	—	3.1
Salty (other)	—	1.2
Chili shrimp	—	67

HERE ARE THE ODDS!!

?!!

WE'LL ANNOUNCE THE RESULTS AFTER YOU TWO KISS!!

Communication 362 — The End

Communication 363: Kiss (Within Comfortable Bounds)

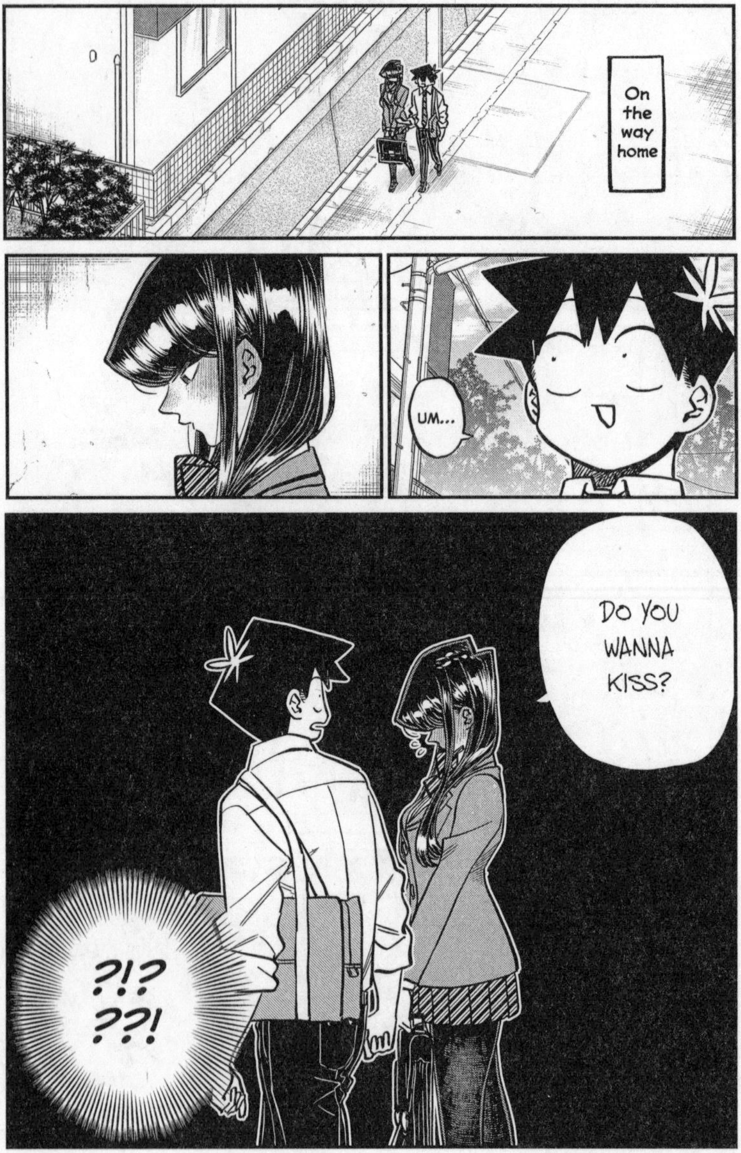
On the way home
UM...
DO YOU WANNA KISS?
?!? ??!

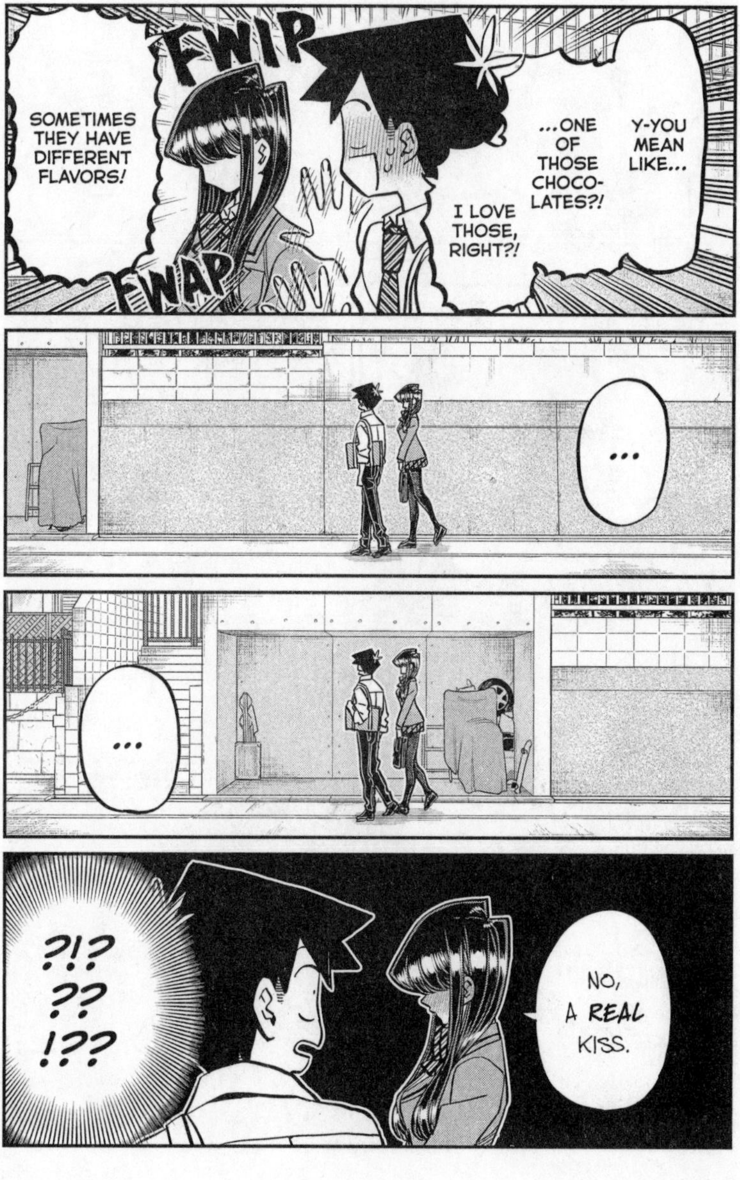
Y-YOU MEAN LIKE...
...ONE OF THOSE CHOCO-LATES?!
I LOVE THOSE, RIGHT?!
FWIP
SOMETIMES THEY HAVE DIFFERENT FLAVORS!
FWAP
...
...
NO, A REAL KISS.
?!? ?? !??

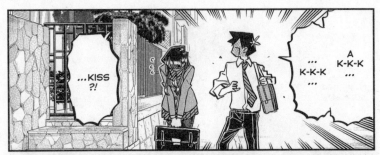

A K-K-K...
...K-K-K...
...KISS?!
NOD
...!!!
YES... ...I DO...
...B-BUT...
...WITHIN COMFORTABLE BOUNDS.
?!
After lengthy deliberation

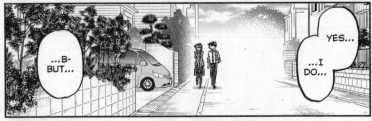

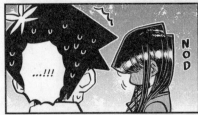

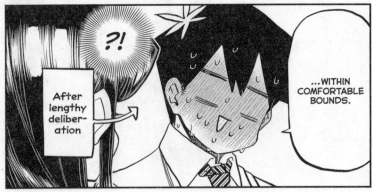

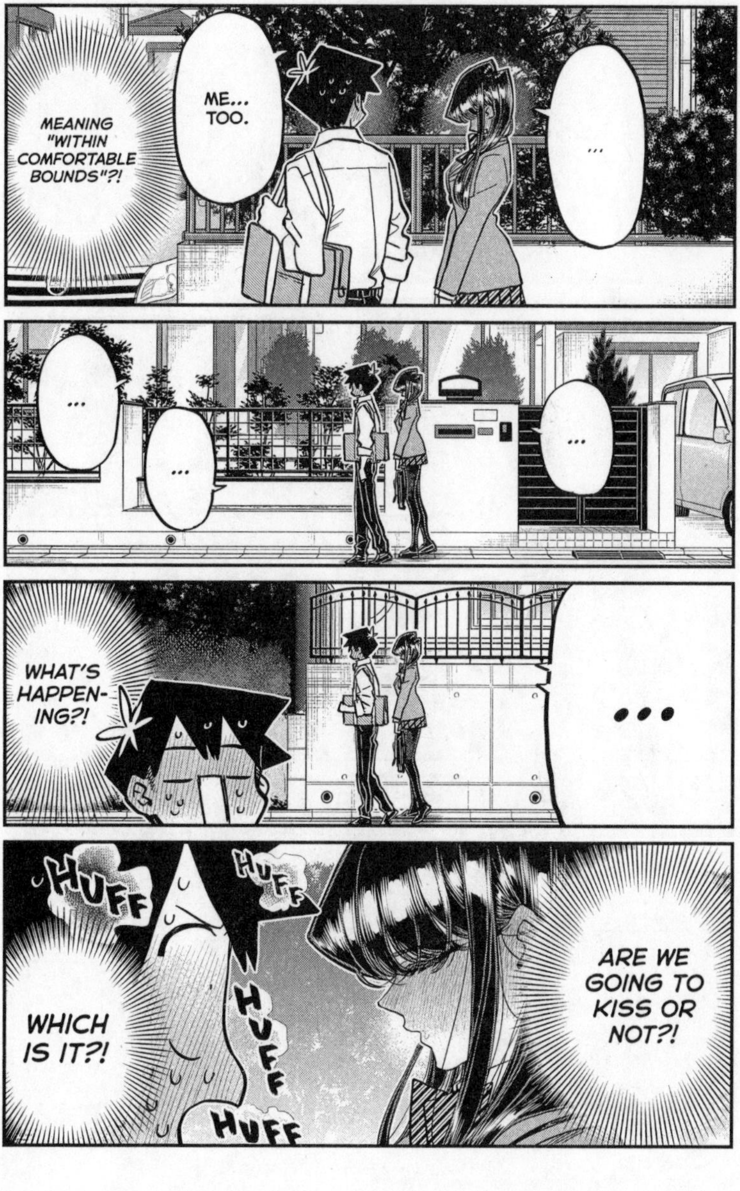
...
ME... TOO.
MEANING "WITHIN COMFORTABLE BOUNDS"?!
...
...
...
•••
WHAT'S HAPPEN-ING?!
ARE WE GOING TO KISS OR NOT?!
HUFF
HUFF
HUFF
HUFF
WHICH IS IT?!

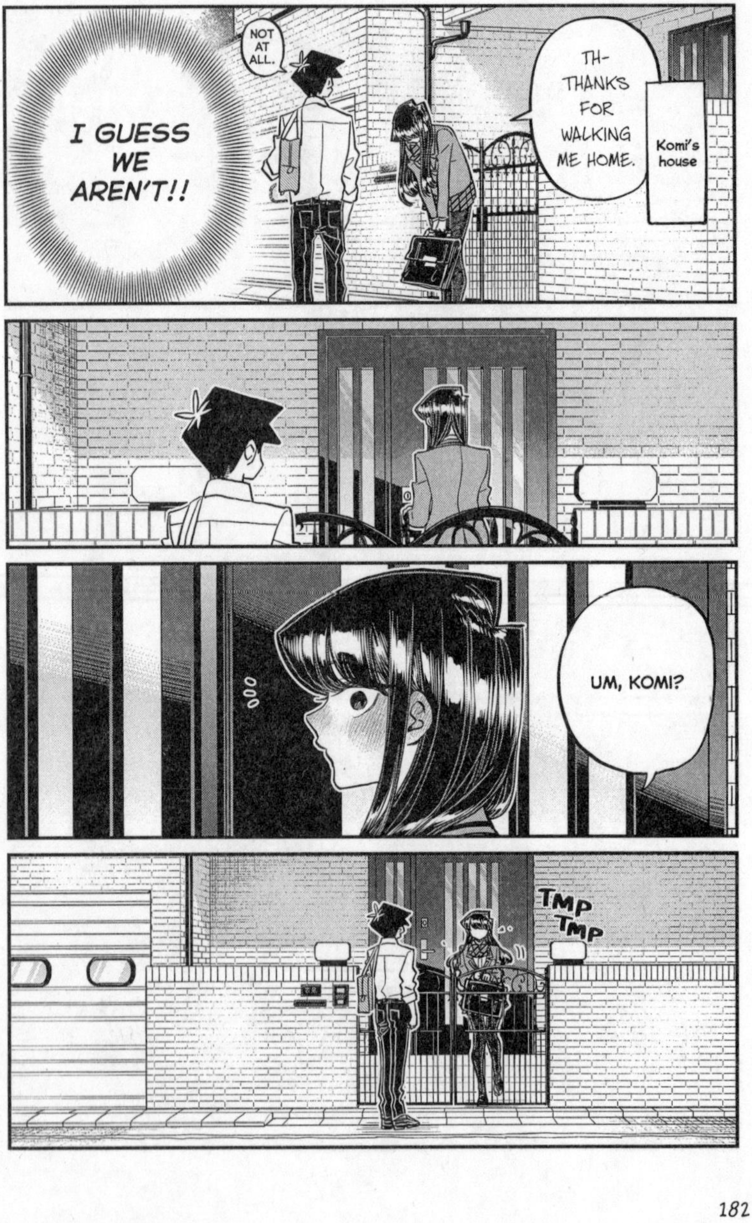
Komi's house
TH-THANKS FOR WALKING ME HOME.
NOT AT ALL.
I GUESS WE AREN'T!!
UM, KOMI?
TMP TMP

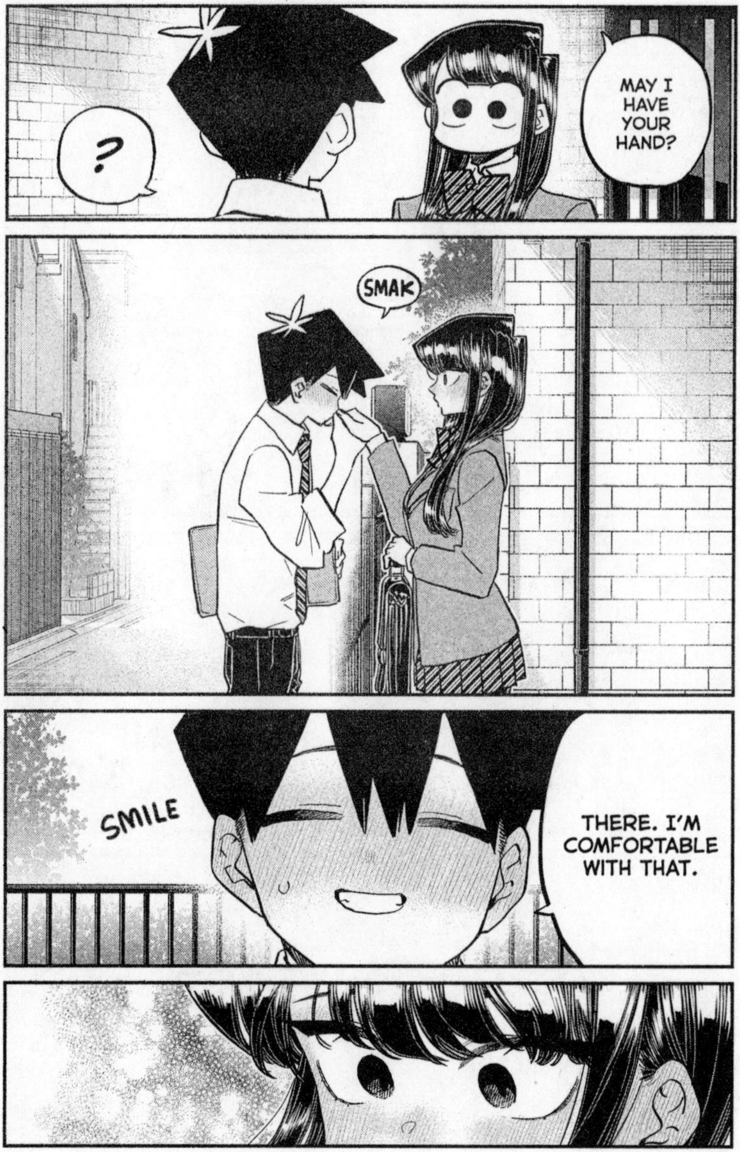
MAY I HAVE YOUR HAND?
?
SMAK
THERE. I'M COMFORTABLE WITH THAT.
SMILE

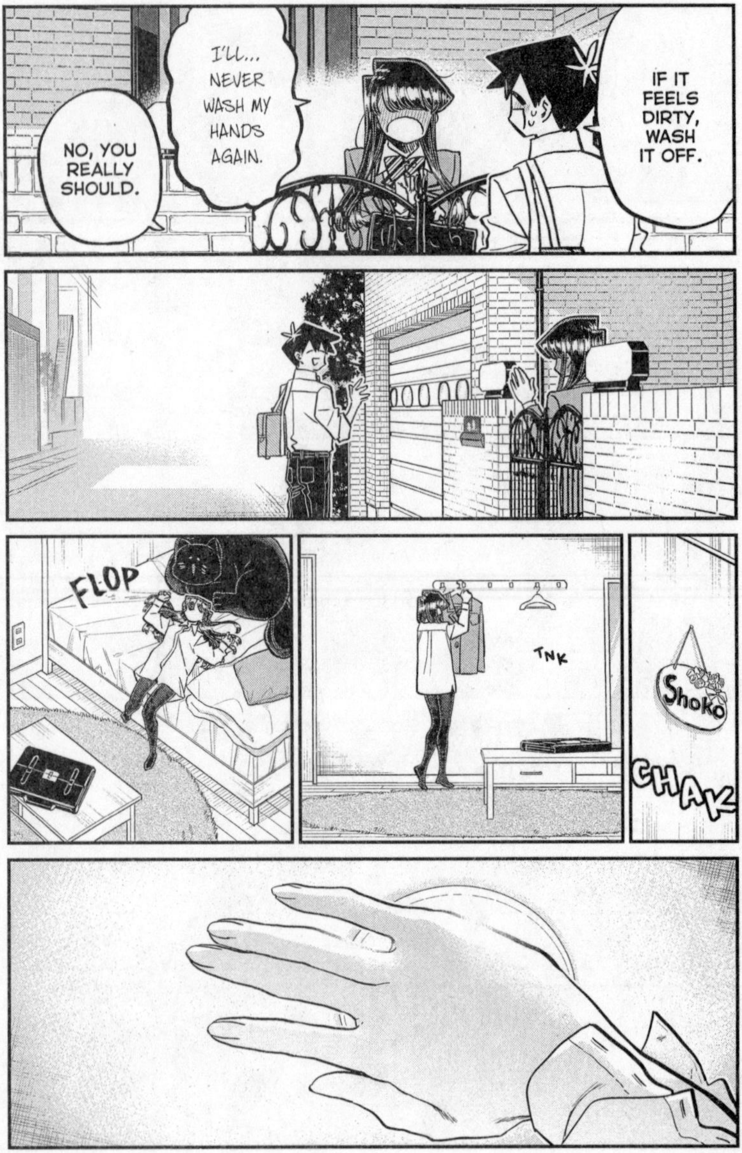
IF IT FEELS DIRTY, WASH IT OFF.
I'LL... NEVER WASH MY HANDS AGAIN.
NO, YOU REALLY SHOULD.
Shoko
CHAK
TNK
FLOP

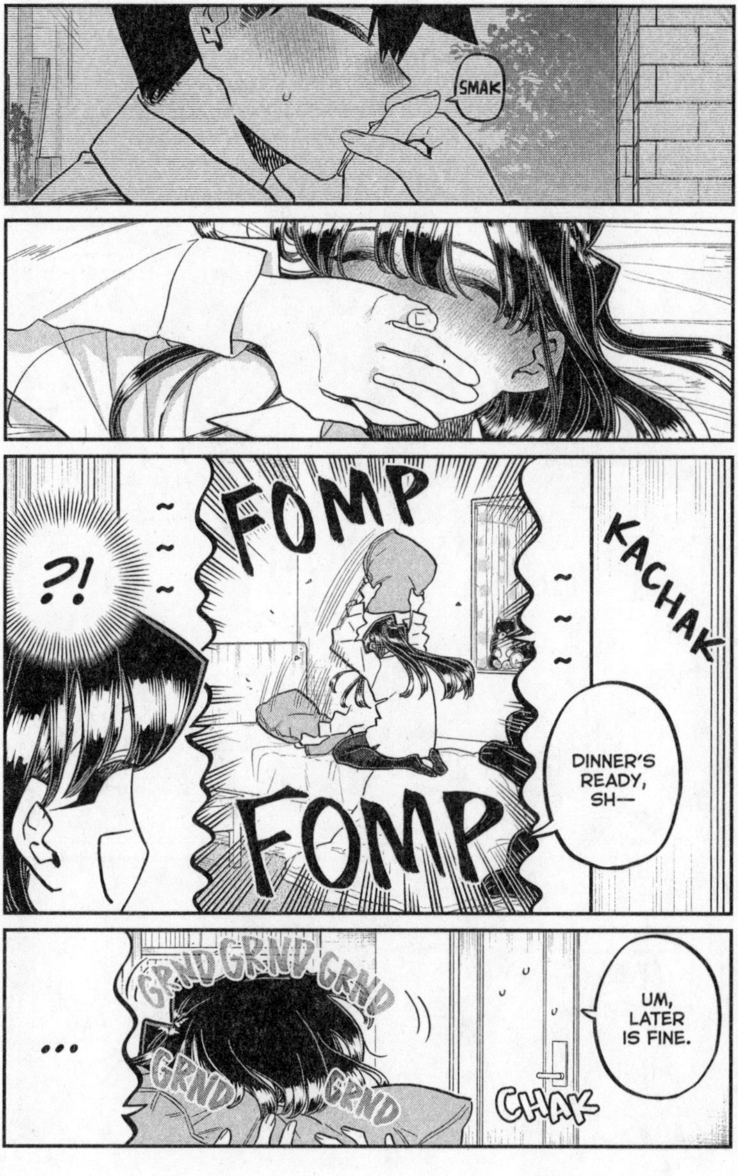
SMAK
KACHAK
DINNER'S READY, SH—
FOMP
FOMP
~ ~ ~
~ ~ ~
?!
UM, LATER IS FINE.
CHAK
GRND GRND GRND GRND
GRND
GRND
...

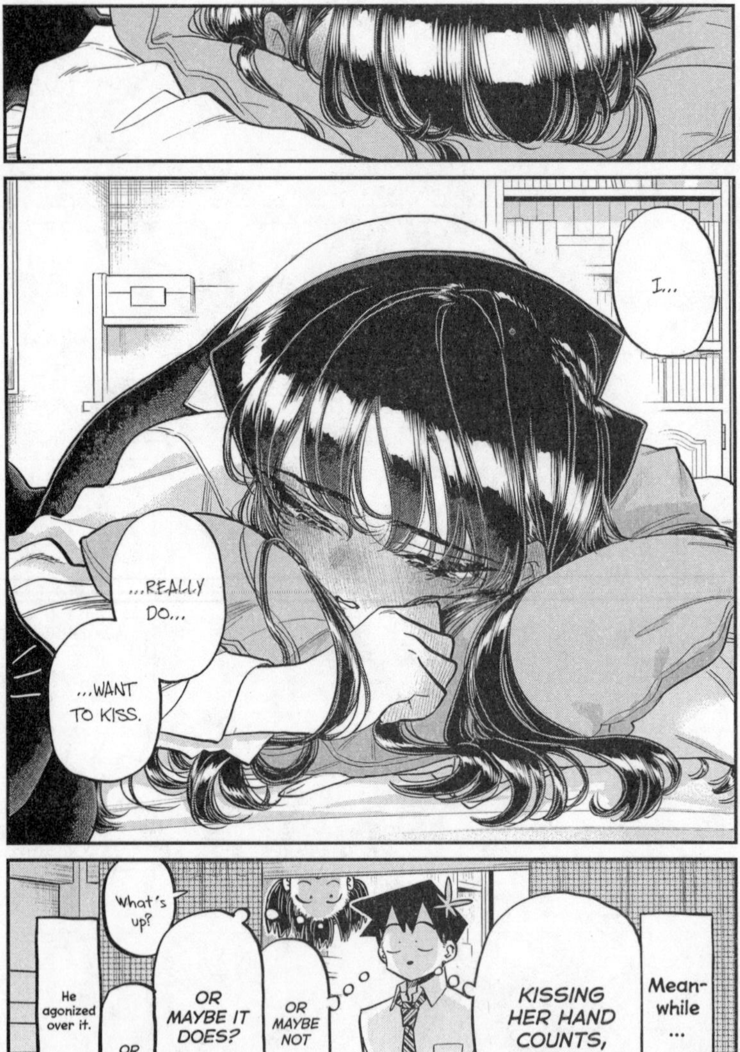
I...
...REALLY DO...
...WANT TO KISS.
Mean-while ...
KISSING HER HAND COUNTS, RIGHT?
OR MAYBE NOT ...
What's up?
OR MAYBE IT DOES?
OR MAYBE NOT.
He agonized over it.

Communication 363 — The End

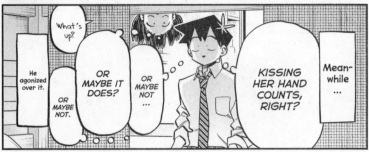

Komi Can't Communicate

Komi Can't Communicate Bonus

Can Komi Make 100 Friends? Muzuka Holds Out, Part 2!!

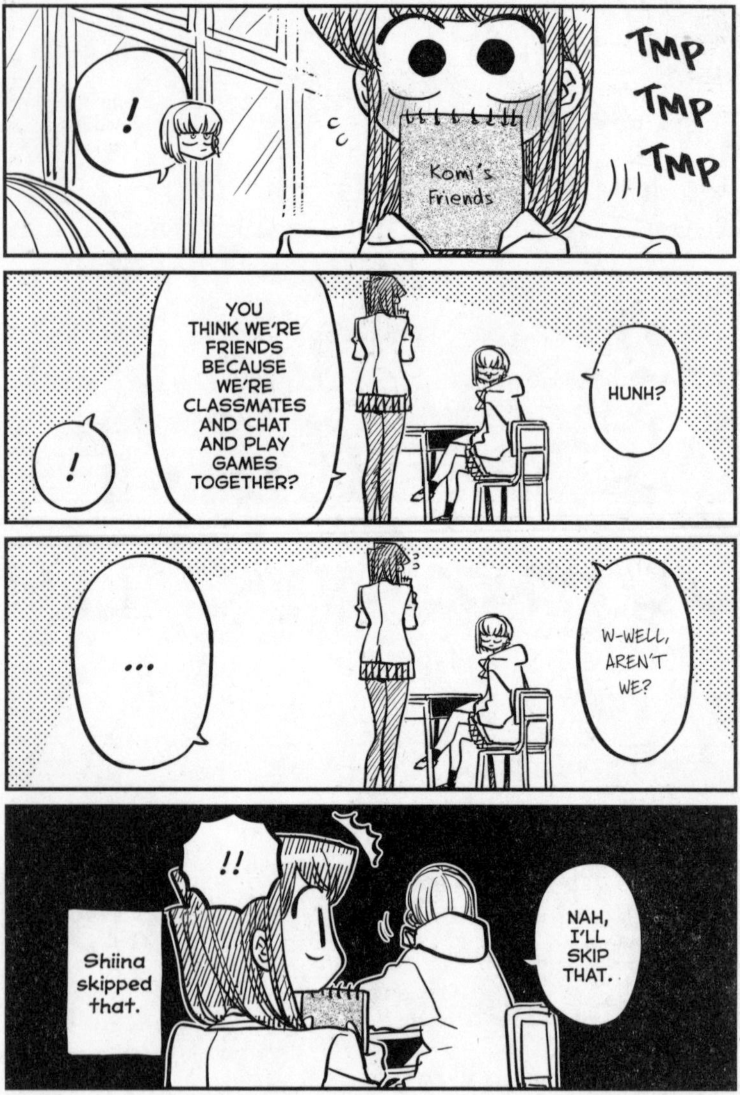
TMP
TMP
TMP
Komi's Friends
!
HUNH?
YOU THINK WE'RE FRIENDS BECAUSE WE'RE CLASSMATES AND CHAT AND PLAY GAMES TOGETHER?
!
W-WELL, AREN'T WE?
...
NAH, I'LL SKIP THAT.
!!
Shiina skipped that.

Komi Can't Communicate Bonus

Can Komi Make 100 Friends? Sisters Not Connected by Blood

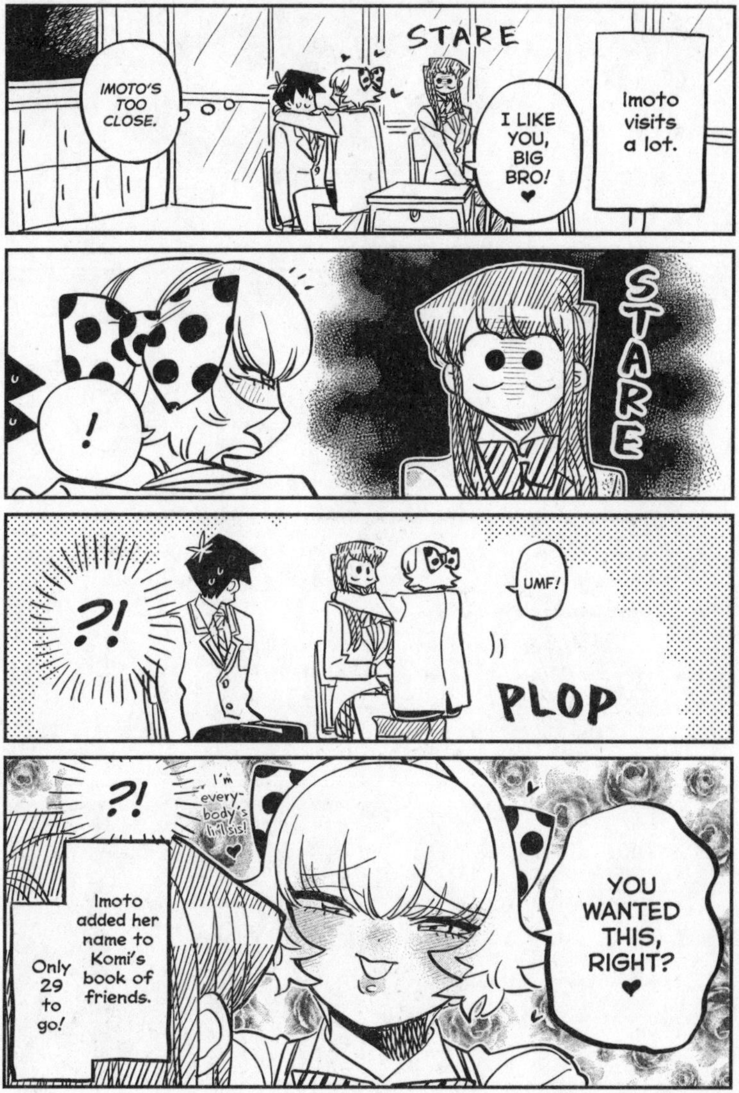

Imoto visits a lot.
I LIKE YOU, BIG BRO! ♥
STARE
IMOTO'S TOO CLOSE.
STARE
!
UMF!
PLOP
?!
YOU WANTED THIS, RIGHT? ♥
I'm everybody's li'l sis! ♥
?!
Imoto added her name to Komi's book of friends.
Only 29 to go!

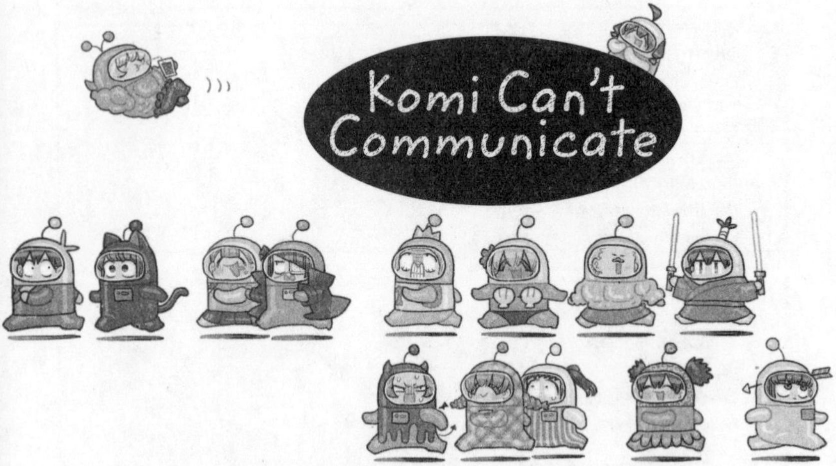
Komi Can't Communicate

Tomohito Oda won the grand prize for *World Worst One* in the 70th Shogakukan New Comic Artist Awards in 2012. Oda's series *Digicon*, about a tough high school girl who finds herself in control of an alien with plans for world domination, ran from 2014 to 2015. In 2015, *Komi Can't Communicate* debuted as a one-shot in *Weekly Shonen Sunday* and was picked up as a full series by the same magazine in 2016.

Komi Can't Communicate

VOL. 27
Shonen Sunday Edition

Story and Art by Tomohito Oda

English Translation & Adaptation/John Werry
Touch-Up Art & Lettering/Kyla Aiko
Additional Lettering/Finn K.
Design/Julian [JR] Robinson
Editor/Pancha Diaz

COMI-SAN WA, COMYUSHO DESU. Vol. 27
by Tomohito ODA
© 2016 Tomohito ODA
All rights reserved.
Original Japanese edition published by SHOGAKUKAN.
English translation rights in the United States of America, Canada, the United
Kingdom, Ireland, Australia and New Zealand arranged with SHOGAKUKAN.

Original Cover Design/Masato ISHIZAWA + Bay Bridge Studio

Printed in the U.S.A.

Published by VIZ Media, LLC
P.O. Box 77010
San Francisco, CA 94107

10 9 8 7 6 5 4 3 2 1
First printing, October 2023

viz.com

shonensunday.com

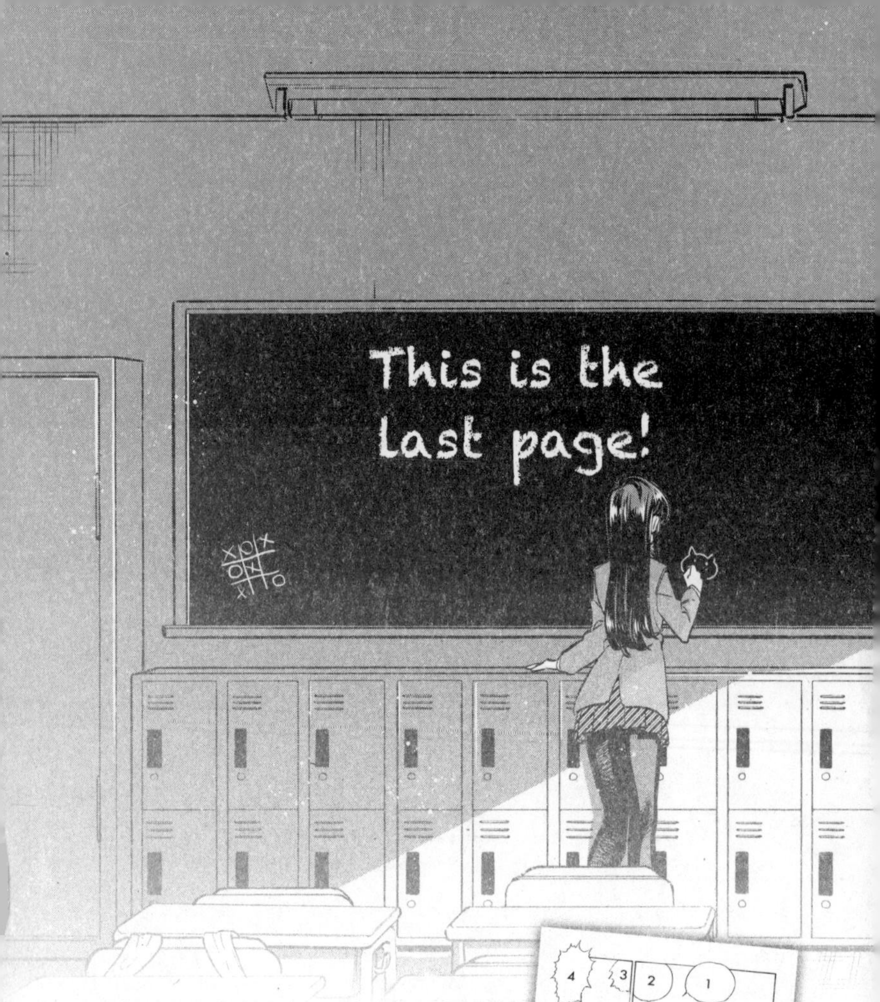
This is the last page!

Komi Can't Communicate has been printed in the original Japanese format to preserve the orientation of the artwork.

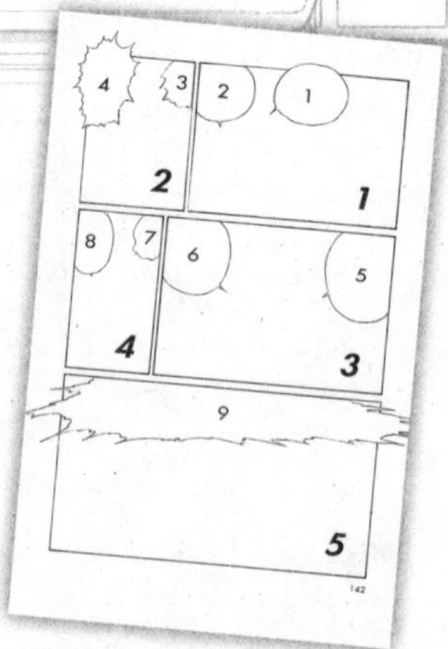
1
2
1
4
3
2
5
6
3
7
8
4
9
5
142

Follow the action this way.